D1691212

Introduction to Asset Management

Introduction to Asset Management

Oliver Hardy

Introduction to Asset Management
Oliver Hardy
ISBN: 978-1-64172-370-1 (Hardback)

© 2020 Larsen & Keller

Larsen & Keller

Published by Larsen and Keller Education,
5 Penn Plaza,
19th Floor,
New York, NY 10001, USA

Cataloging-in-Publication Data

Introduction to asset management / Oliver Hardy.
   p. cm.
Includes bibliographical references and index.
ISBN 978-1-64172-370-1
1. Assets (Accounting). 2. Asset-liability management.
3. Asset requirements. I. Hardy, Oliver.
HF5681.A8 I58 2020
657.7--dc23

This book contains information obtained from authentic and highly regarded sources. All chapters are published with permission under the Creative Commons Attribution Share Alike License or equivalent. A wide variety of references are listed. Permissions and sources are indicated; for detailed attributions, please refer to the permissions page. Reasonable efforts have been made to publish reliable data and information, but the authors, editors and publisher cannot assume any responsibility for the validity of all materials or the consequences of their use.

Trademark Notice: All trademarks used herein are the property of their respective owners. The use of any trademark in this text does not vest in the author or publisher any trademark ownership rights in such trademarks, nor does the use of such trademarks imply any affiliation with or endorsement of this book by such owners.

For more information regarding Larsen and Keller Education and its products, please visit the publisher's website www.larsen-keller.com

TABLE OF CONTENTS

Preface IX

Chapter 1 Introduction 1
- Asset 1
- Asset Management 2

Chapter 2 Current Assets 10
- Cash and Cash Equivalents 11
- Stock Control and Inventory 14
- Accounts Receivable 22
- Marketable Securities 24
- Prepaid Expenses 28
- Current Ratio 30
- Quick Ratio 31
- Cash Ratio 32

Chapter 3 Fixed Assets 35
- Tangible Asset 37
- Intangible Asset 38
- Capital Expenditure 42
- Fixed Assets Management 44
- Fixed-asset Turnover 45
- Revaluation of Fixed Assets 47
- Depreciation in Fixed Asset 52

Chapter 4 Investment Management 56
- Discretionary Investment Management 58
- Investment Risk 59
- Portfolio Management 62
- Investment Strategy 66
- Asset Allocation 68

- Dynamic Asset Allocation ... 72
- Global Tactical Asset Allocation ... 72
- Active Management ... 73
- Benchmark-driven Investment Strategy ... 76
- Fund of Funds ... 79
- Passive Investing ... 81
- Investment Fund ... 83

Chapter 5 Valuation ... 109

- Business Valuation ... 114
- Absolute Valuation Model ... 131
- Relative Valuation Model ... 138
- Inventory Valuation Method ... 139
- Valuation using Multiples ... 140
- Bond Valuation ... 149
- Discounted Cash Flow ... 153
- Valuation using Discounted Cash Flows ... 161
- Deprival Value ... 166
- Market Value ... 167
- Intrinsic Value ... 171
- Terminal Value ... 172
- Liquidation Value ... 174
- Book Value ... 175
- Adjusted Present Value ... 179
- Net Present Value ... 179
- Stock Valuation ... 186

Chapter 6 Diverse Aspects of Asset Management ... 214

- Funds Management ... 214
- Infrastructure Asset management ... 219
- Digital Asset Management ... 223
- Mobile Enterprise Asset Management ... 225
- Capital Appreciation ... 227
- Event Study ... 227
- Asset/Liability Modeling ... 230

- Asset Classes — 231
- Asset Recovery — 234
- Asset Protection — 235
- Asset Tracking — 236
- Asset Swap — 238

Permissions

Index

PREFACE

It is with great pleasure that I present this book. It has been carefully written after numerous discussions with my peers and other practitioners of the field. I would like to take this opportunity to thank my family and friends who have been extremely supporting at every step in my life.

The systematic approach to the governance and realization of value from the things that an entity or a group is responsible for is referred to as asset management. It is applied to both tangible assets including physical objects like buildings or equipment, and to intangible assets such as intellectual property, financial assets or human capital. Asset management is also involved in operating, developing, maintaining, upgrading and disposing of assets in the most cost effective manner. It can be categorized on the basis of the industry in which it is used. The major categories of asset management include financial asset management, physical and infrastructure asset management, enterprise asset management and public asset management. This book outlines the processes and applications of asset management in detail. It traces the progress of this field and highlights some of its key concepts and applications. Those in search of information to further their knowledge will be greatly assisted by this book.

The chapters below are organized to facilitate a comprehensive understanding of the subject:

Chapter - Introduction

A resource of value that can be converted into cash is defined as an asset. Asset management is defined as a systematic approach which is concerned with the governance and management of valuable resources of a group. The topics elaborated in this chapter will help in gaining a better perspective about asset management.

Chapter - Current Assets

Current assets are referred to the assets of a company that are expected to be conveniently sold and utilized through the standard business operations. The cash value of these assets is converted in one year period. This chapter closely examines the key concepts of current assets to provide an extensive understanding of the subject.

Chapter - Fixed Assets

Fixed assets are defined as the assets which are purchased for long term use. The company or firm owns and uses it in its operations to generate revenue. Fixed assets can be categorized into tangible assets and intangible assets. This chapter has been carefully written to provide an easy understanding of the varied facets of fixed assets as well as their management.

Chapter - Investment Management

To meet the investment goals, investment management is the asset management of shares, bonds and other assets. Some of the major aspects of it are portfolio management, asset allocation, investment fund, active management, etc. All these diverse concepts of investment management have been carefully analyzed in this chapter.

Chapter – Valuation

Valuation refers to the process of estimating the present value of an asset. A few of the common business valuation methods include relative valuation, absolute valuation, discounted cash flow, bond valuation, stock valuation etc. This chapter discusses in detail these different business valuation methods.

Chapter – Diverse Aspects of Asset Management

Some of the diverse aspects of asset management are funds management, infrastructure asset management, digital asset management and mobile enterprise asset management. This chapter closely examines these key concepts of asset management to provide an extensive understanding of the subject.

Oliver Hardy

Introduction

CHAPTER 1

A resource of value that can be converted into cash is defined as an asset. Asset management is defined as a systematic approach which is concerned with the governance and management of valuable resources of a group. The topics elaborated in this chapter will help in gaining a better perspective about asset management.

ASSET

An asset is a resource with economic value that an individual, corporation or country owns or controls with the expectation that it will provide a future benefit. Assets are reported on a company's balance sheet and are bought or created to increase a firm's value or benefit the firm's operations.

An asset can be thought of as something that, in the future, can generate cash flow, reduce expenses, or improve sales, regardless of whether it's manufacturing equipment or a patent.

An asset represents an economic resource for a company or represents access that other individuals or firms do not have. A right or other access is legally enforceable, which means economic resources can be used at a company's discretion, and its use can be precluded or limited by an owner.

For an asset to be present, a company must possess a right to it as of the date of the financial statements. An economic resource is something that is scarce and has the ability to produce economic benefit by generating cash inflows or decreasing cash outflows.

Assets can be broadly categorized into short-term (or current) assets, fixed assets, financial investments, and intangible assets.

Examples of Assets

Current Assets

Current assets are short-term economic resources that are expected to be converted into cash within one year. Current assets include cash and cash equivalents, accounts receivable, inventory, and various prepaid expenses.

While cash is easy to value, accountants periodically reassess the recoverability of inventory and accounts receivable. If there is evidence that accounts receivable might be uncollectible, it'll become impaired. Or if inventory becomes obsolete, companies may write off these assets.

Fixed Assets

Fixed assets are long-term resources, such as plants, equipment, and buildings. An adjustment for the aging of fixed assets is made based on periodic charges called depreciation, which may or may not reflect the loss of earning powers for a fixed asset.

Generally accepted accounting principles (GAAP) allow depreciation under two broad methods. The straight-line method assumes that a fixed asset loses its value in proportion to its useful life, while the accelerated method assumes that the asset loses its value faster in its first years of use.

Financial Assets

Financial assets represent investments in the assets and securities of other institutions. Financial assets include stocks, sovereign and corporate bonds, preferred equity, and other hybrid securities. Financial assets are valued depending on how the investment is categorized and the motive behind it.

Intangible Assets

Intangible assets are economic resources that have no physical presence. They include patents, trademarks, copyrights, and goodwill. Accounting for intangible assets differs depending on the type of asset, and they can be either amortized or tested for impairment each year.

ASSET MANAGEMENT

Asset management is the direction of all or part of a client's portfolio by a financial services institution, usually an investment bank, or an individual. Institutions offer investment services along with a wide range of traditional and alternative product offerings that might not be available to the average investor.

Asset management refers to the management of investments on behalf of others. The process essentially has a dual mandate - appreciation of a client's assets over time while mitigating risk. There are investment minimums, which means that this service is generally available to high net-worth individuals, government entities, corporations and financial intermediaries.

The role of an asset manager consists of determining what investments to make, or avoid, that will grow a client's portfolio. Rigorous research is conducted utilizing both macro and micro analytical tools. This includes statistical analysis of the prevailing market trends, interviews with company officials, and anything else that would aid in achieving the stated goal of client asset appreciation. Most commonly, the advisor will invest in products such as equity, fixed income, real estate, commodities, alternative investments and mutual funds.

Accounts held by financial institutions often include check writing privileges, credit cards, debit cards, margin loans, the automatic sweep of cash balances into a money market fund and brokerage services.

When individuals deposit money into the account, it is typically placed into a money market fund that offers a greater return that can be found in regular savings and checking accounts. Account holders can choose between Federal Deposit Insurance Company-backed (FDIC) funds and non-FDIC funds. The added benefit to account holders is all of their banking and investing needs can be serviced by the same institution rather than having separate brokerage account and banking options.

These types of accounts resulted from the passing of the Gramm-Leach-Bliley Act in 1999, which replaced the Glass-Steagall Act. The Glass-Steagall Act of 1933 was created during the Great Depression and did not allow financial institutions to offer both banking and security services.

The Asset Management "Paradigm"

- The capacity to produce output of value to our customers is directly related to sustained performance of our assets using the process of triple bottom line evaluation of the services provided utilizing environmental, social and economic analysis.

- Failures in the asset base directly affect system performance.

- Sustained system performance is the result of successfully managing failure within the asset base.

- The management of failure in the asset base is highly constrained by cost; that is, customers are not typically willing to pay for zero likelihood of failure.

- Different assets have different probabilities of failure, as determined by age, materials and assembly processes, operating environment, demand/usage and maintenance.

- Failures vary substantially in their consequence to the organization, that is, in terms of the production of valued output to the customer.

- Investment in assets (their acquisition, operation, maintenance, renewal and disposal) should be guided by the likelihood of failure and its consequence to the customer and regulator.

- The more we understand about our assets - the demand for our assets, their condition and remaining useful life, their risk and consequence of failure, their feasible renewal options (repair, refurbish, replace) and the cost of those options - the higher the confidence we can have that our investment decisions are indeed the lowest life cycle cost strategies for sustained performance at a level of risk the community is willing to accept.

The AM Framework - Four Views

Think of asset management as an object with multiple faces. Each face presents a different view of the logical framework of asset management.

"Quality Elements Framework" View

Asset management can be seen as an interaction of seven core organizational "quality elements".

Quality elements are fundamental components of an organization's business model that drive its sustained success.

Within the seven elements are "world's best practices" that inform the practitioner as to how best to proceed in strengthening each element. These best practices are under continuous development and refinement, lifting the industry or organization that incorporates them to higher levels of performance.

A successful long-term asset management program is a continuous balancing of these seven elements, built around continuous learning - "the more we understand about our assets, the better we can manage them."

The Quality Elements framework perspective forms the heart of SIMPLE.

"Management Systems" View

To be viable, asset management must drive real results "to the bottom line" - that is, it must make business sense to the organization.

This view is closely related to the question "why do asset management?"

The concepts embedded in this view are:

- Asset management is about creating a management framework that leads to sustained performance at the lowest life cycle cost (while meeting requirements of stakeholders at a level of risk acceptable to the community).

- To achieve the lowest life cycle cost, we must understand how our assets are likely to fail (the failure "mode") and which AM processes and practices to deploy to appropriately manage those failure modes.

- These processes and practices are "bedded down" and supported by good data derived from an integration of asset management information sources.

- This framework drives the production and constant revision of an asset management plan, which is a dynamic strategic framework similar to the agency's budget.

CHAPTER 1 Introduction

- The Total Asset Management Plan, in turn, drives two things:
  - Specific "projects" with declared objectives, resources and timelines that are intended to change or strengthen organizational processes or to solve asset-related problems.
  - The annual CIP and operating budget.

This framework is shown below:

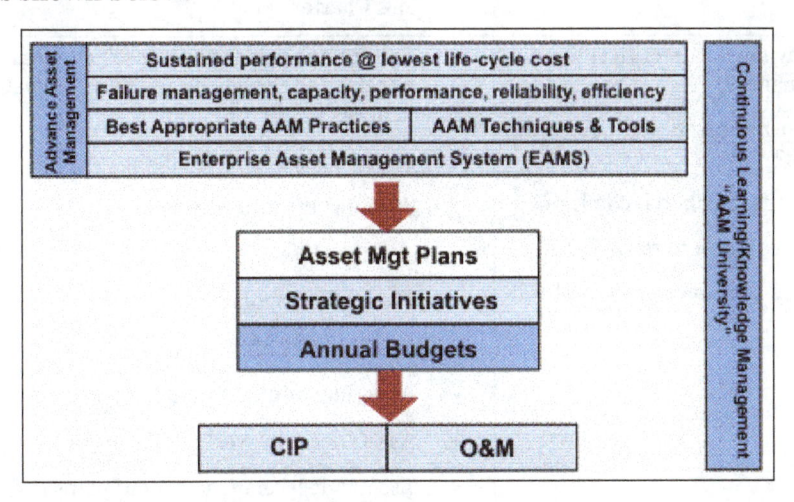

[Framework diagram: Advance Asset Management → Sustained performance @ lowest life-cycle cost; Failure management, capacity, performance, reliability, efficiency; Best Appropriate AAM Practices | AAM Techniques & Tools; Enterprise Asset Management System (EAMS) → Asset Mgt Plans / Strategic Initiatives / Annual Budgets → CIP | O&M. Right side: Continuous Learning/Knowledge Management "AAM University"]

"Five Core Management Questions" View

Successful management can be said to start with asking the right questions. Only by starting with the right questions can we efficiently find good answers.

Asset management's "tool bag" is comprised of literally hundreds of techniques.

This view poses five core questions that all managers of assets should be constantly confronting with their management teams. The questions help impose order on the extensive "tool bag" of techniques, assisting the manager to select the relevant processes and practices that help manage the assets.

The five core questions and their associated techniques are shown below:

Core Questions	Associated Technique / Output
1. What is the current state of my assets? • What do I own? • Where is it? • What condition is it in? • What is its remaining useful life? • What is its economic value?	• Asset registry/inventory. • Data standards / asset hierarchy. • System maps. • Delphi approach to locating other sources of data. • Process diagrams. • "Handover" procedures. • Condition analysis. • Condition rating. • Valuation techniques. • Optimized renewal / replacement cost tables.

2. What is my required sustained Level of Service? • What is the demand for my services from my stakeholders? • What do regulators require? • What is my actual performance?	• Customer demand analysis. • Regulatory requirements analysis. • Level of service statements; LOS "roll-up" hierarchy. • "Balanced scorecard". • Asset functionality statements. • AM Charter.
3. Which of my assets are critical for sustained performance? • How do my assets fail? How can they fail? • What is the likelihood of failure? • What does it cost to repair? • What are the consequences of failure?	• Failure analysis ("root cause" analysis; failure mode, effects and criticality analysis; reliability centered analysis). • Risk / consequence analysis. • Asset list by criticality code. • Failure codes. • Probability of failure. • Business risk exposure. • Asset functionality statements. • Asset "decay curves". • Asset unit-level management plans and guidelines. • Asset knowledge.
4. What are my best minimum lifecycle cost CIP and O&M strategies? • What alternative management options are there? • Which are most feasible for my organization?	• Optimized renewal decision making. • Life-cycle costing. • CIP development and validation. • Condition-based monitoring plans and deployment. • Failure response plans. • Capital "cost compression" strategies. • Operating "cost compression" strategies.
5. Given the above, what is my best long-term funding strategy?	• Over-arching financial impact analysis. • Optimized financial strategy. • Total Asset Management Plan. • Telling the story with confidence.

"Core Processes and Practices" View

Finally, asset management can be viewed as a set of systematic steps that lead to specific deliverables, the most fundamental deliverable being the Total Asset Management Plan.

Certain "best practice" processes and techniques relate directly to the execution of each of these steps.

To successfully execute the steps, an organization must master the basics of the associated practices and processes.

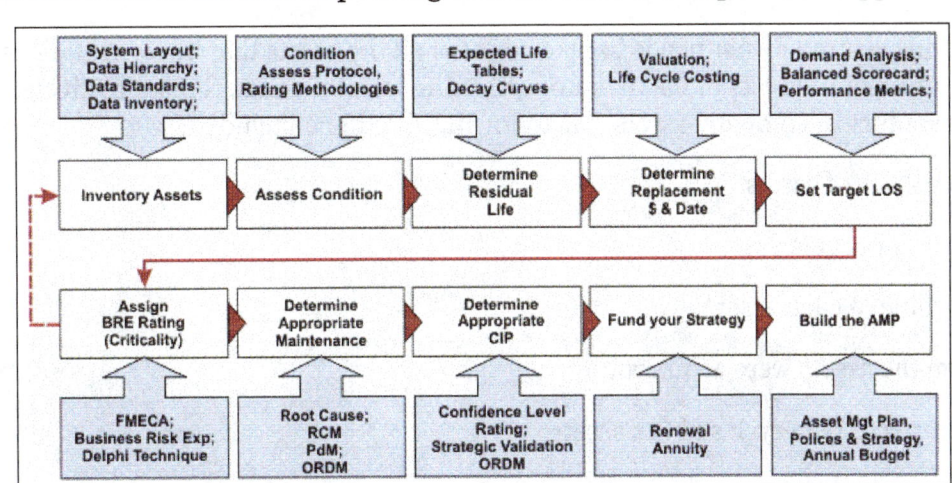

The graphic below shows the core steps along with the basic techniques that support them.

The Importance of Asset Management

There are several reasons why businesses should be concerned about asset management, including:

Enables a Firm to Keep Tabs on all of its Assets

The process makes it easy for organizations to keep track of their assets, whether liquid or fixed. Firm owners will know where the assets are located, how they are being put to use, and whether there are changes made to them. Consequently, the recovery of assets can be done more efficiently, hence, leading to higher returns.

Helps Guarantee the Accuracy of Amortization Rates

Since assets are checked on a regular basis, the process of asset managment ensures that the financial statements associated with them are kept updated.

Helps Identify and Manage Risks

Asset management encompasses the identification and management of risks that arise from the utilization and ownership of certain assets. It means that a firm will always be prepared to counter any risk that comes its way.

Removes Ghost Assets in the Company's Inventory

Instances exist where lost, damaged, or stolen assets are still recorded on the books. With a strategic asset management plan, the firm's owners will be aware of the assets that have been lost and, thus, not keep recording them in the books.

Developing a Strategic Asset Management Plan

Asset ownership is part of any public or private enterprise. To manage the assets effectively, a firm owner needs to develop a strategic plan.

Complete an Asset Inventory

Before anything else, an owner needs to take count of all the assets that he owns. If he is not aware of the exact number of assets in his inventory, then he won't manage them effectively. When preparing an inventory of company assets, the following should be included:

- Total count of assets.
- Where the assets are.
- The value of each asset.
- When the assets were acquired.
- The expected life cycles of the assets.

Compute Life-cycle Costs

If a business owner wants his asset management plan to be precise, then he should calculate the entire life-cycle costs of each asset. Many company owners make the mistake of calculating only the initial purchase costs.

During the asset's life cycle, additional costs are likely to come up such as maintenance expenses, condition and performance modeling, as well as disposal costs.

Set Levels of Service

After computing the life-cycle costs, the next step is to set levels of service. Put simply, it means outlining the overall quality, capacity, and role of the different services that the assets provide. In doing so, a firm's owner can then determine the operating, maintenance, and renewal activities needed to keep the assets in good condition.

Exercise Long-term Financial Planning

Ideally, the asset management process that a firm owner adapts should easily translate into long-term financial plans. With a good financial plan in place, the owner can then assess which objectives are feasible, and which ones need to be prioritized.

Benefits of Asset Management

There are many benefits of adopting an asset management strategy, such as:

Improving Acquisition and Use

By keeping tabs on a company's assets throughout their life cycle, a firm owner can improve their technique of acquiring and using the assets. A good case in point is Cisco Systems, which was able to reduce costs by executing PC asset management. When implementing such a strategy, the company discovered wasteful purchasing practices, which it solved by developing a better strategy for buying the equipment needed by workers.

Improving Compliance

Government agencies, non-profit organizations, and companies are required to provide comprehensive reports on how they acquire, utilize, and dispose of assets. To ease the reporting process, a majority of them record their asset information in a central database. In such a way, when they need to compile the reports at the end of their financial year, they can easily access all the information they need.

Current Assets

CHAPTER 2

Current assets are referred to the assets of a company that are expected to be conveniently sold and utilized through the standard business operations. The cash value of these assets is converted in one year period. This chapter closely examines the key concepts of current assets to provide an extensive understanding of the subject.

Current assets represent all the assets of a company that are expected to be conveniently sold, consumed, utilized or exhausted through the standard business operations, which can lead to their conversion to a cash value over the next one year period. Since current assets is a standard item appearing in the balance sheet, the time horizon represents one year from the date shown in the heading of the company's balance sheet.

Current assets include cash, cash equivalents, accounts receivable, stock inventory, marketable securities, pre-paid liabilities, and other liquid assets. In a few jurisdictions, the term is also known as current accounts.

Current assets contrast with long-term assets, which represent the assets that cannot be feasibly turned into cash in the space of a year. They generally include land, facilities, equipment, copyrights, and other illiquid investments.

Current assets are important to businesses because they can be used to fund day-to-day business operations and to pay for ongoing operating expenses. Since the term is reported as a dollar value of all the assets and resources that can be easily converted to cash in a short period of time, it also represents a company's liquid assets.

However, care should be taken to include only the qualifying assets that are capable of being liquidated at the fair price over the next one year period. For instance, there is a high chance that a lot of commonly used fast-moving consumer goods (FMCG) goods produced by a company can be easily sold over the next one year period, which qualifies inventory to be included in the current assets, but it may be difficult to sell land or heavy machinery, which are excluded from the current assets, easily.

Depending on the nature of the business and the products it markets, current assets can range from barrels of crude oil, fabricated goods, work in progress inventory, raw material, or foreign currency.

Example of Current Assets

For example, leading retailer Walmart Inc.'s (WMT) Total Current Assets for the fiscal year ending

January 2018 is the total of the summation of cash ($6.76 billion), total accounts receivable ($5.61 billion), inventory ($43.78 billion), and other current assets ($3.51 billion), which amount to $59.66 billion.

Similarly, Microsoft Corp. (MSFT) had cash and short-term investments ($133.77 billion), total accounts receivable ($26.48 billion), total inventory ($2.66 billion), and other current Assets ($6.75 billion) for the fiscal year ending June 2018. Thus, the technology leader's Total Current Assets were $169.66 billion.

Uses of Current Assets

The total current assets figure is of prime importance to the company management with regards to the daily operations of a business. As payments towards bills and loans become due at a regular frequency, such as at the end of each month, the management must be able to arrange for the necessary cash in time to pay its obligations. The dollar value represented by the total current assets figure provides a general insight into the company's cash and liquidity position and allows the management to remain prepared for the necessary arrangements to continue business operations.

Additionally, creditors and investors keep a close eye on the current assets of a business to assess the value and risk involved in its operations. Many use a variety of liquidity ratios, which represent a class of financial metrics used to determine a debtor's ability to pay off current debt obligations without raising external capital. Such commonly used ratios include current assets, or its components, as a key ingredient in their calculations.

CASH AND CASH EQUIVALENTS

Cash and cash equivalents refers to the line item on the balance sheet that reports the value of a company's assets that are cash or can be converted into cash immediately. Cash equivalents include bank accounts and marketable securities, which are debt securities with maturities of less than 90 days. However, oftentimes cash equivalents do not include equity or stock holdings because they can fluctuate in value.

Examples of cash equivalents include commercial paper, Treasury bills, and short-term government bonds with a maturity date of three months or less. Marketable securities and money market holdings are considered cash equivalents because they are liquid and not subject to material fluctuations in value.

Cash and cash equivalents are a group of assets owned by a company. For simplicity, the total value of cash on hand includes items with a similar nature to cash. If a company has cash or cash equivalents, the aggregate of these assets is always shown on the top line of the balance sheet. This is because cash and cash equivalents are current assets, meaning they're the most liquid of short-term assets.

Types of Cash and Cash Equivalents

Cash and cash equivalents help companies with their working capital needs since these liquid assets are used to pay off current liabilities, which are short-term debts and bills.

Cash

Cash is money in the form of currency, which includes all bills, coins, and currency notes. A demand deposit is a type of account from which funds may be withdrawn at any time without having to notify the institution. Examples of demand deposit accounts include checking accounts and savings accounts. All demand account balances as of the date of the financial statements are included in cash totals.

Foreign Currency

Companies holding more than one currency can experience currency exchange risk. Currency from foreign countries must be translated to the reporting currency for financial reporting purposes. The conversion should provide results comparable to those that would have occurred if the business had completed operations using only one currency. Translation losses from the devaluation of foreign currency are not reported with cash and cash equivalents. These losses are reported in the financial reporting account called "accumulated other comprehensive income."

Cash Equivalent

Cash equivalents are investments that can readily be converted into cash. The investment must be short term, usually with a maximum investment duration of three months or less. If an investment matures in more than three months, it should be classified in the account named "other investments." Cash equivalents should be highly liquid and easily sold on the market. The buyers of these investments should be easily accessible.

The dollar amounts of cash equivalents must be known. Therefore, all cash equivalents must have a known market price and should not be subject to price fluctuations. The value of the cash equivalents must not be expected to change significantly before redemption or maturity.

Certificates of deposit may be considered a cash equivalent depending on the maturity date. Preferred shares of equity may be considered a cash equivalent if they are purchased shortly before the redemption date and not expected to experience material fluctuation in value.

Cash and Cash Equivalents do not Include

There are some exceptions to short-term assets and current assets being classified as cash and cash equivalents.

Credit Collateral

Exceptions can exist for short-term debt instruments such as Treasury-bills if they're being used as collateral for an outstanding loan or line of credit. Restricted T-bills must be reported separately. In other words, there can be no restrictions on converting any of the securities listed as cash and cash equivalents.

Inventory

Inventory that a company has in stock is not considered a cash equivalent because it might not be readily converted to cash. Also, the value of inventory is not guaranteed, meaning there's no certainty in the amount that'll be received for liquidating the inventory.

Importance of Cash and Cash Equivalents

Liquidity Source

Cash equivalents are held for the purpose of meeting short-term cash commitments rather than for investment or other purposes and are an important source of liquidity. Thus companies want a cash cushion to weather unexpected situations such as a shortfall in revenue, repair or replacement of machinery or other unforeseen circumstances not in the budget.

Liquidity ratio calculations are important to determine the speed with which a company can pay off its short-term debt. Various liquidity ratio includes cash ratio, current ratio quick ratio.

- Cash ratio: (Cash and equivalents + Marketable securities) ÷ Current liabilities.
- Current ratio: Current assets ÷ Current liabilities.
- Quick ratio: (Current asset − inventory) ÷ Current liabilities.

Let us say that if there is a company XYZ with Current ratio: 2.3x, Quick ratio: 1.1x and Cash ratio: 0.6x. Can you comment on the liquidity of the company?

Interpretation: Of the three ratios, cash ratio is the most conservative as it excludes receivables and inventory given that these are not as liquid as a cash. In the example above, the quick ratio of 0.6x means that the company only has $0.6 of liquid assets to pay for every one dollar of current liability.

Speculative Acquisition Strategy

Another good reason for its pile-up is for near-term acquisition. As an example, consider cash balance in 2014 balance sheet of Apple Inc.

- Cash = $13.844 billion.
- Total Assets = $231.839 billions.
- Cash as % of Total Assets = 13.844 / 231.839 ~ 6%.
- Total Sales in 2014 = $182.795.
- Cash as % of Total Sales = 13.844 / 182.795 ~ 7.5%.

Interpretation: Investment of $13.844 bn (cash) + $11.233 bn (short-term investments) + $130.162 bn (long-term investments) totals $155.2 bn. Combination of all these indicates that Apple might be looking for some acquisition in the near term.

View: Annual Date | Quarterly Data			All numbers in thaousands
Period Ending	27-Sep-2014	28-Sep-2014	29-Sep-2014
Assets			
Current Assests			
Cash and Cash Equivalents	13844000	14259000	10746000
Short Term Investments	11233000	26287000	18383000
Net Receivables	31537000	24094000	21275000
Inventory	2111000	1764000	791000
Other Current Assets	9806000	6882000	6458000
Total Current Assets	68531000	73286000	57653000
Long Term Investments	130162000	106215000	92122000
Property Plant And Equipment	20624000	16597000	15452000
Goodwill	4616000	1577000	1135000
Intangible Assets	4142000	4179000	4224000
Accumulated Amortization	-	-	-
Other Assets	3764000	514600	5478000
Deferred Long Term Asset Charges	-	-	-
Total Assets	231839000	207000000	176064000

STOCK CONTROL AND INVENTORY

Stock control, otherwise known as inventory control, is used to show how much stock you have at any one time, and how you keep track of it.

It applies to every item you use to produce a product or service, from raw materials to finished goods. It covers stock at every stage of the production process, from purchase and delivery to using and re-ordering the stock.

Efficient stock control allows you to have the right amount of stock in the right place at the right time. It ensures that capital is not tied up unnecessarily, and protects production if problems arise with the supply chain.

Types of Stock

Everything you use to make your products, provide your services and to run your business is part of your stock.

There are four main types of stock:

- Raw materials and components - ready to use in production.
- Work in progress - stocks of unfinished goods in production.
- Finished goods ready for sale.
- Consumables - for example, fuel and stationery.

The type of stock can influence how much you should keep.

Stock Value

You can categorise stock further, according to its value. For example, you could put items into low, medium and high value categories. If your stock levels are limited by capital, this will help you to plan expenditure on new and replacement stock.

You may choose to concentrate resources on the areas of greatest value.

However, low-cost items can be crucial to your production process and should not be overlooked.

How much Stock should you Keep?

Deciding how much stock to keep depends on the size and nature of your business, and the type of stock involved. If you are short of space, you may be able to buy stock in bulk and then pay a fee to your supplier to store it, calling it off as and when needed.

Keeping little or no stock and negotiating with suppliers to deliver stock as you need it.

Advantages	Disadvantages
Efficient and flexible - you only have what you need, when you need it.	Meeting stock needs can become complicated and expensive.
Lower storage costs.	You might run out of stock if there's a hitch in the system.
You can keep up to date and develop new products without wasting stock.	You are dependent on the efficiency of your suppliers.

This might suit your business if it's in a fast-moving environment where products develop rapidly, the stock is expensive to buy and store, the items are perishable or replenishing stock is quick and easy.

Keeping Lots of Stock

Advantages	Disadvantages
Easy to manage.	Higher storage and insurance costs.
Low management costs.	Certain goods might perish.
You never run out.	Stock may become obsolete before it is used.
Buying in bulk may be cheaper.	Your capital is tied up.

This might suit your business if sales are difficult to predict (and it is hard to pin down how much stock you need and when), you can store plenty of stock cheaply, the components or materials you buy are unlikely to go through rapid developments or they take a long time to re-order.

There are four main types of stock:

Raw Materials and Components

Ask yourself some key questions to help decide how much stock you should keep:
- How reliable is the supply and are alternative sources available?

- Are the components produced or delivered in batches?
- Can you predict demand?
- Is the price steady?
- Are there discounts if you buy in bulk?

Work in Progress - Stocks of Unfinished Goods

Keeping stocks of unfinished goods can be a useful way to protect production if there are problems down the line with other supplies.

Finished Goods Ready for Sale

You might keep stocks of finished goods when:

- Demand is certain.
- Goods are produced in batches.
- You are completing a large order.

Consumables

For example, fuel and stationery. How much stock you keep will depend on factors such as:

- Reliability of supply.
- Expectations of price rises.
- How steady demand is.
- Discounts for buying in bulk.

Stock Control Methods

There are several methods for controlling stock, all designed to provide an efficient system for deciding what, when and how much to order.

You may opt for one method or a mixture of two or more if you have various types of stock:

- Minimum stock level - you identify a minimum stock level, and re-order when stock reaches that level. This is known as the Re-order Level.
- Stock review - you have regular reviews of stock. At every review you place an order to return stocks to a predetermined level.

Just In Time (JIT) - this aims to reduce costs by cutting stock to a minimum. Items are delivered when they are needed and used immediately. There is a risk of running out of stock, so you need to be confident that your suppliers can deliver on demand.

These methods can be used alongside other processes to refine the stock control system. For example:

- Re-order lead time - Allows for the time between placing an order and receiving it.
- Economic Order Quantity (EOQ) - A standard formula used to arrive at a balance between holding too much or too little stock. It's quite a complex calculation, so you may find it easier to use stock control software.
- Batch control - Managing the production of goods in batches. You need to make sure that you have the right number of components to cover your needs until the next batch.

If your needs are predictable, you may order a fixed quantity of stock every time you place an order, or order at a fixed interval - say every week or month. In effect, you're placing a standing order, so you need to keep the quantities and prices under review.

First in, first out - a system to ensure that perishable stock is used efficiently so that it doesn't deteriorate. Stock is identified by date received and moves on through each stage of production in strict order.

Stock Control Systems - Keeping Track Manually

Stocktaking involves making an inventory, or list, of stock, and noting its location and value. It's often an annual exercise - a kind of audit to work out the value of the stock as part of the accounting process.

Codes, including barcodes, can make the whole process much easier but it can still be quite time-consuming. Checking stock more frequently - a rolling inventory - avoids a massive annual exercise, but demands constant attention throughout the year. Radio Frequency Identification (RFID) tagging using handheld readers can offer a simple and efficient way to maintain a continuous check on inventory.

Any stock control system must enable you to:

- Track stock levels.
- Make orders.
- Issue stock.

The simplest manual system is the stock book, which suits small businesses with few stock items. It enables you to keep a log of stock received and stock issued.

It can be used alongside a simple re-order system. For example, the two-bin system works by having two containers of stock items. When one is empty, it's time to start using the second bin and order more stock to fill up the empty one.

Stock cards are used for more complex systems. Each type of stock has an associated card, with information such as:

- Description.
- Value.

- Location.
- Re-order levels, quantities and lead times (if this method is used).
- Supplier details.
- Information about past stock history.

More sophisticated manual systems incorporate coding to classify items. Codes might indicate the value of the stock, its location and which batch it is from, which is useful for quality control.

Stock Control Systems - Keeping Track using Computer Software

Computerised stock control systems run on similar principles to manual ones, but are more flexible and information is easier to retrieve. You can quickly get a stock valuation or find out how well a particular item of stock is moving.

A computerised system is a good option for businesses dealing with many different types of stock. Other useful features include:

- Stock and pricing data integrating with accounting and invoicing systems. All the systems draw on the same set of data, so you only have to input the data once. Sales Order Processing and Purchase Order Processing can be integrated in the system so that stock balances and statistics are automatically updated as orders are processed.
- Automatic stock monitoring, triggering orders when the re-order level is reached.
- Automatic batch control if you produce goods in batches.
- Identifying the cheapest and fastest suppliers.
- Bar coding systems which speed up processing and recording. The software will print and read bar codes from your computer.
- Radio Frequency Identification (RFID) which enables individual products or components to be tracked throughout the supply chain.

The system will only be as good as the data put into it. Run a thorough inventory before it goes "live" to ensure accurate figures. It's a good idea to run the previous system alongside the new one for a while, giving you a back-up and enabling you to check the new system and sort out any problems.

Choose a System

There are many software systems available. Talk to others in your line of business about the software they use, or contact your trade association for advice.

Make a checklist of your requirements. For example, your needs might include:

- Multiple prices for items.
- Prices in different currencies.

- Automatic updating, selecting groups of items to update, single-item updating.
- Using more than one warehouse.
- Ability to adapt to your changing needs.
- Quality control and batch tracking.
- Integration with other packages.
- Multiple users at the same time.

Avoid choosing software that's too complicated for your needs as it will be a waste of time and money.

Using RFID for Inventory Control, Stock Security and Quality Management

Radio Frequency Identification (RFID) allows a business to identify individual products and components, and to track them throughout the supply chain from production to point-of-sale.

An RFID tag is a tiny microchip, plus a small aerial, which can contain a range of digital information about the particular item. Tags are encapsulated in plastic, paper or similar material, and fixed to the product or its packaging, to a pallet or container, or even to a van or delivery truck.

The tag is interrogated by an RFID reader which transmits and receives radio signals to and from the tag. Readers can range in size from a hand-held device to a "portal" through which several tagged devices can be passed at once, e.g. on a pallet. The information that the reader collects is collated and processed using special computer software. Readers can be placed at different positions within a factory or warehouse to show when goods are moved, providing continuous inventory control.

Using RFID tagging for stock control offers several advantages over other methods such as barcodes:

- Tags can be read remotely, often at a distance of several metres.
- Several tags can be read at once, enabling an entire pallet-load of products to be checked simultaneously.
- Tags can be given unique identification codes, so that individual products can be tracked.
- Certain types of tag can be overwritten, enabling information about items to be updated, e.g. when they are moved from one part of a factory to another.

RFID tagging can be used:

- To prevent over-stocking or under-stocking a product or component.
- For stock security, by positioning tag-readers at points of high risk, such as exits, and causing them to trigger alarms.
- For quality control, particularly if you make or stock items with a limited shelf life.

The costs associated with RFID tagging have fallen over recent years, and continue to do so, to bring the process within the reach of more and more businesses. The benefits of more efficient stock control and improved security make it particularly attractive to retailers, wholesalers or distributors who stock a wide range of items, and to manufacturers who produce volume runs of products for different customers.

Stock Security

Keeping stock secure depends on knowing what you have, where it is located and how much it is worth - so good records are essential. Stock that is portable, does not feature the business' logo, or is easy to sell on, is at particular risk.

Thieves and Shoplifters

A thief coming in from outside is an obvious threat. Check the security around your premises to keep the risk to a minimum. In a store, thieves may steal in groups - some providing a distraction while others take goods. Teach your staff to be alert and to recognise behaviour like this. Set up a clear policy and make sure staff are trained in dealing with thieves.

Offering to help a customer if you are suspicious will often prevent a theft. Avoid using confrontational words like "steal" if you do have to approach a suspected thief, and avoid getting into a dangerous situation.

Protect your Stock

- Identify and mark expensive portable equipment (such as computers). If possible, fit valuable stock with security tags - such as Radio Frequency Identification tags - which will sound an alarm if they are moved.

- Don't leave equipment hanging around after delivery. Put it away in a secure place, record it and clear up packaging. It is a good idea to dispose of packaging securely - leaving boxes in view could be an advertisement to thieves.

- Take regular inventories.

- Put CCTV in parking lots and other key locations.

Theft by Staff

Theft by employees can sometimes be a problem. To prevent this:

- Train staff about your security systems and your disciplinary policies and procedures. Training about the cost of stock theft will help, as many people aren't aware of the implications for company turnover and job security.

- Set up procedures to prevent theft. Staff with financial responsibilities should not be in charge of stock records.

- Restrict access to warehouses, stockrooms and stationery cupboards.

- Regularly change staff controlling stock to avoid collusion or bad practice.

Control the Quality of your Stock

Quality control is a vital aspect of stock control - especially as it may affect the safety of customers or the quality of the finished product.

Efficient stock control should incorporate stock tracking and batch tracking. This means being able to trace a particular item backwards or forwards from source to finished product, and identifying the other items in the batch.

Goods should be checked systematically for quality, faults identified and the affected batch weeded out. This will allow you to raise any problems with your supplier and at the same time demonstrate the safety and quality of your product.

With a good computerised stock control system, this kind of tracking is relatively straightforward. Manual stock control methods can also use codes to systematise tracking and make it easier to trace particular batches.

Radio Frequency Identification (RFID) can be used to store information about a product or component's manufacturing date, to ensure that it is sold or processed in time. The system can also be used to trace faulty products quickly and efficiently.

Stock Control Administration

There are many administrative tasks associated with stock control. Depending on the size and complexity of your business, they may be done as part of an administrator's duties, or by a dedicated stock controller.

For security reasons, it's good practice to have different staff responsible for finance and stock.

Typical paperwork to be processed includes:
- Delivery and supplier notes for incoming goods.
- Purchase orders, receipts and credit notes.
- Returns notes.
- Requisitions and issue notes for outgoing goods.

Stock can tie up a large slice of your business capital, so accurate information about stock levels and values is essential for your company's accounting.

Figures should be checked systematically, either through a regular audit of stock -stocktaking - or an ongoing program of checking stock - rolling inventory.

If the figures don't add up, you need to investigate as there could be stock security problems or a failure in the system.

Health and Safety

Health and safety aspects of stock control are related to the nature of the stock itself. Issues such as where and how items are stored, how they are moved and who moves them might be significant - depending on what they are.

You might have hazardous materials on your premises, goods that deteriorate with time or items that are very heavy or awkward to move.

ACCOUNTS RECEIVABLE

Accounts receivable (AR) is the balance of money due to a firm for goods or services delivered or used but not yet paid for by customers. Accounts receivables are listed on the balance sheet as a current asset. AR is any amount of money owed by customers for purchases made on credit.

Accounts receivable refers to the outstanding invoices a company has or the money clients owe the company. The phrase refers to accounts a business has the right to receive because it has delivered a product or service. Accounts receivable, or receivables represent a line of credit extended by a company and normally have terms that require payments due within a relatively short time period. It typically ranges from a few days to a fiscal or calendar year.

Companies record accounts receivable as assets on their balance sheets since there is a legal obligation for the customer to pay the debt. Furthermore, accounts receivable is current assets, meaning the account balance is due from the debtor in one year or less. If a company has receivables, this means it has made a sale on credit but has yet to collect the money from the purchaser. Essentially, the company has accepted a short-term IOU from its client.

Accounts Receivables vs. Accounts Payable

When a company owes debts to its suppliers or other parties, these are accounts payable. Accounts payable are the opposite of accounts receivable. To illustrate, imagine Company A cleans Company B's carpets and sends a bill for the services. Company B owes them money, so it records the invoice in its accounts payable column. Company A is waiting to receive the money, so it records the bill in its accounts receivable column.

Benefits of Accounts Receivable

Accounts receivable is an important aspect of a businesses' fundamental analysis. Accounts receivable is a current asset so it measures a company's liquidity or ability to cover short-term obligations without additional cash flows.

Fundamental analysts often evaluate accounts receivable in the context of turnover, also known as accounts receivable turnover ratio, which measures the number of times a company has collected on its accounts receivable balance during an accounting period. Further analysis would include days sales outstanding analysis, which measures the average collection period for a firm's receivables balance over a specified period.

Example of Accounts Receivable

An example of accounts receivable includes an electric company that bills its clients after the clients received the electricity. The electric company records an account receivable for unpaid invoices as it waits for its customers to pay their bills.

Most companies operate by allowing a portion of their sales to be on credit. Sometimes, businesses offer this credit to frequent or special customers that receive periodic invoices. The practice allows customers to avoid the hassle of physically making payments as each transaction occurs. In other cases, businesses routinely offer all of their clients the ability to pay after receiving the service.

Importance of Accounts Receivable

The businesses usually have invested money in selling a product or delivering a service. After selling the goods, the inventories reduces and in turn businesses need an asset to balance the financial statements. Either that assets are cash-in-hand or receivables in case of credit sales and that's why accounts receivable appear in the assets side of the balance sheet.

As accounts receivables form a major part of the organization's asset, it leads to the generation of cash in-flow in the books of the organization. The idea behind providing a credit facility to the customers is to facilitate and ease the process of the transaction and establish a strong credit relation between the parties involved. It may lead to better deals or increase the chances of improving the working capital management.

Recording Accounts Receivable in the Financial Statements

Usually, the businesses expect to receive money in the future, so it is to be added to the assets in the financial statement of the business. The accurate record keeping of this money that is receivable (accounts receivable) in the books of accounts are required to avoid any default in the payment due.

Few pointers connected to recording accounts receivable are as follows:

Establishing the Practice of Credit Transactions

The business may establish a practice of providing a credit policy to its buyers. This credit can be extended for a specified time period and any default in this payment usually attracts penalty. This practice of credit facility requires two parties to come to an agreement on the terms and conditions for such credit transactions. The provider of this facility should also verify the paying ability of the customer before agreeing to any terms and conditions.to prevent loss of cash inflow.

Generating Invoices for the Customer

The businesses are required to generate invoices of the sales made or services delivered. The invoice should have details of the cost of goods and services sold to the customers. This generating of invoice ensures the recording of the credit transaction clearly in the accounts of the business. Further, a copy of the invoice is given to the customer to make the payment as per the agreed terms.

Tracking the Payments Received and the Payment that is due to be Received

An accountant is required to track the payments received or due from the customers. The details of the method of payment and date of receiving payment have to be recorded in the customer's ledger account. This ensures correctness of accounting of the credit amount. The businesses shall also generate timely reminders for dues pending to the customers.

Accounting for the Accounts Receivable

The accountant or the person responsible for taking due care of the accounts receivables must record all the due dates of the payments to be received. The timely and prompt recording of the accounts receivable leads to receiving the payments on time from the customers. Once the account receivable is recorded and payment is received, the account for the said party can be settled for good.

Accounts Receivable Management

Accounts receivable management is the process of ensuring that customers pay their dues on time. It helps the businesses to prevent themselves from running out of working capital at any point of time. It also prevents overdue payment or non-payment of the pending amounts of the customers. It builds the businesses financial and liquidity position. A good receivable management contributes to the profitability by reducing the risk of any bad debts. Management is not only about reminding the customers and collecting the money on time. It also involves identifying the reasons for such delays and finding a solution to those issues.

Accounts Receivable Management Process

An Account receivable management process involves the following:

- Credit rating i.e the paying ability of the customers shall be reviewed before agreeing to any terms and conditions.
- Continuously monitoring any risk of non-payment or delay in receiving the payments.
- Customer relations should be maintained and thus to reduce the bad debts.
- Addressing the complaints of the customers.
- After receiving the payments, the balances in the particular account receivable should be reduced.
- Preventing any bad debts of the receivables outstanding during a particular period.

MARKETABLE SECURITIES

Securities are a broad category of financial products, defined as any form of non-tangible asset that takes its value from the work of someone else.

A marketable security is a form of security that can be sold or otherwise converted to cash within less than one year. These products are considered relatively liquid compared to products that are locked into long-term positions.

To be considered marketable, a security must have a face value or near-face value transaction within the one-year period. There must also be no restriction on liquidating or selling this product within less than a year.

Virtually any product short of a junk bond will have some short-term sale price. If you purchase a 20-year government bond, you could absolutely sell this product less than a year later. However, you wouldn't get its value at maturity. You would get a sale price that balances the high security of this product against the time value of having that money locked up for 20 years.

This is a salable security, but not a marketable security.

Importance of Marketable Securities

Marketable securities are a measure of how much capital a business can access for any upcoming spending.

When a business calculates its assets and total net worth it has two sections of the balance sheet: Current Assets and Non-current Assets. Anyone who has spent much time overseas might recognize this terminology, as outside of the U.S. most banks also use this language for personal banking. What we call a checking account, the cash intended for immediate access, most other countries call a "current account."

Along with cash holding, a company's current account will include all assets that it could convert into cash for face value within one year. This includes all marketable securities along with any significant property that the company anticipates liquidating in the near future.

A company's non-current account will measure all long term assets that the business either can't or won't sell in the coming year. This typically includes all securities with a longer maturity date as well as any major property that the company doesn't intend to sell right away.

Together this evaluation gives a sense of the company's total holdings and the company's near-term spending power.

It is a valuable figure for multiple forms of analysis. Executives at the company will use it to figure out how aggressively they should spend in the coming year, as well as to understand their flexibility to respond to short-term opportunities. Creditors will use marketable securities when deciding terms on which to extend a loan, as it tells them how easily a company can pay them back without having to devalue assets in a fire sale. Analysts and investors use marketable securities when performing liquidity analyses.

A company will also measure its marketable securities to figure out how many assets it can move from the current to the non-current side of its balance sheet. Over-investing in short term assets can be just as wasteful as under-investing. While a company needs to have enough cash or cash-equivalents to respond to upcoming business expenses, long-term assets typically have significantly higher rates of return. Keeping too much money in marketable securities is wasteful and will mean accepting a lower rate of return for unspent cash that could have been better used elsewhere.

Proper corporate governance, then, looks to find the balance.

Non-Current Marketable Securities

Finally, whether a company marks a product as a marketable security or not may depend on its intentions.

A company might buy a security that could typically be highly liquid but it will intend to keep that product for a longer term. In this case, because the company doesn't intend to sell the asset within the next year, it will list the asset as non-current and will not consider it a marketable security.

A common example of this is when companies purchase shares of another company's stock as part of an acquisition bid.

Shares of stock are highly liquid; you can sell them at any time. As a result, ordinarily a company would consider all of its stock holdings as marketable. However, when a company is trying to acquire a rival it will hold those shares long term and consider them non-marketable.

The same can be said of debt instruments. For example, a bank might extend a 20-year mortgage. How that bank classifies the mortgage will depend entirely on its intentions. Ordinarily this would not be considered a marketable security since it will not fully pay off within the next year. However, if the bank extended this mortgage with the intent to sell it as a securitized asset, it may list the mortgage under current assets and classify the note as marketable.

The mortgage wouldn't meet the standard definition of a marketable security, but the bank will nevertheless build that note's sale price into its business plan and liquidity calculations.

Types of Marketable Securities

There are numerous types of marketable securities, but stocks are the most common type of equity. Bonds and bills are the most common debt securities.

Stocks as Securities

Stock represents an equity investment because shareholders maintain partial ownership in the company in which they have invested. The company can use shareholder investment as equity capital to fund the company's operations and expansion.

In return, the shareholder receives voting rights and periodic dividends based on the company's profitability. The value of a company's stock can fluctuate wildly depending on the industry and the individual business in question, so investing in the stock market can be a risky move. However, many people make a very good living investing in equities.

Bonds as Securities

Bonds are the most common form of marketable debt security and are a useful source of capital to businesses that are looking to grow. A bond is a security issued by a company or government that allows it to borrow money from investors. Much like a bank loan, a bond guarantees a fixed rate of return, called the coupon rate, in exchange for the use of the invested funds.

The face value of the bond is its par value. Each issued bond has a specified par value, coupon rate, and maturity date. The maturity date is when the issuing entity must repay the full par value of the bond.

Because bonds are traded on the open market, they can be purchased for less than par. These bonds trade at a discount. Depending on current market conditions, bonds may also sell for more than par. When this happens, bonds are trading at a premium. Coupon payments are based on the par value of the bond rather than its market value or purchase price. So, an investor who purchases a bond at a discount still enjoys the same interest payments as an investor who buys the security at par value.

Interest payments on discounted bonds represent a higher return on investment than the stated coupon rate. Conversely, the return on investment for bonds purchased at a premium is lower than the coupon rate.

Preferred Shares

There is another type of marketable security that has some of the qualities of both equity and debt. Preferred shares have the benefit of fixed dividends that are paid before dividends to common stockholders, which makes them more like bonds. However, bondholders remain senior to preferred shareholders. In the event of financial difficulties, bonds may continue to receive interest payments while preferred share dividends remain unpaid.

Unlike a bond, the shareholder's initial investment is never repaid, making it a hybrid security. In addition to the fixed dividend, preferred shareholders are granted a higher claim on funds than their common counterparts if the company goes bankrupt.

In exchange, preferred shareholders give up the voting rights that ordinary shareholders enjoy. The guaranteed dividend and insolvency safety net make preferred shares an enticing investment for some people. Preferred shares are particularly appealing to those who find common stocks too risky but don't want to wait around for bonds to mature.

Exchange-Traded Funds (ETFs)

Exchange-traded funds (ETFs) allow investors to buy and sell collections of other assets, including stocks, bonds, and commodities. ETFs are marketable securities by definition because they are traded on public exchanges. The assets held by exchange-traded funds may themselves be marketable securities, such as stocks in the Dow Jones. However, ETFs may also hold assets that are not marketable securities, such as gold and other precious metals.

Other Marketable Securities

Marketable securities can also come in the form of money market instruments, derivatives, and indirect investments. Each of these types contains several different specific securities.

The most reliable liquid securities fall in the money market category. Most money market securities act as short-term bonds and are purchased in vast quantities by large financial entities. These include Treasury bills, banker's acceptances, purchase agreements, and commercial paper.

Many types of derivatives can be considered marketable, such as futures, options, and stock rights and warrants. Derivatives are investments directly dependent on the value of other securities. In the last quarter of the 20th century, derivatives trading began growing exponentially.

Indirect investments include hedge funds and unit trusts. These instruments represent ownership in investment companies. Most market participants have little or no exposure to these types of instruments, but they are common among accredited or institutional investors.

Features of Marketable Securities

The overriding characteristic of marketable securities is their liquidity. Liquidity is the ability to convert assets into cash and use them as an intermediary in other economic activities. The security is further made liquid by its relative supply and demand in the market. The volume of transactions also plays a vital part in liquidity. Because marketable securities can be sold quickly with price quotes available instantly, they typically have a lower rate of return than less liquid assets. However, they are usually perceived as lower risk as well.

From a liquidity standpoint, investments are marketable when they can be bought and sold quickly. If an investor or a business needs some cash in a pinch, it is much easier to enter the market and liquidate marketable securities. For example, common stock is much easier to sell than a nonnegotiable certificate of deposit (CD).

This introduces the element of intent as a characteristic of "marketability." And in fact, many financial experts and accounting courses claim intent as a differentiating feature between marketable securities and other investment securities. Under this classification, marketable securities must satisfy two conditions. The first is ready convertibility into cash. The second condition is that those who purchase marketable securities must intend to convert them when in need of cash. In other words, a note purchased with short-term goals in mind is much more marketable than an identical note bought with long-term goals in mind.

PREPAID EXPENSES

A prepaid expense is a type of asset on the balance sheet that results from a business making advanced payments for goods or services to be received in the future. Prepaid expenses are initially recorded as assets, but their value is expensed over time onto the income statement. Unlike conventional expenses, the business will receive something of value from the prepaid expense over the course of several accounting periods.

Companies make prepayments for goods or services such as leased office equipment or insurance coverage that provide continual benefits over time. Goods or services of this nature cannot be expensed immediately because the expense would not line up with the benefit incurred over time from using the asset.

According to generally accepted accounting principles (GAAP), expenses should be recorded in the same accounting period as the benefit generated from the related asset. For example, if a large Xerox machine is leased by a company for a period of twelve months, the company benefits from its use over the full time period. Recording an advanced payment made for the lease as an expense in the first month would not adequately match expenses with revenues generated from its use. Therefore, it should be recorded as a prepaid expense and allocated out to expense over the full twelve months.

Journal entries that recognize expenses related to previously recorded prepaids are called adjusting entries. They do not record new business transactions but simply adjust previously recorded transactions. Adjusting entries for prepaid expenses are necessary to ensure that expenses are recognized in the period in which they are incurred.

Due to the nature of certain goods and services, prepaid expenses will always exist. For example, insurance is a prepaid expense because the purpose of purchasing insurance is to buy proactive protection in case something unfortunate happens in the future. Clearly, no insurance company would sell insurance that covers an unfortunate event after the fact, so insurance expenses must be prepaid by businesses.

Prepaid Expenses Accounting

Prepayment Accounting

The basic accounting for a prepaid expense follows these steps:

- Upon the initial recordation of a supplier invoice in the accounting system, verify that the item meets the company's criteria for a prepaid expense (asset).
- If the item meets the company's criteria, charge it to the prepaid expenses account. If not, charge the invoiced amount to expense in the current period.
- Record the amount of the expenditure in the prepaid expenses reconciliation spreadsheet.
- At the end of the accounting period, establish the number of periods over which the item will be amortized, and enter this information in the reconciliation spreadsheet. This entry should include the straight-line amount of amortization that will be charged in each of the applicable periods.
- At the end of the accounting period, create an adjusting entry that amortizes the predetermined amount to the most relevant expense account.
- Once all amortizations have been completed, verify that the total in the spreadsheet matches the total balance in the prepaid expenses account. If not, reconcile the two and adjust as necessary.

A best practice is to not record smaller expenditures into the prepaid expenses account, since it takes too much effort to track them over time. Instead, charge these smaller amounts to expense as incurred. To extend this concept further, consider charging remaining balances to expense once they have been amortized down to a certain minimum level. Both of these actions should be governed by a formal accounting policy that states the threshold at which prepaid expenses are to be charged to expense.

Prepaid Expenses Example

A company pays $60,000 in advance for directors and officers liability insurance for the upcoming year. The journal entry is:

	Debit	Credit
Prepaid expenses	$ 60,000	
Cash		$ 60,000

At the end of each period, the company amortizes the prepaid expenses account with the following journal entry, which will charge the entire amount of the prepaid insurance to expense by the end of the year:

	Debit	Credit
Insurance expense	$ 5,000	
Prepaid expenses		$ 5,000

CURRENT RATIO

The current ratio is a liquidity ratio that measures whether a firm has enough resources to meet its short-term obligations. It compares a firm's current assets to its current liabilities, and is expressed as follows:

$$\text{Current ratio} = \frac{\text{Current Assets}}{\text{Current Liabilities}}$$

The current ratio is an indication of a firm's liquidity. Acceptable current ratios vary from industry to industry. In many cases, a creditor would consider a high current ratio to be better than a low current ratio, because a high current ratio indicates that the company is more likely to pay the creditor back. Large current ratios are not always a good sign for investors. If the company's current ratio is too high it may indicate that the company is not efficiently using its current assets or its short-term financing facilities.

If current liabilities exceed current assets the current ratio will be less than 1. A current ratio of less than 1 indicates that the company may have problems meeting its short-term obligations. Some types of businesses can operate with a current ratio of less than one, however. If inventory turns into cash much more rapidly than the accounts payable become due, then the firm's current ratio can comfortably remain less than one. Inventory is valued at the cost of acquiring it and the firm intends to sell the inventory for more than this cost. The sale will therefore generate substantially more cash than the value of inventory on the balance sheet. Low current ratios can also be justified for businesses that can collect cash from customers long before they need to pay their suppliers.

Limitations

- The ratio is only useful when two companies are compared within industry because inter industry business operations differ substantially.

- To determine liquidity, the current ratio is not as helpful as the quick ratio, because it includes all those assets that may not be easily liquidated, like prepaid expenses and inventory.

QUICK RATIO

In finance, the quick ratio, also known as the acid-test ratio is a type of liquidity ratio, which measures the ability of a company to use its *near cash* or quick assets to extinguish or retire its current liabilities immediately. It is defined as the ratio between quickly available or liquid assets and current liabilities. Quick assets are current assets that can presumably be quickly converted to cash at close to their book values.

A normal liquid ratio is considered to be 1:1. A company with a quick ratio of less than 1 cannot currently fully pay back its current liabilities.

The quick ratio is similar to the current ratio, but provides a more conservative assessment of the liquidity position of firms as it excludes inventory, which it does not consider as sufficiently liquid.

Formula

$$\text{Quick Ratio (Acid Test)} = \frac{\text{Liquid Assets}}{\text{Quick Liabilities}}$$

or specifically:

$$\text{Quick Ratio} = \frac{\text{Cash and Cash Equivalent} + \text{Marketable Securities} + \text{Accounts Receivable}}{\text{Current Liabilities}}$$

It can also be expressed as:

$$\text{Quick Ratio} = \frac{\text{Current assets} - \text{Inventory} - \text{Prepaid expenses}}{\text{Current Liabilities}}$$

Ratios are tests of viability for business entities but do not give a complete picture of the business' health. If a business has large amounts in accounts receivable which are due for payment after a long period (say 120 days), and essential business expenses and accounts payable due for immediate payment, the quick ratio may look healthy when the business is actually about to run out of cash. In contrast, if the business has negotiated fast payment or cash from customers, and long terms from suppliers, it may have a very low quick ratio and yet be very healthy.

More detailed analysis of all major payables and receivables in line with market sentiments and adjusting input data accordingly shall give more sensible outcomes which shall give actionable insights.

Generally, the acid test ratio should be 1:1 or higher; however, this varies widely by industry. In general, the higher the ratio, the greater the company's liquidity (i.e., the better able to meet current obligations using liquid assets).

CASH RATIO

Cash ratio is the ratio of very liquid current assets such as cash and short-term marketable securities of a company to its current liabilities.

Cash ratio is the most conservative liquidity ratio because it takes only the near-cash current assets and compare them with current liabilities. This ratio is most relevant for companies in crisis situations. Since cash and cash equivalents are readily available and short-term marketable securities can be easily converted to cash in very short time, cash ratio assesses a company's liquidity position in worst-case scenario, a scenario in which it is unable to generate any cash from receivables and inventories and must pay current liabilities out of very liquid assets.

Formula

Cash ratio is calculated using the following formula:

$$\text{Cash Ratio} = \frac{\text{Cash} + \text{Marketable Securities}}{\text{Current Liabilities}}$$

Cash includes cash in hand and cash at bank while marketable securities are very short-term investments which can be converted to cash quickly without any significant loss of value.

Current liabilities are those liabilities which are to be settled within 12 months or in one operating cycle.

Interpretation

A high cash ratio is preferred by creditors because it means that more liquid assets are available to pay current liabilities when they become due all at once. However, it is naive to expect companies to maintain a cash ratio of close to 1. It is because cash and short-term marketable securities generate very little return when compared with long-term investments and expansion projects. Hence, businesses tend to minimize their idle cash balance. This means that a normal value of cash ratio is well below 1.00.

Even cash ratio is not fail-safe in all situations. In financial crises, liquidity generally dries up which means that companies are not able to sell their short-term marketable securities without significant loss of value. It means that in distress situations, a smaller proportion of current liabilities can be effectively paid out of the liquid assets than otherwise projected by the cash ratio.

Analysis

The cash ratio shows how well a company can pay off its current liabilities with only cash and cash equivalents. This ratio shows cash and equivalents as a percentage of current liabilities.

A ratio of 1 means that the company has the same amount of cash and equivalents as it has current debt. In other words, in order to pay off its current debt, the company would have to use all of its cash and equivalents. A ratio above 1 means that all the current liabilities can be paid with cash and equivalents. A ratio below 1 means that the company needs more than just its cash reserves to pay off its current debt.

As with most liquidity ratios, a higher cash coverage ratio means that the company is more liquid and can more easily fund its debt. Creditors are particularly interested in this ratio because they want to make sure their loans will be repaid. Any ratio above 1 is considered to be a good liquidity measure.

Limitations of the Cash Ratio

The cash ratio is seldom used in financial reporting or by analysts in the fundamental analysis of a company. It is not realistic for a company to maintain excessive levels of cash and near-cash assets to cover current liabilities. It is often seen as poor asset utilization for a company to hold large amounts of cash on its balance sheet, as this money could be returned to shareholders or used elsewhere to generate higher returns. While providing an interesting liquidity perspective, the usefulness of this ratio is limited.

The cash ratio is more useful when it is compared with industry averages and competitor averages, or when looking at changes in the same company over time. A cash ratio lower than 1 does sometimes indicate that a company is at risk of having financial difficulty. However, a low cash ratio may also be an indicator of a company's specific strategy that calls for maintaining low cash reserves—because funds are being used for expansion, for example.

Certain industries tend to operate with higher current liabilities and lower cash reserves, so cash ratios across industries may not be indicative of trouble.

Examples

1. A company has following assets and liabilities at the year ended December 31, 20X9:

Cash	$ 34,390
Marketable Securities	12,000
Accounts Receivable	56,200
Prepaid Insurance	9,000
Total Current Liabilities	73,780

Calculate cash ratio from the above information.

Solution:

$$\text{Cash ratio} = \frac{34,390 + 12,000}{73,780} = \frac{46,390}{73,780} = 0.63$$

2. Calculate cash ratio from the following information.

Cash	$ 21,720
Treasury Bills	18,500
Accounts Receivable	35,930
Total Current Liabilities	82,960

Solution:

Since treasury bills are marketable securities thus we will calculate cash ratio as follows:

$$\text{Cash ratio} = \frac{21{,}720 + 18{,}500}{82{,}960} = \frac{40{,}220}{82{,}960} = 0.48$$

Cash ratio should be complemented by current ratio, quick ratio and cash conversion cycle to get a company's complete liquidity profile.

References

- Currentassets: investopedia.com, Retrieved 26 January, 2019
- Cash-equivalents: wallstreetmojo.com, Retrieved 05 March, 2019
- Stock-control-and-inventory: infoentrepreneurs.org, Retrieved 19 April, 2019
- Accounts-receivable-management: cleartax.in, Retrieved 25 May, 2019
- What-are-marketable-securities-14992523: thestreet.com, Retrieved 18 January, 2019
- What-are-some-common-examples-marketable-securities-033015: investopedia.com, Retrieved 05 August, 2019

Fixed Assets

CHAPTER 3

Fixed assets are defined as the assets which are purchased for long term use. The company or firm owns and uses it in its operations to generate revenue. Fixed assets can be categorized into tangible assets and intangible assets. This chapter has been carefully written to provide an easy understanding of the varied facets of fixed assets as well as their management.

A fixed asset is a long-term tangible piece of property or equipment that a firm owns and uses in its operations to generate income. Fixed assets are not expected to be consumed or converted into cash within a year. Fixed assets most commonly appear on the balance sheet as property, plant, and equipment (PP&E). They are also referred to as capital assets.

A company's balance sheet statement consists of its assets, liabilities, and shareholders' equity. Assets are divided into current assets and noncurrent assets, the difference for which lies in their useful lives. Current assets are typically liquid assets which will be converted into cash in less than a year. Noncurrent assets refer to assets and property owned by a business which are not easily converted to cash. The different categories of noncurrent assets include fixed assets, intangible assets, long-term investments, and deferred charges.

A fixed asset is bought for production or supply of goods or services, for rental to third parties, or for use in the organization. The term "fixed" translates to the fact that these assets will not be used up or sold within the accounting year. A fixed asset typically has a physical form and is reported on the balance sheet as property, plant, and equipment (PP&E).

When a company acquires or disposes of a fixed asset, this is recorded on the cash flow statement under the cash flow from investing activities. The purchase of fixed assets represents a cash outflow to the company, while a sale is a cash inflow. If the value of the asset falls below its net book value, the asset is subject to an impairment write-down. This means that its recorded value on the balance sheet is adjusted downward to reflect that its overvalued compared to the market value.

When a fixed asset has reached the end of its useful life, it is usually disposed of by selling it for a salvage value, which is the estimated value of the asset if it was broken down and sold in parts. In some cases, the asset may become obsolete and may no longer have a market for it, and will, therefore, be disposed of without receiving any payment in return. Either way, the fixed asset is written off the balance sheet as it is no longer in use by the company.

Fixed assets lose value as they age. Because they provide long-term income, these assets are expensed differently than other items. Tangible assets are subject to periodic depreciation, as intangible assets are subject to amortization. A certain amount of an asset's costs is expensed annually. The asset's value decreases along with its depreciation amount on the company's balance sheet. The corporation can then match the asset's cost with its long-term value.

How a business depreciates an asset can cause its book value—the asset value that appears on the balance sheet—to differ from the current market value at which the asset could sell. Land cannot be depreciated unless it contains natural resources, in which case depletion would be recorded.

Fixed Assets vs. Current Assets

Both current assets and fixed assets appear on the balance sheet, with current assets meant to be used or converted to cash in the short-term (less than one year) and fixed assets meant to be utilized for the longer-term (greater than one year). Current assets include cash and cash equivalents, accounts receivable, inventory, and prepaid expenses. Fixed assets are depreciated, while current assets are not.

Fixed Assets vs. Noncurrent Assets

Fixed assets are a noncurrent asset. Other noncurrent assets include long-term investments and intangibles. Intangible assets are fixed assets, meant to be used over the long-term, but they lack physical existence. Examples of intangible assets include goodwill, copyrights, trademarks, and intellectual property. Meanwhile, long-term investments can include bond investments that will not be sold or mature within a year.

Benefits of Fixed Assets

Information about a corporation's assets helps create accurate financial reporting, business valuations, and thorough financial analysis. Investors and creditors use these reports to determine a company's financial health and to decide whether to buy shares in or lend money to the business. Because a company may use a range of accepted methods for recording, depreciating, and disposing of its assets, analysts need to study the notes on the corporation's financial statements to find out how the numbers were determined.

Fixed assets are particularly important to capital-intensive industries, such as manufacturing, that require large investments in PP&E. When a business is reporting persistently negative net cash flows for the purchase of fixed assets, this could be a strong indicator that the firm is in growth or investment mode.

Examples of Fixed Assets

Fixed assets can include buildings, computer equipment, software, furniture, land, machinery, and vehicles. For example, if a company sells produce, the delivery trucks it owns and uses are fixed assets. If a business creates a company parking lot, the parking lot is a fixed asset. Note that a fixed asset does not necessarily have to be "fixed" in all sense of the word. Some of these types of assets can be moved from one location to another, such as furniture and computer equipment.

Example:

Company ABC is a construction company that plans to purchase a second building for $15 million. The building is a tangible asset and, if the company keeps the building for more than one year, it becomes a fixed asset. After closing the legal agreement with the buyer, company ABC will own the main building where it will run its core operations and a second building, which can be rented and earn the company an extra revenue. However, the value of the building, $15 million, will be reported as a fixed asset on the balance sheet.

Companies usually report their non-current assets as property, plant and equipment on the balance sheet. Yet, as assets lose value as time progresses, companies also report the depreciation and amortization expenses. Regardless of their physical form, the assets of a company must be accurately valued so that investors and financial analysts can properly assess the intrinsic value of the company. Regulatory bodies such as the Financial Accounting Standards Board (FASB) and the Securities and Exchange Commission (SEC) determine when and how companies should report their assets, including depreciation.

TANGIBLE ASSET

A tangible asset is a physical property that has value. Such an asset can be seen and touched by anyone. From a company's perspective, this type of asset is available for the use of a company and is not for sale to customers.

A tangible asset may also be known as a hard asset or real asset.

Tangible assets are classified based on their properties, such as reproducible or non-reproducible, depending on the nature of its use. In this case, buildings or machinery are reproducible assets because they can be used to produce specific products. On the other hand, non-reproducible assets are those that cannot be used for the direct production of any product and examples of such assets include land or a piece of art work.

From an accounting perspective, tangible assets receive special treatment. When a company uses these assets for more than one year, a process called depreciation is used to divide the expense of the asset across its useful lifespan. For example, if the value of an asset is $50,000 and its useful lifespan is 10 years, then the company can claim a depreciation of $5,000 for each year. This depreciation allows for certain accounting and tax benefits for the company.

Tangible assets are opposite to intangible assets which cannot be seen or felt. Examples of intangible assets include copyright, brand recognition, goodwill and patents. All companies have a combination of both tangible and intangible assets as part of their business assets. These items are not available for sale to its customers.

In the case of companies that engage in the sale of fixed items, such as land, these items are viewed as the product of the company and not its assets; therefore, they do not appear in a company's balance sheet.

Current and Long-Term Tangible Assets

Tangible assets can be either current assets or long-term assets. Current assets may or may not have a physical onsite presence but they will have a finite transaction value. A company's most liquid, tangible current assets include cash, cash equivalents, marketable securities, and accounts receivable. All of these tangible assets are included in the calculation of a company's quick ratio. Other current assets are included in the calculation of a company's current ratio. The current ratio shows how well a company can cover its current liabilities with its current assets. Current ratio assets include inventory which is not as liquid as cash equivalents but has a finite market value and could be sold for cash if needed in a liquidation.

Long-term assets, sometimes called fixed assets, comprise the second portion of the asset section on the balance sheet. These assets include things like real estate properties, manufacturing plants, manufacturing equipment, vehicles, office furniture, computers, and office supplies. The costs of these assets may or may not be part of a company's cost of goods sold but regardless they are assets that hold real transactional value for the company.

Tangible assets are recorded on the balance sheet at the cost incurred to acquire them. Long-term tangible assets are reduced in value over time through depreciation. Depreciation is a noncash balance sheet notation that reduces the value of assets by a scheduled amount over time. Current assets are converted to cash within one year and therefore do not need to be devalued over time. For example, inventory is a current asset that is usually sold within one year.

Tangible vs. Intangible Assets

Asset values are important for managing shareholders' equity and the return on equity ratio metric. Tangible and intangible assets are the two types of assets that makeup the full list of assets comprehensively for a firm. As such, both values are recorded on the balance sheet and analyzed in total performance management.

Intangible assets include non-physical assets that usually have a theoretical value generated by a firm's own valuation. These assets include things like copyrights, trademarks, patents, licenses, and brand value. Intangible assets are recorded on a balance sheet as long-term assets. There are some itemized values associated with intangible assets that can help form the basis of their balance sheet value such as their registration and renewal costs. Generally though, expenses associated with intangible assets will fall under general and much of intangible value must be determined by the firm itself.

Intangible assets cannot usually be sold individually in an open market but in some cases they may be acquired from other companies. They may also be paid for and transferred as part of an acquisition or merger deal. Intangible assets do contribute to a firm's net worth and total value if they are recorded on the balance sheet but it is up to the firm to decide on any carrying value.

INTANGIBLE ASSET

An intangible asset is an asset that lacks physical substance; in contrast to physical assets, such as machinery and buildings, and financial assets such as government securities. An intangible asset is usually very hard to evaluate. Examples are patents, copyright, franchises, goodwill, trademarks, and trade names. The general interpretation also includes software and other intangible computer based assets; these are all examples of intangible assets. Intangible assets generally—though not necessarily—suffer from typical market failures of non-rivalry and non-excludability.

Intangible assets may be one possible contributor to the disparity between "company value as per their accounting records", as well as "company value as per their market capitalization". Considering this argument, it is important to understand what an intangible asset truly is in the eyes of an accountant. A number of attempts have been made to define intangible assets:

- Prior to 2005 the Australian Accounting Standards Board issued the Statement of Accounting Concepts number 4 (SAC 4). This statement did not provide a formal definition of an intangible asset but did provide that tangibility was not an essential characteristic of asset.

- International Accounting Standards Board standard 38 (IAS 38) defines an intangible asset as: "an identifiable non-monetary asset without physical substance." This definition is in addition to the standard definition of an asset which requires a past event that has given rise to a resource that the entity controls and from which future economic benefits are expected to flow. Thus, the extra requirement for an intangible asset under IAS 38 is identifiability. This criterion requires that an intangible asset is separable from the entity or that it arises from a contractual or legal right.

- The Financial Accounting Standards Board Accounting Standard Codification 350 (ASC 350) defines an intangible asset as an asset, other than a financial asset, that lacks physical substance.

The lack of physical substance would therefore seem to be a defining characteristic of an intangible asset. Both the IASB and FASB definitions specifically preclude monetary assets in their definition of an intangible asset. This is necessary in order to avoid the classification of items such as accounts receivable, derivatives and cash in the bank as an intangible asset. IAS 38 contains examples of intangible assets, including: computer software, copyright and patents.

Research and Development

Research and Development (known also as R&D) is considered to be an intangible asset (about 16 percent of all intangible assets in the US)), even though most countries treat R&D as current expenses for both legal and tax purposes. Most countries report some intangibles in their National Income and Product Accounts (NIPA), yet no country has included a comprehensive measure of intangible assets. The contribution of intangible assets in long-term GDP growth has been recognized by economists.

IAS 38 requires any project that results in the generation of a resource to the entity be classified into two phases: a research phase, and a development phase.

The classification of research and development expenditure can be highly subjective, and it is important to note that organisations may have an ulterior motive in its classification of research and development expenditure. Less scrupulous directors may manipulate financial statements through their classification of research and development expenditure.

An example of research (as defined as "the original and planned investigation undertaken with the prospect of gaining new scientific or technical knowledge and understanding"): a company can carry a research on one of its products which it will use in the entity of which results in future economic income.

Development is defined as "the application of research findings to a plan or design for the production of new or substantially improved materials, devices, products, processes, systems, or services, before the start of commercial production or use."

Accounting treatment of expenses depends on whether they are classified as research or development. Where the distinction cannot be made, IAS 38 requires that the entire project be treated as research and expensed through the Statement of Comprehensive Income.

Research expenditure is highly speculative. There is no certainty that future economic benefits will flow to the entity. Prudence dictates that research expenditure be expensed through the Statement of Comprehensive Income. Development expenditure, however, is less speculative and it becomes possible to predict the future economic benefits that will flow to the entity. The matching principle dictates that development expenditure be capitalised, as the expenditure is expected to generate future economic benefit to the entity.

Financial Accounting

General Standards

The International Accounting Standards Board (IASB) offers some guidance (IAS 38) as to how intangible assets should be accounted for in financial statements. In general, legal intangibles that are developed internally are not recognized and legal intangibles that are purchased from third parties are recognized. Wordings are similar to IAS 9.

Under US GAAP, intangible assets are classified into: Purchased vs. internally created intangibles, and Limited-life vs. indefinite-life intangibles.

Expense Allocation

Intangible assets are typically expensed according to their respective life expectancy. Intangible assets have either an identifiable or an indefinite useful life. Intangible assets with identifiable useful lives are amortized on a straight-line basis over their economic or legal life, whichever is shorter. Examples of intangible assets with identifiable useful lives are copyrights and patents. Intangible assets with indefinite useful lives are reassessed each year for impairment. If an impairment has occurred, then a loss must be recognized. An impairment loss is determined by subtracting the asset's fair value from the asset's book/carrying value. Trademarks and goodwill are examples of intangible assets with indefinite useful lives. Goodwill has to be tested for impairment rather than amortized. If impaired, goodwill is reduced and loss is recognized in the Income statement.

Taxation

For personal income tax purposes, some costs with respect to intangible assets must be capitalized rather than treated as deductible expenses. Treasury regulations in the USA generally require capitalization of costs associated with acquiring, creating, or enhancing intangible assets. For example, an amount paid to obtain a trademark must be capitalized. Certain amounts paid to facilitate these transactions are also capitalized. Some types of intangible assets are categorized based on whether the asset is acquired from another party or created by the taxpayer. The regulations contain many provisions intended to make it easier to determine when capitalization is required.

Given the growing importance of intangible assets as a source of economic growth and tax revenue, and because their non-physical nature makes it easier for taxpayers to engage in tax strategies such as income-shifting or transfer pricing, tax authorities and international organizations have been designing ways to link intangible assets to the place where they were created, hence defining nexus. Intangibles for corporations are amortized over a 15-year period, equivalent to 180 months.

Definition of "intangibles" differs from standard accounting, in some US state governments. These governments may refer to stocks and bonds as "intangibles".

Identifiable and Unidentifiable Intangible Assets

Identifiable intangible assets are those that can be separated from other assets and can even be sold by the company. These are assets such as intellectual property, patents, copyrights, trademarks, and trade names. Software and other computer-related assets outside of hardware also classify as identifiable intangible assets.

Unidentifiable intangible assets are those that cannot be physically separated from the company. The most commonplace unidentifiable intangible asset is goodwill. Internally generated goodwill is expensed as a loss, but externally generated goodwill when a company acquires or merges with another company is capitalized as an asset. This means that when a company pays above the fair value of another company to acquire it, the difference is goodwill. This asset is not depreciated like PP&E. However, it is instead tested for impairment regularly. A company will record an impairment loss if it deems the goodwill's value has decreased from its recorded book value.

Another key unidentifiable asset is branding and reputation. While a company can sell its trademark, logos, and such, it can be very difficult to separate good branding and reputation from a strong company. Nonetheless, brand recognition and reputation are expected to generate good economic returns for the company in the future.

Amortization Expense

While PP&E is depreciated, intangible assets are amortized (except for goodwill). These assets are amortized over the useful life of the asset. Generally, intangible assets are simply amortized using the straight-line expense method.

If an intangible asset has a perpetual life, it is not amortized. Consequently, if an intangible asset has a useful life but can be renewed easily and without substantial cost, it is considered perpetual and is not amortized.

Example:

McRonald's has two intangible assets. The first is a patent worth $25,000,000 and with a useful life of 50 years. The patent expires and cannot be renewed. The second is a trademark worth $1,000,000 and with a useful life of 10 years, after which it expires. However, the trademark can be renewed at a marginal cost. What is McRonald's amortization expense per year?

The trademark is not amortized, as it virtually has a perpetual life. The patent, however, is amortized on the straight-line scale over its 50-year life. The amortization expense is $25,000,000 / 50 = $500,000. Thus, the yearly amortization expense for McRonald's is $500,000.

Goodwill

Referring to the identifiable intangible asset definition, goodwill does not meet the IFRS definition, as it is not identifiable/not separable. However, goodwill is still an intangible asset, treated as a separate class. The main difference concerning goodwill, as compared to other intangibles, is that goodwill is never amortized. In accounting, goodwill represents the difference between the purchase price of a business and the fair value of its assets, net of liabilities.

What this essentially means is the difference represents how much the buyer is willing to pay for the business as a whole, over and above the value of its individual assets alone. For example, if XYZ Company paid $50 million to acquire a sporting goods business and $10 million was the value of its assets net of liabilities, then $40 million would be goodwill. Companies can only have goodwill on their balance sheets if they have acquired another business.

Government Grants

Finally, another type of intangible asset is government grants. For several reasons, governments at all levels may choose to provide financial assistance to companies that engage in certain activities. The accounting treatment for grants involves two methods: the net method and the gross method. The net method deducts the grant to arrive at the carrying amount of the asset, while the gross method sets up the grant as deferred income.

Government grants may be in the form of a specific grant that includes specific requirements/stipulations such as employment levels or pollution control levels. If these stipulations are not met, then the grants may need to be refunded by the company. Government grants may also include forgivable loans in situations where companies meet certain conditions. As the name implies, the loan does not need to be repaid. In terms of recognition, government grants should be recognized only if:

- The entity will comply with the stipulations/requirements attached to them; and
- The grants will actually be received.

CAPITAL EXPENDITURE

Capital expenditure or capital expense (capex or CAPEX) is the money an organization or corporate entity spends to buy, maintain, or improve its fixed assets, such as buildings, vehicles, equipment, or land. It is considered a capital expenditure when the asset is newly purchased or when money is used towards extending the useful life of an existing asset, such as repairing the roof.

Capital expenditures contrast with operating expenses (opex), which are ongoing expenses that are inherent to the operation of the asset. Opex includes items like electricity or cleaning. The difference between opex and capex may not be immediately obvious for some expenses; for instance, repaving the parking lot may be thought of inherent to the operation of a shopping mall. The dividing line for items like these is that the expense is considered capex if the financial benefit of the expenditure extends beyond the current fiscal year.

Usage

Capital expenditures are the funds used to acquire or upgrade a company's fixed assets, such as expenditures towards property, plant, or equipment (PP&E). In the case when a capital expenditure constitutes a major financial decision for a company, the expenditure must be formalized at an annual shareholders meeting or a special meeting of the Board of Directors. In accounting, a capital expenditure is added to an asset account, thus increasing the asset's basis (the cost or value of an asset adjusted for tax purposes). Capex is commonly found on the cash flow statement under "Investment in Plant, Property, and Equipment" or something similar in the Investing subsection.

Accounting Rules

For tax purposes, capex is a cost that cannot be deducted in the year in which it is paid or incurred and must be capitalized. The general rule is that if the acquired property's useful life is longer than the taxable year, then the cost must be capitalized. The capital expenditure costs are then amortized or depreciated over the life of the asset in question. Further to the above, capex creates or adds basis to the asset or property, which once adjusted, will determine tax liability in the event of sale or transfer. In the US, Internal Revenue Code §§263 and 263A deal extensively with capitalization requirements and exceptions.

Included in capital expenditures are amounts spent on:

- Acquiring fixed, and in some cases, intangible assets.
- Repairing an existing asset so as to improve its useful life.
- Upgrading an existing asset if it results in a superior fixture.
- Preparing an asset to be used in business.
- Restoring property or adapting it to a new or different use.
- Starting or acquiring a new business.

An ongoing question for the accounting of any company is whether certain costs incurred should be capitalized or expensed. Costs which are expensed in a particular month simply appear on the financial statement as a cost incurred that month. Costs that are capitalized, however, are amortized or depreciated over multiple years. Capitalized expenditures show up on the balance sheet. Most ordinary business costs are either expensable or capitalizable, but some costs could be treated either way, according to the preference of the company. Capitalized interest if applicable is also spread out over the life of the asset.

The counterpart of capital expenditure is operating expense or operational cost (opex).

FIXED ASSETS MANAGEMENT

Fixed assets management is an accounting process that seeks to track fixed assets for the purposes of financial accounting, preventive maintenance, and theft deterrence.

Organizations face a significant challenge to track the location, quantity, condition, maintenance and depreciation status of their fixed assets. A popular approach to tracking fixed assets uses serial numbered asset tags, which are labels often with bar codes for easy and accurate reading. The owner of the assets can take inventory with a mobile bar code reader and then produce a report.

Off-the-shelf software packages for fixed asset management are marketed to businesses small and large. Some enterprise resource planning systems are available with fixed assets modules.

Some tracking methods automate the process, such as by using fixed scanners to read bar codes on railway freight cars or by attaching a radio-frequency identification (RFID) tag to an asset.

Fixed Asset Tracking Software

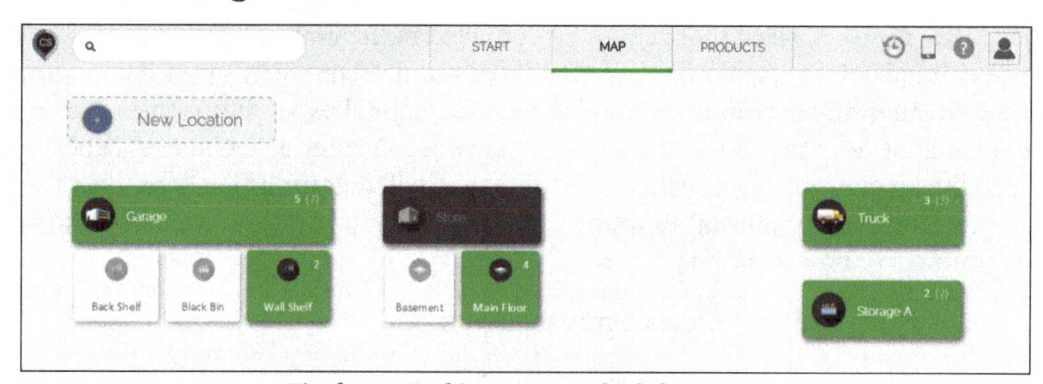

Fixed asset tracking across multiple locations.

Tracking assets is an important concern of every company, regardless of size. Fixed assets are defined as any 'permanent' object that a business uses internally including but not limited to computers, tools, software, or office equipment. While employees may use a specific tool or tools, the asset ultimately belongs to the company and must be returned. And therefore without an accurate method of keeping track of these assets it would be very easy for a company to lose control of them.

Asset tracking software allows companies to track what assets it owns, where each is located, who has it, when it was checked out, when it is due for return, when it is scheduled for maintenance, and the cost and depreciation of each asset.

The reporting option that is built into most asset tracking solutions provides pre-built reports, including assets by category and department, check-in/check-out, net book value of assets, assets past due, audit history, and transactions.

All of this information is captured in one program and can be used on PCs as well as mobile devices. As a result, companies reduce expenses through loss prevention and improved equipment maintenance. They reduce new and unnecessary equipment purchases, and they can more accurately calculate taxes based on depreciation schedules.

The most commonly tracked assets are:
- Plant and equipment,
- Buildings,
- Fixtures and fittings,
- Long term investment,
- Machinery,
- Vehicles and heavy equipments.

Asset tracking software is often used to track both the information about an asset for financial reporting purposes as well as the physical location of an asset. The financial reporting elements of tracking often relate to accounting procedures and valuation needs but may or may not relate to location information.

Asset location tracking software often takes one of two approaches to monitoring asset locations. The first approach is to use a physical tracking device to provide data on physical location. This can take the form of a Bluetooth tracking beacon or a GPS tracking unit. The second approach is to track a location by the "responsible party". In this approach the software uses peer to peer assign and accept procedures to allow individuals to accept responsibility for assets. The asset location is then inferred based upon the person who has accepted responsibility.

FIXED-ASSET TURNOVER

Fixed-asset turnover is the ratio of sales (on the profit and loss account) to the value of fixed assets (on the balance sheet). It indicates how well the business is using its fixed assets to generate sales.

$$\text{Fixed Asset Turnover} = \frac{\text{Net sales}}{\text{Average net fixed assets}}$$

Generally speaking, the higher the ratio, the better, because a high ratio indicates the business has less money tied up in fixed assets for each unit of currency of sales revenue. A declining ratio may indicate that the business is over-invested in plant, equipment, or other fixed assets.

In A.A.T. assessments this financial measure is calculated in two different ways:
- Total Asset Turnover Ratio = Revenue / Total Assets.
- Net Asset Turnover Ratio = Revenue / (Total Assets - Current Liabilities).

Fixed Asset Turnover Ratio

The fixed asset turnover ratio is an efficiency ratio that measures a companies return on their investment in property, plant, and equipment by comparing net sales with fixed assets. In other words, it calculates how efficiently a company is a producing sales with its machines and equipment.

Investors and creditors use this formula to understand how well the company is utilizing their equipment to generate sales. This concept is important to investors because they want to be able to measure an approximate return on their investment. This is particularly true in the manufacturing industry where companies have large and expensive equipment purchases. Creditors, on the other hand, want to make sure that the company can produce enough revenues from a new piece of equipment to pay back the loan they used to purchase it.

Analysis

Good Fixed Assets Turnover

A high turn over indicates that assets are being utilized efficiently and large amount of sales are generated using a small amount of assets. It could also mean that the company has sold off its equipment and started to outsource its operations. Outsourcing would maintain the same amount of sales and decrease the investment in equipment at the same time.

A low turn over, on the other hand, indicates that the company isn't using its assets to their fullest extent. This could be due to a variety of factors. For example, they might be producing products that no one wants to buy. Also, they might have overestimated the demand for their product and overinvested in machines to produce the products. It might also be low because of manufacturing problems like a bottleneck in the value chain that held up production during the year and resulted in fewer than anticipated sales.

Keep in mind that a high or low ratio doesn't always have a direct correlation with performance. There are a few outside factors that can also contribute to this measurement.

Use of Fixed Asset Turnover

Accelerated depreciation is one of the main factors. Remember we always use the net PPL by subtracting the depreciation from gross PPL. If a company uses an accelerated depreciation method like double declining depreciation, the book value of their equipment will be artificially low making their performance look a lot better than it actually is.

Similarly, if a company doesn't keep reinvesting in new equipment, this metric will continue to rise year over year because the accumulated depreciation balance keeps increasing and reducing the denominator. Thus, if the company's PPL are fully depreciated, their ratio will be equal to their sales for the period. Investors and creditors have to be conscious of this fact when evaluating how well the company is actually performing.

Example:

Jeff's Car Restoration is a custom car shop that builds custom hotrods and restores old cars to their former glory. Jeff is applying for a loan to build a new facility and expand his operations. His sales for the year are $250,000 using equipment he paid $100,000 for. The accumulated deprecation on the equipment is $50,000.

How is the Fixed Assets Turnover Ratio Calculated?

Here's how the bank would calculate Jeff's turn over.

Fixed Asset Turnover,

$$5 = \frac{\$250,000}{\$100,000 - 50,000}$$

As you can see, Jeff generates five times more sales than the net book value of his assets. The bank should compare this metric with other companies similar to Jeff's in his industry. A 5x metric might be good for the architecture industry, but it might be horrible for the automotive industry that is dependent on heavy equipment.

It's always important to compare ratios with other companies' in the industry.

Limitations of using the Fixed Asset Ratio

Companies with cyclical sales may have worse ratios in slow periods, so the ratio should be looked at during several different time periods. Additionally, management could be outsourcing production to reduce reliance on assets and improve its FAT ratio, while still struggling to maintain stable cash flows and other business fundamentals.

Companies with strong asset turnover ratios can still lose money because the amount of sales generated by fixed assets speaks nothing of the company's ability to generate solid profits or healthy cash flow.

REVALUATION OF FIXED ASSETS

In finance, a revaluation of fixed assets is an action that may be required to accurately describe the true value of the capital goods a business owns. This should be distinguished from planned depreciation, where the recorded decline in value of an asset is tied to its age.

Fixed assets are held by an enterprise for the purpose of producing goods or rendering services, as opposed to being held for resale for the normal course of business. An example, machines, buildings, patents or licenses can be fixed assets of a business.

The purpose of a revaluation is to bring into the books the fair market value of fixed assets. This may be helpful in order to decide whether to invest in another business. If a company wants to sell one of its assets, it is revalued in preparation for sales negotiations.

Reasons for Revaluation

It is common to see companies revaluing their fixed assets. It is important to make the distinctions between a 'private' revaluation to a 'public' revaluation which is carried out in the financial reports. The purposes are varied:

- To show the true rate of return on capital employed.

- To conserve adequate funds in the business for replacement of fixed assets at the end of their useful lives. Provision for depreciation based on historic cost will show inflated profits and lead to payment of excessive dividends.

- To show the fair market value of assets which have considerably appreciated since their purchase such as land and buildings.

- To negotiate fair price for the assets of the company before merger with or acquisition by another company.

- To enable proper internal reconstruction, and external reconstruction.

- To issue shares to existing shareholders (rights issue or follow-on offering).

- To get fair market value of assets, in case of sale and leaseback transaction.

- When the company intends to take a loan from banks/financial institutions by mortgaging its fixed assets. Proper revaluation of assets would enable the company to get a higher amount of loan.

- Sale of an individual asset or group of assets.

- In financial firms revaluation reserves are required for regulatory reasons. They are included when calculating a firm's funds to give a fairer view of resources. Only a portion of the firm's total funds (usually about 20%) can be loaned or in the hands of any one counterparty at any one time (large exposures restrictions).

- To decrease the leverage ratio (the ratio of debt to equity).

Methods of Revaluation of Fixed assets

The common methods used in revaluing assets are:

Indexation

Under this method, indices are applied to the cost value of the assets to arrive at the current cost of the assets. The Indices by the country's departments of Statistical Bureau or Economic Surveys may be used for the revaluation of assets.

Current Market Price (CMP)

- Land values can be estimated by using recent prices for similar plots of land sold in the area. However, certain adjustments will have to be made for the plus and minus points of the land possessed by the company. This may be done with the assistance of brokers and agencies dealing in land, or by a licensed appraiser.

- Buildings values can be estimated by a realtor (real estate dealer) or Chartered Surveyor (in the UK) in a similar manner to land.

- Plant & Machinery: The CMP can be obtained from suppliers of the assets concerned. This may not be possible if brands are not available in the market due to the closure of companies manufacturing them. Similarly, a direct CMP may not be available for a model that has been discontinued or changed by the manufacturer. Comparison of assets to most similar types available for sale, new or used, can provide an estimate of value.

CMP of an existing asset = CMP of comparable new asset x Remaining useful life of asset / Original useful life of asset.

Appraisal Method

Under this method, technical experts are called in to carry out a detailed examination of the assets with a view to determining their fair market value. A proper appraisal is necessary when the company is taking out an insurance policy for protection of its fixed assets. It ensures that the fixed assets are neither over-insured nor under-insured. The factors which are considered in determining the value of an asset, are as follows:

- Date of purchase.
- Extent of use i.e. single shift, double shift, triple shift.
- Type of asset. Whether the asset is a general purpose or special purpose asset?
- Repairs & Maintenance policy of the enterprise.
- Availability of spares in the future, mainly in the case of imported machines.
- Future demand for the product manufactured by an asset.
- If the asset is part of a bigger fixed asset, the life of the latter is crucial.

Selective Revaluation

Selective revaluation can be defined as the revaluation of specific assets within a class or all assets within a specific location.

A manufacturing company may have its manufacturing facilities spread over different locations. Suppose it decides to undertake a revaluation of its plant & machinery. Selective revaluation will mean revaluing specific assets (such as the boiler, heater, central air-conditioning system) at all locations, or revaluing all items of Plant & Machinery at a particular location only. Such revaluation will lead to unrepresentative amounts being shown in the Fixed Assets Register (FAR). In case of revaluation of specific assets of a class, while some assets will be shown at a revalued amount others will be shown at historical cost. The same will happen in case of revaluation of all assets of plant & machinery at a particular location only.

It is not consistent to value and depreciate fixed assets using different bases. Therefore, selective revaluation is generally not considered best practice.

Preliminary Considerations

Revaluation will typically require liaison between the company's Production Department, Accounts Department, Technical Department and external appraisers. To commission the project they should set out their conclusions to the following questions:

- Why is the revaluation necessary?

- What is the most suitable method, taking into account the type of fixed assets, statutory requirements, availability of required information? Should the values arrived at by one method be crosschecked with the values derived from another method?

- What assets are to be revalued?

- What is the period within which the revaluation has to be completed?

- What guidelines should be laid down for the revaluation?

- What modifications will be required in the FAR to show revalued figures in place of historical figures? Similarly, depreciation will be computed twice. One takes into account the historical cost, and the other as per revalued figures.

Upward Revaluation

The FASB in the U.S. does not allow upward revaluation of fixed assets to reflect fair market values although it is compulsory to account for impairment costs in fixed assets (downward revaluation of fixed assets) as per FASB Statement No. 144, Accounting for the Impairment or Disposal of Long-Lived Assets.

In other countries, upward revaluation is mainly done for fixed assets such as land, and real estate whose value keeps rising from year to year. It seems the concept of upward revaluation of fixed assets such as real estate has not been widely welcomed by a majority of companies in USA on account of fear of paying higher property and capital gains taxes. Further, the provision against upward restatement ensures conservative valuation.

The United Kingdom, Australia, and India allow upward revaluation in the values of fixed assets to bring them in consonance with fair market values. However, the law requires disclosure of the basis of revaluation, amount of revaluation made to each class of assets (for a specified period after the financial year in which revaluation is made), and other information. Similarly, the law prohibits payment of dividend out of any reserve created as a result of the upward revaluation of fixed assets. The law in Australia has been amended recently to allow for the payment of dividends from the increase in the value of non-current assets in certain instances where a company meets other liquidity tests.

Important Points

- Increase in the value of fixed assets because of revaluation of fixed assets is credited to 'Revaluation Reserve', and is not available for distribution as dividend. Revaluation Reserve is treated as a Capital Reserve.

- The increase in depreciation arising out of revaluation of fixed assets is debited to revaluation reserve and the normal depreciation to Profit and Loss account.

- Selection of the most suitable method of revaluation is extremely important. The most used method is the appraisal method. Methods such as indexation and reference to current market prices are also used. However, when these methods are used they are crosschecked with the values arrived at by using the appraisal method.

- When an asset is sold that has previously been revalued, the revaluation within the carrying value is debited to the Revaluation Reserve.

- When assets are revalued, every Balance Sheet shall show for a specified period of years, the amount of increase/decrease made in respect of each class of assets. Similarly, the increased/decreased value shall be shown in place of the original cost.

- In case of land and buildings, revaluation is desirable as their value generally increases over time, and is carried out every 3 to 5 years. In case of plant & machinery, revaluation is carried out only if there is a strong case for it. In case of depreciable assets such as vehicles, furniture & fittings or office equipment, revaluation is not carried out.

- Revaluation should not result in the net book value of an asset exceeding its recoverable value.

Downward Revaluation

Revaluation does not mean only an upward revision in the book values of the asset. It can also mean a downward revision (also called impairment) in the book values of the assets. However, any downward revision in the book values of the assets is immediately written off to the Profit & Loss account. Under IFRS, an asset is considered to be impaired (and is thus written down) if its carrying amount is greater than its recoverable amount. The recoverable amount is the greater of the asset's value in use (present value of future values) or net realizable value.

Successive Revaluations

An upward revaluation of a fixed asset which has been previously subject to downward revaluation, an amount of the upward revaluation equal to the amount previously expensed is credited back to the Profit & Loss Account.

Example:

Machinery 'A' is purchased on 01-04-1999 for $100,000. It is depreciated using the Straight Line Method at the rate of 10% p.a.:

Particulars	First Revaluation	Second Revaluation
Nature of Revaluation	▼	▲
Date of Revaluation	01-04-2001	01-04-2004
Gross Cost	100,000	93,750
Less: Depreciation	20,000	46,875
Net Book Value	80,000	46,875
Revalued – Appraisal Method	75,000	55,000
Increase / (Decrease) in Net Book Value	(5,000)	8,125
Debit to Profit & Loss a/c	5,000	0
Credit to Profit & Loss a/c	0	5,000
Credit to Revaluation Reserve	0	3,125

DEPRECIATION IN FIXED ASSET

What is Depreciation?

In accounting terms, depreciation is defined as the reduction of recorded cost of a fixed asset in a systematic manner until the value of the asset becomes zero or negligible.

An example of fixed assets are buildings, furniture, office equipment, machinery etc.. A land is the only exception which cannot be depreciated as the value of land appreciates with time.

Depreciation allows a portion of the cost of a fixed asset to the revenue generated by the fixed asset. This is mandatory under the matching principle as revenues are recorded with their associated expenses in the accounting period when the asset is in use. This helps in getting a complete picture of the revenue generation transaction.

An example of Depreciation – If a delivery truck is purchased a company with a cost of $ 100,000 and the expected usage of the truck are 5 years, the business might depreciate the asset under depreciation expense as $ 20,000 every year for a period of 5 years.

Calculating Depreciation in Small Business

There are three methods commonly used to calculate depreciation. They are:

- Straight line method.
- Unit of production method.
- Double-declining balance method.

Three main inputs are required to calculate depreciation:

- Useful life – this is the time period over which the organisation considers the fixed asset to be productive. Beyond its useful life, the fixed asset is no longer cost-effective to continue the operation of the asset.
- Salvage value – Post the useful life of the fixed asset, the company may consider selling it at a reduced amount. This is known as the salvage value of the asset.
- The cost of the asset – this includes taxes, shipping, and preparation/setup expenses.

Unit of production method needs the number of units used during production.

Types of Depreciation

Straight-line Depreciation Method

This is the simplest method of all. It involves simple allocation of an even rate of depreciation every year over the useful life of the asset. The formula for straight line depreciation is:

Annual Depreciation expense = (Asset cost – Residual Value) / Useful life of the asset.

Example – Suppose a manufacturing company purchases a machinery for $ 100,000 and the useful life of the machinery are 10 years and the residual value of the machinery is $ 20,000.

Annual Depreciation expense = (100,000-20,000) / 10 = $ 8,000.

Thus the company can take $ 8000 as the depreciation expense every year over the next ten years as shown in depreciation table below:

Year	Original cost – Residual value	Depreciation expense
1	$ 80000	$ 8000
2	$ 80000	$ 8000
3	$ 80000	$ 8000
4	$ 80000	$ 8000
5	$ 80000	$ 8000
6	$ 80000	$ 8000
7	$ 80000	$ 8000
8	$ 80000	$ 8000
9	$ 80000	8000
10	$ 80000	$ 8000

Unit of Production Method

This is a two-step process, unlike straight line method. Here, equal expense rates are assigned to each unit produced. This assignment makes the method very useful in assembly for production lines. Hence, the calculation is based on output capability of the asset rather than the number of years.

The steps are:

Step 1: Calculate per unit depreciation:

Per unit Depreciation = (Asset cost – Residual value) / Useful life in units of production.

Step 2: Calculate the total depreciation of actual units produced:

Total Depreciation Expense = Per Unit Depreciation * Units Produced.

Example: ABC company purchases a printing press to print flyers for $ 40,000 with a useful life of 1,80,000 units and residual value of $ 4000. It prints 4000 flyers.

Step 1: Per unit Depreciation = (40,000-4000)/180,000 = $ 0.2.

Step 2: Total Depreciation expense = $ 0.2 * 4000 flyers = $ 800.

So the total Depreciation expense is $ 800 which is accounted. Once the per unit depreciation is found out, it can be applied to future output runs.

Double Declining Method

This is one of the two common methods a company uses to account for the expenses of a fixed asset. This is an accelerated depreciation method. As the name suggests, it counts expense twice as much as the book value of the asset every year.

The formula is:

Depreciation = 2 * Straight line depreciation percent * book value at the beginning of the accounting period

Book value = Cost of the asset – accumulated depreciation

Accumulated depreciation is the total depreciation of the fixed asset accumulated up to a specified time.

Example: On April 1, 2012, company X purchased an equipment for $ 100,000. This is expected to have 5 useful life years. The salvage value is $ 14,000. Company X considers depreciation expense for the nearest whole month. Calculate the depreciation expenses for 2012, 2013, 2014 using a declining balance method.

Useful life = 5

Straight line depreciation percent = 1/5 = 0.2 or 20% per year

Depreciation rate = 20% * 2 = 40% per year

Depreciation for the year 2012 = $ 100,000 * 40% * 9/12 = $ 30,000

Depreciation for the year 2013 = ($ 100,000 - $ 30,000) * 40% * 12/12 = $ 28,000

Depreciation for the year 2014 = ($ 100,000 – $ 30,000 – $ 28,000) * 40% * 9/12 = $ 16,800

Depreciation table is shown below:

Year	Book value at the beginning	Depreciation rate	Depreciation Expense	Book value at the end of the year
2012	$ 100,000	40%	$ 30,000 * (1)	$ 70,000
2013	$ 70,000	40%	$ 28,000 * (2)	$ 42,000
2014	$ 42,000	40%	$ 16,800 * (3)	$ 25,200
2015	$ 25,200	40%	$ 10,080 * (4)	$ 15,120
2016	$ 15,120	40%	$ 1,120 * (5)	$ 14,000

Depreciation for 2016 is $ 1,120 to keep the book value same as salvage value.

$ 15,120 – $ 14,000 = $ 1,120 (At this point the depreciation should stop).

Need of Recording Depreciation for Small Businesses

So now we know the meaning of depreciation, the methods used to calculate them, inputs required to calculate them and also we saw examples of how to calculate them. Let's find out as to why the small businesses should care to record depreciation.

As we already know the purpose of depreciation is to match the cost of the fixed asset over its productive life to the revenues the business earns from the asset. It is very difficult to directly link the cost of the asset to revenues, hence, the cost is usually assigned to the number of years the asset is productive.

Over the useful life of the fixed asset, the cost is moved from balance sheet to income statement. Alternatively, it is just an allocation process as per matching principle instead of a technique which determines the fair market value of the fixed asset.

Accounting entry – DEBIT depreciation expense account and CREDIT accumulated depreciation account.

If we do not use depreciation in accounting, then we have to charge all assets to expense once they are bought. This will result in huge losses in the following transaction period and in high profitability in periods when the corresponding revenue is considered without an offset expense. Hence, companies which do not use the depreciation expense in their accounts will incur front-loaded expenses and highly variable financial results.

References

- Fixed-assets, accounting-dictionary: myaccountingcourse.com, Retrieved 28 April, 2019
- Tangible-asset-5331: divestopedia.com, Retrieved 08 July, 2019
- Intangible-assets, accounting: corporatefinanceinstitute.com, Retrieved 16 June, 2019
- Fixed-asset-turnover, financial-ratios: myaccountingcourse.com, Retrieved 15 May, 2019
- What-is-depreciation: profitbooks.net, Retrieved 05 August, 2019

Investment Management

CHAPTER 4

To meet the investment goals, investment management is the asset management of shares, bonds and other assets. Some of the major aspects of it are portfolio management, asset allocation, investment fund, active management, etc. All these diverse concepts of investment management have been carefully analyzed in this chapter.

Investment management is the activity of overseeing and making decisions regarding the investments of an individual, company, or other institution. Individuals having personal investments in the form of either physical assets (such as real estate) or paper assets (such as bonds and stock shares) may take on the tasks of managing their investments on their own, or they may use an investment manager to make decisions about their investments. Usually companies and other large organizations employ investment managers to guide and oversee all aspects of the company's investments. In addition to corporations, institutions such as insurance companies and pension funds may rely on professionals to handle their investments. The investment manager may be an individual or a firm.

One reason companies regard investment management as important is that they often rely on investments to help expand their business. For example, if an airline desires to expand operations into a new market, it will need a large amount of ready cash to pay for building a new customer base, advertising, and other requirements. In this situation, the airline's investment manager will examine the company's investment portfolio (the collection of investments held by the company) to determine which investments, when converted to cash, could provide the funding the firm needs for the new operation. The company may own stocks or bonds and may have invested in certain funds such as mutual funds.

Investment management goes by a variety of names that can depend on the type of investors and investments involved. Private individuals with investments of large value usually refer to the investment management services they use as wealth management or portfolio management. When financial firms such as banks and insurance companies manage investments, it is usually called fund management. Asset management is the name for the management of mutual funds, managed funds, and other funds that allow large numbers of shareholders (investors) to participate in a range of investment opportunities. As an industry, investment management is a crucial part of the global corporate culture.

Investment management in the United States has developed rapidly in the few decades it has existed. Until the 1970s, most wealth in the United States was managed by money managers in Europe or by private trust companies. Families in possession of wealth that required management typically employed private portfolio managers.

The Employee Retirement Income Security Act of 1974 required a new process for the statistical measurement of retirement portfolios, which resulted in the emergence of investment management firms to oversee such corporate investments as employee-benefit-fund assets. In the late 1980s these management firms, which until then had served only institutions, started providing services to individual investors. In 1985 the Investment Management Consultants Association (IMCA) was established, which advocated high standards for the education of professional investment managers.

Growth in the amount and value of assets is important to the overall worth of a company and the wealth of its stockholders. Among the various types of assets a company may possess, most require investment management. Fixed assets (also known as long-term assets) are generally forms of physical property that are held for a long time (for instance, buildings, equipment, and heavy machinery) and that are used to generate revenue. Most fixed assets lose their value over time due to wear and tear, a process called depreciation. Bonds are another kind of fixed asset. A bond is a long-term loan an investor makes to the entity that issues the bond, for example, the United States government. Current assets (also called liquid assets) are held by an investor for relatively short time spans, typically less than 12 months, and they can be easily converted to cash, sold, or consumed. Examples of a company's current assets are cash, tradable stock, and inventory.

When a group of assets have similar characteristics, generally perform similarly when invested in, and are regulated in the same way by laws, they are said to be in the same asset class. Equities, which are public stocks, are in one such asset class. Fixed-income bonds are in another, and cash equivalents such as bank certificates of deposit are in yet another.

Investment portfolios are typically managed through decisions about purchases and sales of assets. Investment managers must be able to analyze the finances of investors, understand how to select different types of assets, set realistic investment goals, and know how to monitor investments and make adjustments when changing economic situations require them.

When an investment manager is first engaged by an investor, the manager generally begins by analyzing the investor's current financial situation to create a profile. This activity involves assessing the net worth of the investor, which is the value of all property owned (assets), less any debts or obligations (liabilities). It also involves determining the cash flow of the investor, which is the amount of cash earned in a certain time period after paying all expenses and taxes.

After the investment manager has established the investor's financial profile, the manager and the investor work together to identify and define investment goals. Goals depend on many factors, including the percentage of wealth the investor wants to commit, the level of investment risk appropriate to the investor, the desired rate of return (the earnings expected from an investment over a specific time period), and the relative percentages of the total investment that should be put long-term and short-term assets.

Next, the investment manager employs financial models that assess the likelihood of achieving the investment goals. These models, which are run on a computer, use statistics, mathematics, logic, economic information, and other resources to construct a representation of a particular investment strategy over time. Results from the models give the investor and the manager and idea of how realistic the investment goals are. If they have concerns about realizing these goals, they can adjust their overall strategy.

DISCRETIONARY INVESTMENT MANAGEMENT

Discretionary Investment Management is a form of professional investment management that invests on behalf of their clients through a variety of securities. The term "discretionary" refers to the fact that investment decisions are made at the investment manager's judgement. The major aim of the services offered is to outperform benchmarks listed in the mandate; this is called providing alpha.

The services provided are usually tailored for institutional business, pension funds and high-net worth individuals. The investment management company has a continuing responsibility to ensure that an investment portfolio is suitable for the client's attitude to risk and investment objectives.

Investment Products

Discretionary Investment Managers have access to every security in the market place. It is up to the investment manager's strategy to decide what securities best fit in a client's portfolio. The most common investment products are stocks, bonds, ETFs and financial derivatives. All the investment products in the scope of the investment manager's strategy must be outlined in the investment mandate.

Investment Process

Due to the nature of the service, discretionary investment management firms provide a mandate in order to ensure that the services offered meet the aims of the client's financial goals.

The process is structured in a way for clients capital to be invested in the specified strategies in the investment mandate. Clients choosing a specific strategy will get the same strategy – there is no investment tailoring for the client. This means clients monies will be pooled together and invested at the same time. The actual client account is segregated and the monies invested will be weighted to the individuals capital. E.g) 1% investment in a £10,000,000 account will contribute £100,000 to the transaction whilst a £1,000,000 will contribute £10,000.

The most common process you will encounter is using a systematic approach which is important for investment managers to demonstrate their strategies and will help you understand their decisions better. This process is widely used because it allows the investment strategies to be exercised in a specific way and makes it easier to report results.

Investment Management Fees

Assets Under Management Fees

Most discretionary investment management companies charge an assets under management (AUM) fee. This is to keep the companies interests aligned with their investors. The more they grow the assets under management, the more they'll receive from the AUM fee. The fee can range from anything between 0.1%-4% AUM.

Transactional Fees

In addition to an AUM fee, a transactional fee is another type of fee provided by investment managers.

This is a fee that is charged every time the investment manager makes a transaction on your behalf. This can vary between 0.01%-0.5% of the amount invested.

High-Water Mark Fees (% of Profits)

A more attractive fee is when a company receives a share of the profits generated for their clients. This usually ranges between 10% - 30% of the profits. The high-water mark is used to prevent clients from paying when the fund is performing poorly, or below their mandate.

INVESTMENT RISK

Investment risk can be defined as the probability or likelihood of occurrence of losses relative to the expected return on any particular investment.

All investments involve risks including possible loss of principal. The following are some general risks associated with various asset classes. Each specific investment approach and product will have its own specific risks and risks will vary.

Alternatives risks: Alternative investments tend to use leverage, which can serve to magnify potential losses. Additionally, they can be subject to increased illiquidity, volatility and counterparty risks, among other risks.

Below investment grade risks: Lower-rated securities have a significantly greater risk of default in payments of interest and/or principal than the risk of default for investment-grade securities. The secondary market for lower-rated securities is typically much less liquid than the market for investment-grade securities, frequently with significantly more volatile prices and larger spreads between bid and asked price in trading.

Capital risk: Investment markets are subject to economic, regulatory, market sentiment, and political risks. All investors should consider the risks that may impact their capital, before investing. The value of your investment may become worth more or less than at the time of the original investment.

Commodities risk: Exposure to the commodities markets may be more volatile than investments in traditional equity or fixed income securities. The value of commodity-linked derivative instruments may be affected by changes in overall market movements, commodity index volatility, interest-rate changes, or events affecting a particular commodity or industry.

Common stock risk: Common stock are subject to many factors, including economic conditions, government regulations, market sentiment, local and international political events, and environmental and technological issues as well as the profitability and viability of the individual company. Equity security prices may decline as a result of adverse changes in these factors, and there is no assurance that a portfolio manager will be able to predict these changes. Some equity markets are more volatile than others and may present higher risks of loss. Common stock represents an equity or ownership interest in an issuer.

Concentration risk: Concentration of investments in a relatively small number of securities, sectors or industries, or geographical regions may significantly affect performance.

Credit risk: The value of fixed income security may decline, or the issuer or guarantor of that security may fail to pay interest or principal when due, as a result of adverse changes to the issuer's or guarantor's financial status and/or business. In general, lower-rated securities carry a greater degree of credit risk than higher-rated securities.

Currency risk: Investments in currencies, currency derivatives, or similar instruments, as well as in securities that are denominated in foreign currency, are subject to the risk that the value of a particular currency will change in relation to one or more other currencies.

Equity market risks: Equity markets are subject to many factors, including economic conditions, government regulations, market sentiment, local and international political events, and environmental and technological issues.

Fixed income securities market risks: Fixed income securities markets are subject to many factors, including economic conditions, government regulations, market sentiment, and local and international political events. In addition, the market value of fixed income securities will fluctuate in response to changes in interest rates, currency values, and the creditworthiness of the issuer.

Foreign and emerging markets risk: Investments in foreign markets may present risks not typically associated with domestic markets. These risks may include changes in currency exchange rates; less-liquid markets and less available information; less government supervision of exchanges, brokers, and issuers; increased social, economic, and political uncertainty; and greater price volatility. These risks may be greater in emerging markets, which may also entail different risks from developed markets.

Interest-rate risk: Generally, the value of fixed income securities will change inversely with changes in interest rates. The risk that changes in interest rates will adversely affect investments will be greater for longer-term fixed income securities than for shorter-term fixed income securities.

Issuer-specific risk: A security issued by a particular issuer may be impacted by factors that are unique to that issuer and thus may cause that security's return to differ from that of the market.

Leverage risk: Use of leverage exposes the portfolio to a higher degree of additional risk, including (i) greater losses from investments than would otherwise have been the case had leverage not been used to make the investments, (ii) margin calls that may force premature liquidations of investment positions.

Repo and reverse-repo risk: Both repurchase and reverse repurchase transactions involve counterparty risk. A reverse repurchase transaction also involves the risk that the market value of the securities the investor is obligated to repurchase may decline below the repurchase price.

Risks of derivative instruments: Derivatives, which are often used in alternative investments, can be volatile and involve various degrees of risk. The value of derivative instruments may be affected by changes in overall market movements, the business or financial condition of specific companies, index volatility, changes in interest rates, or factors affecting a particular industry or region. Other relevant risks include the possible default of the counterparty to the transaction and the potential liquidity risk with respect to particular derivative instruments. Moreover, because many derivative instruments provide significantly more market exposure than the money paid or deposited when the transaction is entered into, a relatively small adverse market movement can not only result in the loss of the entire investment, but may also expose a portfolio to the possibility of a loss exceeding the original amount invested.

Risks of investments in other pools: Investors in a fund that has invested in another fund will be subject to the same risks, in direct proportion to the amount of assets the first fund has invested in the second, as direct investors in that second fund.

Smaller capitalization stock risks: The share prices of small and mid-cap companies may exhibit greater volatility than the share prices of larger capitalization companies. In addition, shares of small and mid-cap companies are often less liquid than larger capitalization companies.

Additional Risks

Liquidity risk: Investments with low liquidity can have significant changes in market value, and there is no guarantee that these securities could be sold at fair value.

Manager risk: Investment performance depends on the portfolio management team and the team's investment strategies. If the investment strategies do not perform as expected, if opportunities to implement those strategies do not arise, or if the team does not implement its investment strategies successfully, an investment portfolio may underperform or suffer significant losses.

Importance of Investment Risk

When you invest, you expect to get a return on your money. You're probably also hoping you'll be able to buy more with your money in the future than you can today. If so, your return needs to be higher than the rate of inflation.

This is how the amount of risk you take on can affect your investment outcomes:

- No risk - You can hold on to cash and eliminate risk but your money will be going backwards because inflation will increase the cost of goods and services so you'll be able to buy less with your money over time.

- Low risk - If you choose a low-risk investment, such as a bank account or government bond when interest rates are low, your returns may not be much higher than the rate of inflation, so you'll probably be standing still financially.

- Higher risk - If you want your money to grow, you'll need to take on more risk. This means putting some money into growth assets like shares and property. You will usually get higher returns, on average, over the longer term, but the trade-off is that they may lose value over the shorter term.

Market and economic conditions can change rapidly, but a knee-jerk reaction to change your investment strategy can make things worse.

Any investment decision should be based on your long-term investment plans, not short-term market fluctuations. Review your goals and risk tolerance and, if your investment still fits into your long-term plan, you would need a good reason to change it.

Minimising Investment Risk

Volatility in financial markets can affect your confidence but it's important to remember the principles of good risk management when it comes to investing:

- Diversification - Having a diversified portfolio means you'll be less exposed to a particular economic event. You can diversify across and within asset classes, industry sectors and geographic regions. If your investment portfolio is well diversified, a fall in the value of one asset may be offset by an increase in the value of another.

- Focus on your investment goals - Usually when you buy growth investment assets you expect some short-term volatility, so it's important not to panic when markets drop. Consider whether the assets you hold are still appropriate to achieve your long-term goals. Look at how market volatility has affected your investment in the past and consider whether there is any information available that suggests any short-term losses won't be regained.

- Monitor your investments - As assets gain or lose value, the balance of your assets may change and reduce the diversity of your portfolio. If the percentage of any asset strays too far from its target weighting you may need to rebalance your portfolio. This usually involves selling some of one asset type and buying more of another.

- Consider financial advice - If you need assistance with developing a financial plan or selecting financial products that are appropriate for your risk appetite, it can help to seek professional financial advice.

- Beware of scams - When markets are volatile scammers try to take advantage of investors. Find out how to avoid investment scams.

PORTFOLIO MANAGEMENT

A portfolio can be defined as different investments tools namely stocks, shares, mutual funds, bonds, cash all combined together depending specifically on the investor's income, budget, risk appetite and the holding period. It is formed in such a way that it stabilizes the risk of nonperformance of different pools of investments.

Portfolio Management is defined as the art and science of making decisions about the investment mix and policy, matching investments to objectives, asset allocation for individuals and institutions, and balancing risk against performance.

Simply put it, someone has given you their hard earned money and you need to help them increase the capital in the best of diversified ways. This should be in a way in which the risk-return ratio is aptly maintained considering the profits in mind and the holding period of investments.

Portfolio management refers to managing an individual's investments in the form of bonds, shares, cash, mutual funds etc so that he earns the maximum profits within the stipulated time frame. It is the art of managing the money of an individual under the expert guidance of portfolio managers.

It is the detailed SWOT analysis (strengths, weaknesses, opportunities, and threats) of an investment avenue, which could be in the form of debt/equity, domestic/international, with the goal of maximizing return at a given appetite for risk.

Objectives of Portfolio Management

- It is aptly put as the customization of the investment needs catered by the portfolio managers as per the defined requirements.
- Portfolio management helps in providing the best options for investments to individuals as per the defined criterions of their income, budget, age, holding period and risk taking capacity.
- This is mainly done by the Portfolio managers who understand the investors' financial needs and accordingly suggest the investment policy that would have maximum returns with minimum risks involved. Aptly put, it is risk reduction through diversification.
- This is the method preferred by those who believe in having liquidity in investments so that one can get the money back when needed.
- Some of the portfolio management schemes are also done for tax saving purposes.
- It helps the investors maintain the purchasing power.

Key Elements of Portfolio Management

- Asset Allocation: The key to effective portfolio management is the long-term mix of assets. Asset allocation is based on the understanding that different types of assets do not move in concert, and some are more volatile than others. Asset allocation seeks to optimize the risk/return profile of an investor by investing in a mix of assets that have low correlation to each other. Investors with a more aggressive profile can weight their portfolio toward more volatile investments. Investors with a more conservative profile can weight their portfolio toward more stable investments. Indexed portfolios may employ modern portfolio theory (MPT) to aid in building an optimized portfolio, while active managers may use any number of quantitative and/or qualitative models.
- Diversification: The only certainty in investing is it is impossible to consistently predict the winners and losers, so the prudent approach is to create a basket of investments that provide broad exposure within an asset class. Diversification is the spreading of risk and reward

within an asset class. Because it is difficult to know which particular subset of an asset class or sector is likely to outperform another, diversification seeks to capture the returns of all of the sectors over time but with less volatility at any one time. Proper diversification takes place across different classes of securities, sectors of the economy and geographical regions.

Rebalancing is a method used to return a portfolio to its original target allocation at annual intervals. It is important for retaining the asset mix that best reflects an investor's risk/return profile. Otherwise, the movements of the markets could expose the portfolio to greater risk or reduced return opportunities. For example, a portfolio that starts out with a 70% equity and 30% fixed-income allocation could, through an extended market rally, shift to an 80/20 allocation that exposes the portfolio to more risk than the investor can tolerate. Rebalancing almost always entails the sale of high-priced/low-value securities and the redeployment of the proceeds into low-priced/high-value or out-of-favor securities. The annual iteration of rebalancing enables investors to capture gains and expand the opportunity for growth in high potential sectors while keeping the portfolio aligned with the investor's risk/return profile.

Active Portfolio Management

Investors who implement an active management approach use fund managers or brokers to buy and sell stocks in an attempt to outperform a specific index, such as the Standard & Poor's 500 Index or the Russell 1000 Index.

An actively managed investment fund has an individual portfolio manager, co-managers, or a team of managers actively making investment decisions for the fund. The success of an actively managed fund depends on combining in-depth research, market forecasting, and the experience and expertise of the portfolio manager or management team.

Portfolio managers engaged in active investing pay close attention to market trends, shifts in the economy, changes to the political landscape, and factors that may affect specific companies. This data is used to time the purchase or sale of investments in an effort to take advantage of irregularities. Active managers claim that these processes will boost the potential for returns higher than those achieved by simply mimicking the stocks or other securities listed on a particular index.

Since the objective of a portfolio manager in an actively managed fund is to beat the market, he or she must take on additional market risk to obtain the returns necessary to achieve this end. Indexing eliminates this, as there is no risk of human error in terms of stock selection. Index funds are also traded less frequently, which means that they incur lower expense ratios and are more tax-efficient than actively managed funds. Active management traditionally charges high fees, and recent research has cast doubts on managers' ability to consistently outperform the market.

Passive Portfolio Management

Passive management, also referred to as index fund management, involves the creation of a portfolio intended to track the returns of a particular market index or benchmark as closely as possible. Managers select stocks and other securities listed on an index and apply the same weighting. The purpose of passive portfolio management is to generate a return that is the same as the chosen index instead of outperforming it.

A passive strategy does not have a management team making investment decisions and can be structured as an exchange-traded fund (ETF), a mutual fund, or a unit investment trust. Index funds are branded as passively managed because each has a portfolio manager replicating the index, rather than trading securities based on his or her knowledge of the risk and reward characteristics of various securities. Because this investment strategy is not proactive, the management fees assessed on passive portfolios or funds are often far lower than active management strategies.

Index mutual funds are easy to understand and offer a relatively safe approach to investing in broad segments of the market.

Types of Portfolio Management

- Active Portfolio Management: When the portfolio managers actively participate in the trading of securities with a view to earning a maximum return to the investor, it is called active portfolio management.

- Passive Portfolio Management: When the portfolio managers are concerned with a fixed portfolio, which is created in alignment with the present market trends, is called passive portfolio management.

- Discretionary Portfolio Management: The Portfolio Management in which the investor places the fund with the manager, and authorizes him to invest them as per his discretion, on the investor's behalf. The portfolio manager looks after all the investment needs, documentation, etc.

- Non-Discretionary Portfolio Management: Non-discretionary portfolio management is one in which the portfolio managers gives advice to the investor or client, who can accept or reject it.

The outcome, i.e. profit received or loss sustained belongs to the investor himself, whereas the service provider receives an adequate consideration in the form of fee for rendering services.

Activities Involved in Portfolio Management

- Selection of securities in which the amount is to be invested.

- Creation of appropriate portfolio, with the securities chosen for investment.

- Making decision regarding the proportion of various securities in the portfolio, to make it an ideal portfolio for the concerned investor.

These activities aim at constructing an optimal portfolio of investment, that is compatible with the risk involved in it.

Process of Portfolio Management

- Security Analysis: It is the first stage of portfolio creation process, which involves assessing the risk and return factors of individual securities, along with their correlation.

- Portfolio Analysis: After determining the securities for investment and the risk involved, a number of portfolios can be created out of them, which are called as feasible portfolios.

- Portfolio Selection: Out of all the feasible portfolios, the optimal portfolio, that matches the risk appetite, is selected.

- Portfolio Revision: Once the optimal portfolio is selected, the portfolio manager, keeps a close watch on the portfolio, to make sure that it remains optimal in the coming time, in order to earn good returns.

- Portfolio Evaluation: In this phase, the performance of the portfolio is assessed over the stipulated period, concerning the quantitative measurement of the return obtained and risk involved in the portfolio, for the whole term of the investment.

The portfolio management services are provided by the financial companies, banks, hedge funds and money managers.

INVESTMENT STRATEGY

In finance, an investment strategy is a set of rules, behaviors or procedures, designed to guide an investor's selection of an investment portfolio. Individuals have different profit objectives, and their individual skills make different tactics and strategies appropriate. Some choices involve a tradeoff between risk and return. Most investors fall somewhere in between, accepting some risk for the expectation of higher returns.

Strategies

No strategy: Investors who don't have a strategy have been called Sheep. Arbitrary choices modeled on throwing darts at a page (referencing earlier decades when stock prices were listed daily in the newspapers) have been called Blind Folded Monkeys Throwing Darts. This famous test had debatable outcomes.

Active vs Passive: Passive strategies like buy and hold and passive indexing are often used to minimize transaction costs. Passive investors don't believe it is possible to time the market. Active strategies such as momentum trading are an attempt to outperform benchmark indexes. Active investors believe they have the better than average skills.

Momentum Trading: One strategy is to select investments based on their recent past performance. Stocks that had higher returns for the recent 3 to 12 months tend to continue to perform better for the next few months compared to the stocks that had lower returns for the recent 3 to 12 months. There is evidence both for and against this strategy.

Buy and Hold: This strategy involves buying company shares or funds and holding them for a long period. It is a long term investment strategy, based on the concept that in the long run equity markets give a good rate of return despite periods of volatility or decline. This viewpoint also holds that market timing, that one can enter the market on the lows and sell on the highs, does not work for small investors, so it is better to simply buy and hold.

Long Short Strategy: A long short strategy consists of selecting a universe of equities and ranking them according to a combined alpha factor. Given the rankings we long the top percentile and short the bottom percentile of securities once every re-balancing period.

Indexing: Indexing is where an investor buys a small proportion of all the shares in a market index such as the S&P 500, or more likely, an index mutual fund or an exchange-traded fund (ETF). This can be either a passive strategy if held for long periods, or an active strategy if the index is used to enter and exit the market quickly.

Pairs Trading: Pairs trade is a trading strategy that consists of identifying similar pairs of stocks and taking a linear combination of their price so that the result is a stationary time-series. We can then compute Altman_Z-score for the stationary signal and trade on the spread assuming mean reversion: short the top asset and long the bottom asset.

Value vs Growth: Value investing strategy looks at the intrinsic value of a company and value investors seek stocks of companies that they believed are undervalued. Growth investment strategy looks at the growth potential of a company and when a company that has expected earning growth that is higher than companies in the same industry or the market as a whole, it will attract the growth investors who are seeking to maximize their capital gain.

Dividend growth investing: This strategy involves investing in company shares according to the future dividends forecast to be paid. Companies that pay consistent and predictable dividends tend to have less volatile share prices. Well-established dividend-paying companies will aim to increase their dividend payment each year, and those who make an increase for 25 consecutive years are referred to as a dividend aristocrat. Investors who reinvest the dividends are able to benefit from compounding of their investment over the longer term, whether directly invested or through a Dividend Reinvestment Plan (DRIP).

Dollar cost averaging: The dollar cost averaging strategy is aimed at reducing the risk of incurring substantial losses resulted when the entire principal sum is invested just before the market falls.

Contrarian investment: A contrarian investment strategy consists of selecting good companies in time of down market and buying a lot of shares of that company in order to make a long-term profit. In time of economic decline, there are many opportunities to buy good shares at reasonable prices. But, what makes a company good for shareholders? A good company is one that focuses on the long term value, the quality of what it offers or the share price. This company must have a durable competitive advantage, which means that it has a market position or branding which either prevents easy access by competitors or controls a scarce raw material source. Some examples of companies that response to these criteria are in the field of insurance, soft drinks, shoes, chocolates, home building, furniture and many more. We can see that there is nothing "fancy" or special about these fields of investment: they are commonly used by each and every one of us. Many variables must be taken into consideration when making the final decision for the choice of the company. Some of them are:

- The company must be in a growing industry.
- The company cannot be vulnerable to competition.
- The company must have its earnings on an upward trend.

- The company must have a consistent returns on invested capital.
- The company must be flexible to adjust prices for inflation.

Smaller companies: Historically medium-sized companies have outperformed large cap companies on the Stock market. Smaller companies again have had even higher returns. The very best returns by market cap size historically are from micro-cap companies. Investors using this strategy buy companies based on their small market cap size on the stock exchange. One of the greatest investors Warren Buffett made money in small companies early in his career combining it with value investing. He bought small companies with low P/E ratios and high assets to market cap.

ASSET ALLOCATION

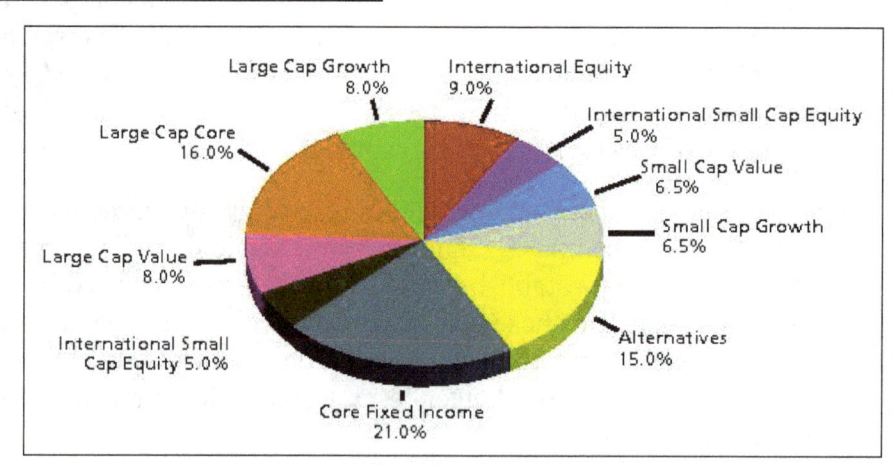

Investment portfolio with a diverse asset allocation.

Asset allocation is the implementation of an investment strategy that attempts to balance risk versus reward by adjusting the percentage of each asset in an investment portfolio according to the investor's risk tolerance, goals and investment time frame. The focus is on the characteristics of the overall portfolio. Such a strategy contrasts with an approach that focuses on individual assets.

Many financial experts argue that asset allocation is an important factor in determining returns for an investment portfolio. Asset allocation is based on the principle that different assets perform differently in different market and economic conditions.

A fundamental justification for asset allocation is the notion that different asset classes offer returns that are not perfectly correlated, hence diversification reduces the overall risk in terms of the variability of returns for a given level of expected return. Asset diversification has been described as "the only free lunch you will find in the investment game". Academic research has painstakingly explained the importance and benefits of asset allocation and the problems of active management.

Although risk is reduced as long as correlations are not perfect, it is typically forecast (wholly or in part) based on statistical relationships (like correlation and variance) that existed over some past period. Expectations for return are often derived in the same way. Studies of these forecasting methods constitute an important direction of academic research.

When such backward-looking approaches are used to forecast future returns or risks using the traditional mean-variance optimization approach to asset allocation of modern portfolio theory (MPT), the strategy is, in fact, predicting future risks and returns based on history. As there is no guarantee that past relationships will continue in the future, this is one of the "weak links" in traditional asset allocation strategies as derived from MPT. Other, more subtle weaknesses include seemingly minor errors in forecasting leading to recommended allocations that are grossly skewed from investment mandates and/or impractical—often even violating an investment manager's "common sense" understanding of a tenable portfolio-allocation strategy.

Asset Classes

An asset class is a group of economic resources sharing similar characteristics, such as riskiness and return. There are many types of assets that may or may not be included in an asset allocation strategy.

Traditional Assets

The "traditional" asset classes are *stocks*, *bonds*, and *cash*:

- Stocks: value, dividend, growth, or sector-specific (or a "blend" of any two or more of the preceding); large-cap versus mid-cap, small-cap or micro-cap; domestic, foreign (developed), emerging or frontier markets.
- Bonds (fixed income securities more generally): investment-grade or junk (high-yield); government or corporate; short-term, intermediate, long-term; domestic, foreign, emerging markets.
- Cash and cash equivalents (e.g., deposit account, money market fund).

Allocation among these three provides a starting point. Usually included are hybrid instruments such as convertible bonds and preferred stocks, counting as a mixture of bonds and stocks.

Alternative Assets

Other alternative assets that may be considered include:

- Commodities: precious metals, nonferrous metals, agriculture, energy, others.
- Commercial or residential real estate (also REITs).
- Collectibles such as art, coins, or stamps.
- Insurance products (annuity, life settlements, catastrophe bonds, personal life insurance products, etc.)
- Derivatives such as long-short or market neutral strategies, options, collateralized debt, and futures.

- Foreign currency.
- Venture capital.
- Private equity.
- Distressed securities.
- Infrastructure.
- Hedge funds.

Allocation Strategy

There are several types of asset allocation strategies based on investment goals, risk tolerance, time frames and diversification. The most common forms of asset allocation are: strategic, dynamic, tactical, and core-satellite.

Strategic Asset Allocation

The primary goal of strategic asset allocation is to create an asset mix that seeks to provide the optimal balance between expected risk and return for a long-term investment horizon. Generally speaking, strategic asset allocation strategies are agnostic to economic environments, i.e., they do not change their allocation postures relative to changing market or economic conditions.

Dynamic Asset Allocation

Dynamic asset allocation is similar to strategic asset allocation in that portfolios are built by allocating to an asset mix that seeks to provide the optimal balance between expected risk and return for a long-term investment horizon. Like strategic allocation strategies, dynamic strategies largely retain exposure to their original asset classes; however, unlike strategic strategies, dynamic asset allocation portfolios will adjust their postures over time relative to changes in the economic environment.

Tactical Asset Allocation

Tactical asset allocation is a strategy in which an investor takes a more active approach that tries to position a portfolio into those assets, sectors, or individual stocks that show the most potential for perceived gains. While an original asset mix is formulated much like strategic and dynamic portfolio, tactical strategies are often traded more actively and are free to move entirely in and out of their core asset classes.

Core-Satellite Asset Allocation

Core-satellite allocation strategies generally contain a 'core' strategic element making up the most significant portion of the portfolio, while applying a dynamic or tactical 'satellite' strategy that makes up a smaller part of the portfolio. In this way, core-satellite allocation strategies are a hybrid of the strategic and dynamic/tactical allocation strategies.

Return versus Risk Trade-off

In asset allocation planning, the decision on the amount of stocks versus bonds in one's portfolio is a very important decision. Simply buying stocks without regard of a possible bear market can result in panic selling later. One's true risk tolerance can be hard to gauge until having experienced a real bear market with money invested in the market. Finding the proper balance is key.

Cumulative return after inflation from 2000-to-2002 bear market	
80% stock / 20% bond	−34.35%
70% stock / 30% bond	−25.81%
60% stock / 40% bond	−19.99%
50% stock / 50% bond	−13.87%
40% stock / 60% bond	−7.46%
30% stock / 70% bond	−0.74%
20% stock / 80% bond	+6.29%

Projected 10-year Cumulative return after inflation (stock return 8% yearly, bond return 4.5% yearly, inflation 3% yearly	
80% stock / 20% bond	52%
70% stock / 30% bond	47%
60% stock / 40% bond	42%
50% stock / 50% bond	38%
40% stock / 60% bond	33%
30% stock / 70% bond	29%
20% stock / 80% bond	24%

The tables show why asset allocation is important. It determines an investor's future return, as well as the bear market burden that he or she will have to carry successfully to realize the returns.

Problems with Asset Allocation

There are various reasons why asset allocation fails to work.

- Investor behavior is inherently biased. Even though investor chooses an asset allocation, implementation is a challenge.
- Investors agree to asset allocation, but after some good returns they decide that they really wanted more risk.
- Investors agree to asset allocation, but after some bad returns they decide that they really wanted less risk.
- Investors' risk tolerance is not knowable ahead of time.
- Security selection within asset classes will not necessarily produce a risk profile equal to the asset class.
- The long-run behavior of asset classes does not guarantee their shorter-term behavior.

DYNAMIC ASSET ALLOCATION

Dynamic asset allocation is a strategy used by investment products such as hedge funds, mutual funds, credit derivatives, index funds, principal protected notes (also known as guaranteed linked notes) and other structured investment products to achieve exposure to various investment opportunities and provide 100% principal protection.

Dynamic asset allocation includes CPPI, which consists of a guarantee, notionally related to a zero-coupon bond and an underlying investment. Assets are dynamically shifted (or allocated) between these two components depending largely on the performance of the underlying investments.

In some cases, certain products can use a borrowing facility to enhance exposure if the underlying investments experience strong returns. If the underlying investments decline in value, CPPI automatically deleverages, reducing exposure in falling markets.

The term 'Dynamic Asset Allocation' (DAA) can also refer to an investment strategy that seeks to produce high total returns irrespective of the performance of market indices using the tools of Tactical asset allocation/Global tactical asset allocation (TAA/GTAA) around a strategic benchmark. Indeed, many investment firms and commentators use the terms TAA, DAA, and GTAA interchangeably.

In the arena of institutional asset management DAA mandates tend to have absolute return targets that are not related to market index returns (e.g. USD LIBOR + 500bps), while TAA mandates will tend to have performance targets that reference market indices (e.g. 50% S&P 500/ 50% Barclays Capital Aggregate Bond Index + 200bps).

GLOBAL TACTICAL ASSET ALLOCATION

Global Tactical Asset Allocation, or GTAA, is a top-down investment strategy that attempts to exploit short-term mis-pricings among a global set of assets. The strategy focuses on general movements in the market rather than on performance of individual securities.

Hedge Funds and Asset Allocation

GTAA is believed to be derived from, and share some characteristics of, global macro hedge funds and tactical asset allocation (TAA). Global macro hedge funds, like GTAA, seek to profit from taking positions in major world equity, bond or currency markets. However, the two differ in the fact that global macro has been characterized by large, undiversified bets, while modern GTAA strategies are generally well-diversified and operate with risk controls. TAA decisions undertaken by managers of multi-asset funds, like GTAA decisions, are intended to enhance investment outcomes by overweighting and underweighting asset classes based on their expected performance over relatively short time periods (usually 3 to 6 months). While TAA, within multi-asset funds, is restricted to the asset classes contained in the fund's strategic asset allocation, GTAA strategies enjoys the privilege of accessing a broader opportunity set.

Strategies

The modern global tactical asset allocation program is composed of two separate strategies: strategic rebalancing and overlay. The strategic rebalancing element of GTAA program is designed to remove any unintentional asset allocation risk which can be caused by various factors, including: drift risk, which occurs when the value of underlying portfolio holdings moves away from the strategic benchmark due to differences in asset class returns, due to changes in asset valuation, cash holdings, currency deviations from stock selection, unintentional country deviations within underlying stock/bond portfolios, manager of benchmark transitions, and contributions to and redemptions from the portfolio. The overlay element of GTAA program is designed to capture excess return through intentional, opportunistic, long and short positions in asset classes and countries. The GTAA strategy can be viewed as making two major types of decisions: The first type is asset class timing, including stocks vs. bonds vs. cash, small-cap vs. large-cap stocks, value vs. growth stocks, emerging vs. developed stocks and bonds, etc. This kind of decision making is often referred to as TAA. The second type of decision is known as country or sector decisions within asset classes, including country selection in developed and emerging equity, as well as fixed income and currency markets. These are the global relative-value decisions which give meaning to the "G" in GTAA and distinguish the strategy from traditional market timing.

Portfolios

It is widely known that many institutional investment portfolios remain dominated by equity and interest rate risk, and that these allocations tend to remain motionless regardless of market conditions. Therefore, there is reason to establish a portfolio of alternative alpha sources, and GTAA represents just that, for myriad reasons: the performance differentials between asset classes are frequently substantial, the derivative instruments used in GTAA are, for the most part, highly liquid and transaction costs are low. The volume of assets managed with a focus on relative performance of asset classes is low compared to that focused on finding opportunities within asset classes, and a number of managers with very impressive teams, processes and track records can be identified. Furthermore, the analysis and decision making involved in GTAA is focused on cross-market comparisons which proves to differ from the comparison of securities within given markets. Accordingly, GTAA should be a good diversifier, particularly within an alpha portfolio.

GTAA strategies provide investors with a series of exposures that may not otherwise be prevalent in their portfolios. Managing these exposures provides an opportunity for the generation of returns that share low correlations with other sources of active return, and they can also be expected to lead to more reliable added value.

ACTIVE MANAGEMENT

Active management (also called *active investing*) refers to a portfolio management strategy where the manager makes specific investments with the goal of outperforming an investment benchmark index or target return. In passive management, investors expect a return that closely replicates the investment weighting and returns of a benchmark index and will often invest in an index fund.

Ideally, the active manager exploits market inefficiencies by purchasing securities (stocks etc.) that are undervalued or by short selling securities that are overvalued. Either of these methods may be used alone or in combination. Depending on the goals of the specific investment portfolio, hedge fund or mutual fund, active management may also serve to create less volatility (or risk) than the benchmark index. The reduction of risk may be instead of, or in addition to, the goal of creating an investment return greater than the benchmark.

Active portfolio managers may use a variety of factors and strategies to construct their portfolio(s). These include quantitative measures such as price–earnings ratios and PEG ratios, sector investments that attempt to anticipate long-term macroeconomic trends (such as a focus on energy or housing stocks), and purchasing stocks of companies that are temporarily out-of-favor or selling at a discount to their intrinsic value. Some actively managed funds also pursue strategies such as risk arbitrage, short positions, option writing, and asset allocation.

Using the concept of asset allocation, researchers divide active management into two parts; one part is selecting securities within an asset class, while the other part is selecting between asset classes (often called tactical asset allocation). For example, a large-cap U.S. stock fund might decide which large-cap U.S. stocks to include in the fund. Then those stocks will do better or worse than the class in general. Another fund may choose to move money between bonds and stocks, or some country versus a different one, et cetera. Then one class will do worse or better than the other class.

The case where a fund changes its class of assets is called style drift. An example would be where a fund that normally invests in government bonds switches into stocks of small companies in emerging markets. Although this gives the most discretion to the manager, it also makes it difficult for the investor (portfolio manager) if he also has a target of asset allocation.

Performance

The effectiveness of an actively managed investment portfolio depends on the skill of the manager and research staff but also on how the term active is defined. Many mutual funds purported to be actively managed stay fully invested regardless of market conditions, with only minor allocation adjustments over time. Other managers will retreat fully to cash, or use hedging strategies during prolonged market declines. These two groups of active managers will often have very different performance characteristics.

Approximately 20% of all mutual funds are pure index funds. The balance are actively managed in some respect. In reality, a large percentage of actively managed mutual funds rarely outperform their index counterparts over an extended period of time because 45% of all mutual funds are "closet indexers" — funds whose portfolios look like indexes and whose performance is very closely correlated to an index but call themselves active to justify higher management fees. Prospectuses of closet indexers will often include language such as "80% of holdings will be large cap growth stocks within the S&P 500" causing the majority of their performance to be directly dependent upon the performance of the growth stock index they are benchmarking, less the larger fees.

The Standard & Poor's Index Versus Active (SPIVA) quarterly scorecards demonstrate that only a minority of actively managed mutual funds have gains better than the Standard & Poor's (S&P) index benchmark. As the time period for comparison increases, the percentage of actively managed funds whose gains exceed the S&P benchmark declines further. This may be due to the preponderance of closet-index funds in the study.

Only about 30% of mutual funds are active enough that the manager has the latitude to move completely out of an asset class in decline, which is what many investors expect from active management. Of these 30% of funds there are out-performers and under-performers, but this group that outperforms is also the same group that outperforms passively managed portfolios over long periods of time.

Due to mutual fund fees and/or expenses, it is possible that an active or passively managed mutual fund could under-perform compared to the benchmark index, even though the securities that comprise the mutual fund are outperforming the benchmark, because indexes themselves have no expenses whatsoever. However, since many investors are not satisfied with a benchmark return, a demand for active management continues to exist. In addition, many investors find active management an attractive investment strategy in volatile or declining markets or when investing in market segments that are less likely to be profitable when considered as a whole. These kinds of sectors might include a sector such as small cap stocks.

Advantages of Active Management

The primary attraction of active management is that it allows selection of a variety of investments instead of investing in the market as a whole. Investors may have a variety of motivations for following such a strategy:

- An investor may believe that actively managed funds do better in general than passively managed funds.

- Investors believe that they have some skill for picking which active managers will do better after they have invested.

- They may be skeptical of the efficient-market hypothesis, or believe that some market segments are less efficient in creating profits than others.

- They may want to manage volatility by investing in less-risky, high-quality companies rather than in the market as a whole, even at the cost of slightly lower returns.

- Conversely, some investors may want to take on additional risk in exchange for the opportunity of obtaining higher-than-market returns.

- Investments that are not highly correlated to the market are useful as a portfolio diversifier and may reduce overall portfolio volatility.

- Some investors may wish to follow a strategy that avoids or underweights certain industries compared to the market as a whole, and may find an actively managed fund more in line with their particular investment goals. (For instance, an employee of a high-technology growth company who receives company stock or stock options as a benefit might prefer not to have additional funds invested in the same industry.)

- Investors may gain some psychic benefit from firing a manager that has underperformed, and replacing them with a different manager.

Several of the actively managed mutual funds with strong long-term records invest in value stocks. Passively managed funds that track broad market indices such as the S&P 500 have money invested in all the securities in that index i.e. both growth and value stocks.

The use of managed funds in certain emerging markets has been recommended by Burton Malkiel, a proponent of the efficient market theory who normally considers index funds to be superior to active management in developed markets.

Disadvantages of Active Management

The most obvious disadvantage of active management is that the fund manager may make bad investment choices or follow an unsound theory in managing the portfolio. Unless active management is performed by a robo-advisor the fees associated with active management are generally also higher than those associated with passive management, even if frequent trading is not present, reflecting in part the additional research costs associated with active investing. Those who are considering investing in an actively managed mutual fund should evaluate the fund's prospectus carefully. Data from recent decades demonstrates that the majority of actively managed large and mid-cap stock funds in United States fail to outperform their passive stock index counterparts.

Active fund management strategies that involve frequent trading generate higher transaction costs which diminish the fund's return. In addition, the short-term capital gains resulting from frequent trades often have an unfavorable income tax impact when such funds are held in a taxable account.

When the asset base of an actively managed fund becomes too large, it begins to take on index-like characteristics because it must invest in an increasingly diverse set of investments instead of those limited to the fund manager's best ideas. Many mutual fund companies close their funds before they reach this point, but there is potential for a conflict of interest between mutual fund management and shareholders because closing the fund will result in a loss of income (management fees) for the mutual fund company.

Real Active Management

Most mutual funds do not have board members and directors with an equity stake in the mutual fund that their manager(s) are administrating. In other words, the directors and board members don't directly impact the future performance of the fund. Real active management, then, is when every manager and director has a vested interest in the success of the fund. Private equity is often real active management since a privately owned company usually has just one owner that make strategy decisions at the board level.

BENCHMARK-DRIVEN INVESTMENT STRATEGY

Benchmark-driven investment strategy is an investment strategy where the target return is usually linked to an index or combination of indices of the sector or any other like S&P 500. With the Benchmarks approach the investor chooses an index of the market (benchmark). The goal of the fund manager is to try to beat the index performance-wise.

A benchmark is a standard against which the performance of a security, mutual fund or investment manager can be measured. Generally, broad market and market-segment stock and bond indexes are used for this purpose. It's an element of a Sigma Six black belt.

Benchmarks are indexes created to include multiple securities representing some aspect of the total market. Benchmark indexes have been created across all types of asset classes. In the equity market, the S&P 500 and Dow Jones Industrial Average are two of the most popular large cap stock benchmarks. In fixed income, examples of top benchmarks include the Barclays Capital U.S. Aggregate Bond Index, the Barclays Capital U.S. Corporate High Yield Bond Index and the Barclays Capital U.S. Treasury Bond Index. Mutual fund investors may use Lipper indexes, which use the 30 largest mutual funds in a specific category, while international investors may use MSCI Indexes. The Wilshire 5000 is also a popular benchmark representing all of the publicly traded stocks in the U.S. When evaluating the performance of any investment, it's important to compare it against an appropriate benchmark.

Identifying and setting a benchmark can be an important aspect of investing for individual investors. In addition to traditional benchmarks representing broad market characteristics such as large cap, mid cap, small cap, growth and value. Investors will also find indexes based on fundamental characteristics, sectors, dividends, market trends and much more. Having an understanding or interest in a specific type of investment will help an investor identify appropriate investment funds and also allow them to better communicate their investment goals and expectations to a financial advisor.

When seeking investment benchmarks, an investor should also consider risk. An investor's benchmark should reflect the amount of risk he or she is willing to take. Other investment factors around benchmark considerations may include the amount to be invested and the cost the investor is willing to pay.

Investment Industry Fund Management

The number of benchmarks has been expanding with product innovation. Benchmarks are often used as the central factor for portfolio management in the investment industry. Passive investment funds and smart beta funds are two strategies that are derived from benchmark investing. Replication strategies following customized benchmarks are also becoming more prevalent. Active managers are also in the market deploying actively managed strategies using indexes in the most traditional form, as benchmarks they seek to beat.

Passive

Benchmarks are created to include multiple securities representing some aspect of the total market. Passive investment funds were created to provide investors exposure to a benchmark since it is expensive for an individual investor to invest in each of the indexes' securities. In passive funds the investment manager uses a replication strategy to match the holdings and returns of the benchmark index providing investors with a low cost fund for targeted investing. A leading example of this type of fund is the SPDR S&P 500 ETF (SPY) which replicates the S&P 500 Index with a management fee of 0.09%. Investors can easily find large cap, mid cap, small cap, growth and value mutual funds and ETFs deploying this strategy.

Smart Beta

Smart Beta strategies were developed as an enhancement to passive index funds. They seek to enhance the returns an investor could achieve by investing in a standard passive fund by choosing stocks based on certain variables or by taking long and short positions to obtain alpha. State Street Global Advisors' enhanced index strategies provide an example of this. The SSGA Enhanced Small Cap Fund (SESPX) seeks to marginally outperform its Russell 2000 benchmark by taking long and short positions in the small cap stocks of the index.

Market Segment Benchmarks

Market segment benchmarks can provide investors with other options for benchmark investing based on specific market segments such as sectors. The State Street Global Advisors SPDR ETFs provide investors the opportunity to invest in each of the individual sectors in the S&P 500. One example is the Technology Select Sector SPDR Fund (XLK).

Fundamental and Thematic Benchmarks

With the challenges of beating the market, many investment managers have created customized benchmarks that use a replication strategy. These types of funds are becoming more prevalent as top performers. These funds benchmark to customized indexes based on fundamentals, style and market themes. The Global X Robotics & Artificial Intelligence Thematic ETF (BOTZ) is one of the best performing non leveraged thematic ETFs in the investable universe. It uses an index replication strategy and seeks to track the Indxx Global Robotics & Artificial Intelligence Thematic Index. The Index is a customized index benchmark that includes companies involved in robotic and artificial intelligence solutions.

Active Management

Active management becomes more challenging with the growing number of benchmark replication strategies. Thus, for investors it becomes more challenging to find active managers consistently beating their benchmarks. In 2017, the ARK Innovation ETF (ARKK) is one of the top performing ETFs in the investable market. Year-to-date as of November 3 it had a return of 76.06%. Its benchmarks are the S&P 500 with a comparable return of 15.59% and the MSCI World Index with a comparable return of 17.55%.

The Value of Benchmarks

The value of benchmarks has been an ongoing topic for debate bringing about a number of innovations that center around investing in the actual benchmark indexes directly. Debates are primarily derived from the demands for benchmark exposure, fundamental investing and thematic investing. Managers who subscribe to the efficient market hypothesis (EMH) claim that it is essentially impossible to beat the market, and then by extension, the idea of trying to beat a benchmark isn't a realistic goal for a manager to meet. Thus, the evolving number of portfolio strategies centered around index benchmark investing. Nonetheless, there are active managers who do consistently beat benchmarks. These strategies do require extensive monitoring and often include high management fees. However, successful active managers are becoming more prevalent as artificial intelligence quantitative models integrate more variables with greater automation into the portfolio management process.

Benchmark Error

Benchmark error is a situation in which the wrong benchmark is selected in a financial model. This error can create large dispersions in an analyst or academic's data, but can easily be avoided by selecting the most appropriate benchmark at the onset of an analysis. Tracking error can be confused for benchmark error, but the two measures have distinctly different utilities.

To avoid benchmark error, it is important to use the most appropriate benchmark, or market, in your calculations, when creating a market portfolio under the capital asset pricing model (CAPM). If, for example, you want to create a portfolio of American stocks using the CAPM, you would not use the Nikkei — a Japanese index — as your benchmark. Accordingly, if you want to compare your portfolio returns, you should use an index that contains similar stocks. For example, if your portfolio is tech-heavy, you should use the Nasdaq as your benchmark, rather than the S&P 500.

FUND OF FUNDS

A "fund of funds" (FOF) is an investment strategy of holding a portfolio of other investment funds rather than investing directly in stocks, bonds or other securities. This type of investing is often referred to as multi-manager investment. A fund of funds may be "fettered", meaning that it invests only in funds managed by the same investment company, or "unfettered", meaning that it can invest in external funds run by other managers.

There are different types of FOF, each investing in a different type of collective investment scheme (typically one type per FOF), for example a mutual fund FOF, a hedge fund FOF, a private equity FOF, or an investment trust FOF. The original Fund of Funds was created by Bernie Cornfeld in 1962. It went bankrupt after being looted by Robert Vesco.

Features

Investing in a collective investment scheme may increase diversity compared with a small investor holding a smaller range of securities directly. Investing in a fund of funds may achieve greater diversification. According to modern portfolio theory, the benefit of diversification can be the reduction of volatility while maintaining average returns. However, this is countered by the increased fees paid both at FOF level and at the level of the underlying investment fund.

Considerations

Management fees for FOFs are typically higher than those on traditional investment funds because they include the management fees charged by the underlying funds.

"Historically, a fund of funds showed an expense figure that didn't always include the fees of the underlying funds. As of January 2007, the SEC began requiring that these fees be disclosed in a line called 'Acquired Fund Fees and Expenses' (AFFE)."

After allocation of the levels of fees payable and taxation, returns on FOF investments will generally be lower than what single-manager funds can yield. However, some FOFs waive the second level of fees (the FOF fee) so that investors only pay the expenses of the underlying mutual funds.

Pension funds, endowments and other institutions often invest in funds of hedge funds for part or all of their "alternative asset" programs, i.e., investments other than traditional stock and bond holdings.

The due diligence and safety of investing in FOFs has come under question as a result of the Bernie Madoff scandal, where many FOFs put substantial investments into the scheme. It became clear that a motivation for this was the lack of fees by Madoff, which gave the illusion that the FOF was performing well. The due diligence of the FOFs apparently did not include asking why Madoff was not making this charge for his services. 2008 and 2009 saw FOFs take a battering from investors and the media on all fronts from the hollow promises made by over-eager marketers to the strength (or lack) of their due diligence processes to those carefully explained and eminently justifiable extra layers of fees, all reaching their zenith with the Bernie Madoff fiasco.

These strategic and structural issues have caused fund-of-funds to become less and less popular. Nonetheless, fund-for-funds remain important in particular asset classes, including venture capital and for particular investors in order for them to be able to diversify their too low or too high level of assets under management appropriately.

Asset Allocation

The FOF structure may be useful for asset-allocation funds, that is, an "exchange-traded fund (ETF) of ETFs" or "mutual fund of mutual funds". For example, iShares has asset-allocation ETFs, which own other iShares ETFs. Similarly, Vanguard has asset-allocation mutual funds, which own other Vanguard mutual funds. The "parent" funds may own the same "child" funds, with different proportions to allow for "aggressive" to "conservative" allocation. This structure simplifies management by separating allocation from security selection.

Target-date Fund

A target-date fund is similar to an asset-allocation fund, except that the allocation is designed to change over time. The same structure is useful here. iShares has target-date ETFs that own other iShares ETFs; Vanguard has target-date mutual funds that own other Vanguard mutual funds. In both cases, the same funds are used as the asset-allocation funds. Since a provider may have many target dates, this can greatly reduce duplication of work.

Fund of Hedge Funds

A fund of hedge funds is a fund of funds that invests in a portfolio of different hedge funds to provide broad exposure to the hedge fund industry and to diversify the risks associated with a single investment fund. Funds of hedge funds select hedge fund managers and construct portfolios based upon those selections. The fund of hedge funds is responsible for hiring and firing the managers in the fund. Some funds of hedge funds might have only one hedge fund in them, which lets ordinary investors into a highly acclaimed fund, or many hedge funds.

Funds of hedge funds generally charge a fee for their services, always in addition to the hedge fund's management and performance fees, which can be 1.5% and 15-30%, respectively. Fees can reduce an investor's profits and potentially reduce the total return below what could be achieved through a less expensive mutual fund or exchange-traded fund (ETF).

Fund of Venture Capital Funds

A fund of venture capital funds is a fund of funds that invests in a portfolio of different venture capital funds for access to private capital markets. Clients are usually university endowments and pension funds.

PASSIVE INVESTING

Passive investing is an investment strategy to maximize returns by minimizing buying and selling. Index investing in one common passive investing strategy whereby investors purchase a representative benchmark, such as the S&P 500 index, and hold it over a long time horizon.

Passive investing methods seek to avoid the fees and limited performance that may occur with frequent trading. Passive investing's goal is to build wealth gradually. Also known as a buy-and-hold strategy, passive investing means buying a security to own it long-term. Unlike active traders, passive investors do not seek to profit from short-term price fluctuations or market timing. The underlying assumption of passive investment strategy is that the market posts positive returns over time.

Passive managers generally believe it is difficult to out-think the market, so they try to match market or sector performance. Passive investing attempts to replicate market performance by constructing well-diversified portfolios of single stocks, which if done individually, would require extensive research. The introduction of index funds in the 1970s made achieving returns in line with the market much easier. In the 1990s, exchange-traded funds, or ETFs, that track major indices, such as the SPDR S&P 500 ETF (SPY), simplified the process even further by allowing investors to trade index funds as though they were stocks.

Passive Investing Benefits and Drawbacks

Maintaining a well-diversified portfolio is important to successful investing, and passive investing via indexing is an excellent way to achieve diversification. Index funds spread risk broadly in holding all, or a representative sample of the securities in their target benchmarks. Index funds track a target benchmark or index rather than seeking winners, so they avoid constantly buying and selling securities. As a result, they have lower fees and operating expenses than actively managed funds. An index fund offers simplicity as an easy way to invest in a chosen market because it seeks to track an index. There is no need to select and monitor individual managers, or chose among investment themes.

However, passive investing is subject to total market risk. Index funds track the entire market, so when the overall stock market or bond prices fall, so do index funds. Another risk is the lack of flexibility. Index fund managers usually are prohibited from using defensive measures such as reducing a position in shares, even if the manager thinks share prices will decline. Passively managed index funds face performance constraints as they are designed to provide returns that closely track their benchmark index, rather than seek outperformance. They rarely beat the return on the index, and usually return slightly less due to fund operating costs.

Some of the key benefits of passive investing are:

- Ultra-low fees: There's nobody picking stocks, so oversight is much less expensive. Passive funds follow the index they use as their benchmark.

- Transparency: It's always clear which assets are in an index fund.

- Tax efficiency: Their buy-and-hold strategy doesn't typically result in a massive capital gains tax for the year.

- Simplicity: Owning an index, or group of indices is far easier to implement and comprehend than a dynamic strategy that requires constant research and adjustment.

Proponents of active investing would say that passive strategies have these weaknesses:

- Too limited: Passive funds are limited to a specific index or predetermined set of investments with little to no variance; thus, investors are locked into those holdings, no matter what happens in the market.

- Smaller potential returns: By definition, passive funds will pretty much never beat the market, even during times of turmoil, as their core holdings are locked in to track the market. Sometimes, a passive fund may beat the market by a little, but it will never post the big returns active managers crave unless the market itself booms. Active managers, on the other hand, can bring bigger rewards, although those rewards come with greater risk as well.

Benefits and Limitations

To contrast the pros and cons of passive investing, active investing also have its benefits and limitations to consider:

- Flexibility: Active managers aren't required to follow a specific index. They can buy those "diamond in the rough" stocks they believe they've found.

- Hedging: Active managers can also hedge their bets using various techniques such as short sales or put options, and they're able to exit specific stocks or sectors when the risks become too big. Passive managers are stuck with the stocks that the index they track holds, regardless of how they are doing.

- Tax management: Even though this strategy could trigger a capital gains tax, advisors can tailor tax management strategies to individual investors, such as by selling investments that are losing money to offset the taxes on the big winners.

But active strategies have these shortcomings:

- Very expensive: Thomson Reuters Lipper pegs the average expense ratio at 1.4 percent for an actively managed equity fund, compared to only 0.6 percent for the average passive equity fund. Fees are higher because all that active buying and selling triggers transaction costs, not to mention that you're paying the salaries of the analyst team researching equity picks. All those fees over decades of investing can kill returns.

- Active risk: Active managers are free to buy any investment they think would bring high returns, which is great when the analysts are right but terrible when they're wrong.

- Poor track record: The data show that very few actively managed portfolios beat their passive benchmarks, especially after taxes and fees are accounted for. Indeed, over medium to long time frames, only a small handful of actively managed mutual funds surpass their benchmark index.

INVESTMENT FUND

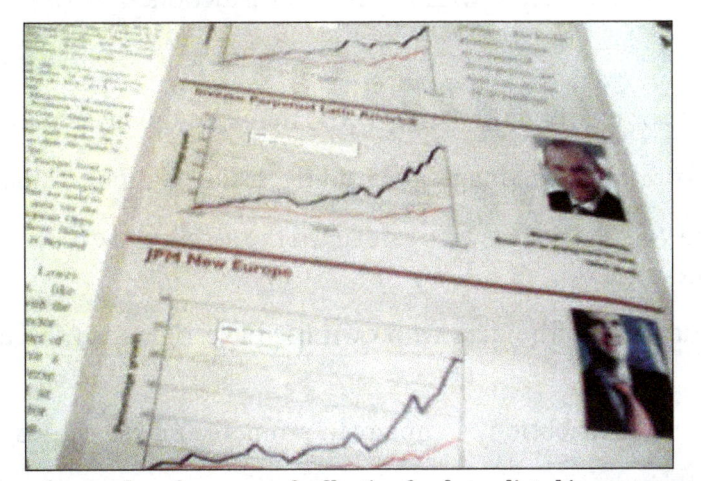

The values and performance of collective funds are listed in newspapers.

An investment fund is a way of investing money alongside other investors in order to benefit from the inherent advantages of working as part of a group. These advantages include an ability to:

- Hire professional investment managers, which may potentially be able to offer better returns and more adequate risk management.

- Benefit from economies of scale, i.e., lower transaction costs.

- Increase the asset diversification to reduce some unsystematic risk.

It remains unclear whether professional active investment managers can reliably enhance risk adjusted returns by an amount that exceeds fees and expenses of investment management. Terminology varies with country but investment funds are often referred to as investment pools, collective investment vehicles, collective investment schemes, managed funds, or simply funds. The regulatory term is undertaking for collective investment in transferable securities, or short collective investment undertaking (cf. Law). An investment fund may be held by the public, such as a mutual fund, exchange-traded fund, special-purpose acquisition company or closed-end fund, or it may be sold only in a private placement, such as a hedge fund or private equity fund. The term also includes specialized vehicles such as collective and common trust funds, which are unique bank-managed funds structured primarily to commingle assets from qualifying pension plans or trusts.

Investment funds are promoted with a wide range of investment aims either targeting specific geographic regions (*e.g.*, emerging markets or Europe) or specified industry sectors (*e.g.*, technology). Depending on the country there is normally a bias towards the domestic market due to familiarity, and the lack of currency risk. Funds are often selected on the basis of these specified investment aims, their past investment performance, and other factors such as fees.

Generic Information—Structure

Constitution and Terminology

Collective investment vehicles may be formed under company law, by legal trust or by statute. The nature of the vehicle and its limitations are often linked to its constitutional nature and the associated tax rules for the type of structure within a given jurisdiction.

Typically there is:

- A fund manager or investment manager who manages the investment decisions.
- A fund administrator who manages the trading, reconciliations, valuation and unit pricing.
- A board of directors or trustees who safeguard the assets and ensure compliance with laws, regulations and rules.
- The shareholders or unitholders who own (or have rights to) the assets and associated income.
- A "marketing" or "distribution" company to promote and sell shares/units of the fund.

Net Asset Value

The net asset value or NAV is the value of a vehicle's assets minus the value of its liabilities. The method for calculating this varies between vehicle types and jurisdiction and can be subject to complex regulation.

Open-end Fund

An open-end fund is equitably divided into shares which vary in price in direct proportion to the variation in value of the fund's net asset value. Each time money is invested, new shares or units are created to match the prevailing share price; each time shares are redeemed, the assets sold match the prevailing share price. In this way there is no supply or demand created for shares and they remain a direct reflection of the underlying assets.

Closed-end Fund

A closed-end fund issues a limited number of shares (or units) in an initial public offering (or IPO) or through private placement. If shares are issued through an IPO, they are then traded on an exchange or directly through the fund manager to create a secondary market subject to market forces. If demand for the shares is high, they may trade at a *premium* to net asset value. If demand is low they may trade at a *discount* to net asset value. Further share (or unit) offerings may be made by the vehicle if demand is high although this may affect the share price.

For listed funds, the added element of market forces tends to amplify the performance of the fund increasing investment risk through increased volatility.

Gearing and Leverage

Some collective investment vehicles have the power to borrow money to make further investments; a process known as gearing or leverage. If markets are growing rapidly this can allow the vehicle to take advantage of the growth to a greater extent than if only the subscribed contributions were invested. However this premise only works if the cost of the borrowing is less than the increased growth achieved. If the borrowing costs are more than the growth achieved a net loss is achieved.

This can greatly increase the investment risk of the fund by increased volatility and exposure to increased capital risk.

Gearing was a major contributory factor in the collapse of the split capital investment trust debacle in the UK in 2002.

Availability and Access

Collective investment vehicles vary in availability depending on their intended investor base:

- Public-availability vehicles: Are available to most investors within the jurisdiction they are offered. Some restrictions on age and size of investment may be imposed.
- Limited-availability vehicles: Are limited by laws, regulations, and/or rules to experienced and/or sophisticated investors and often have high minimum investment requirements.
- Private-availability vehicles: May be limited to family members or whomever set up the fund. They are not publicly traded and may be arranged for tax or estate planning purposes.

Limited Duration

Some vehicles are designed to have a limited term with enforced redemption of shares or units on a specified date.

Unit or Share Class

Many collective investment vehicles split the fund into multiple classes of shares or units. The underlying assets of each class are effectively pooled for the purposes of investment management, but classes typically differ in the fees and expenses paid out of the fund's assets.

These differences are supposed to reflect different costs involved in servicing investors in various classes; for example:

- One class may be sold through a stockbroker or financial adviser with an initial commission (front-end load) and might be called *retail* shares.

- Another class may be sold with no commission (load) direct to the public called direct shares.
- Still a third class might have a high minimum investment limit and only be open to financial institutions, and called institutional shares.

In some cases, by aggregating regular investments by many individuals, a retirement plan (such as a 401(k) plan) may qualify to purchase "institutional" shares (and gain the benefit of their typically lower expense ratios) even though no members of the plan would qualify individually. These also include Unit Trusts.

Generic Information—Advantages

Diversity and Risk

One of the main advantages of collective investment is the reduction in investment risk (capital risk) by diversification. An investment in a single equity may do well, but it may collapse for investment or other reasons (e.g., Marconi). If your money is invested in such a failed holding you could lose your capital. By investing in a range of equities (or other securities) the capital risk is reduced.

The more diversified your capital, the lower the capital risk. This investment principle is often referred to as spreading risk.

Collective investments by their nature tend to invest in a range of individual securities. However, if the securities are all in a similar type of asset class or market sector then there is a systematic risk that all the shares could be affected by adverse market changes. To avoid this systematic risk investment managers may diversify into different non-perfectly-correlated asset classes. For example, investors might hold their assets in equal parts in equities and fixed income securities.

Reduced Dealing Costs

If one investor had to buy a large number of direct investments, the amount this person would be able to invest in each holding is likely to be small. Dealing costs are normally based on the number and size of each transaction, therefore the overall dealing costs would take a large chunk out of the capital (affecting future profits).

Generic Information—Disadvantages

Costs

The fund manager managing the investment decisions on behalf of the investors will of course expect remuneration. This is often taken directly from the fund assets as a fixed percentage each year or sometimes a variable (performance based) fee. If the investor managed their own investments, this cost would be avoided.

Often the cost of advice given by a stockbroker or financial adviser is built into the vehicle. Often referred to as commission or load (in the U.S.) this charge may be applied at the start of the plan or as an ongoing percentage of the fund value each year. While this cost will diminish your returns it could be argued that it reflects a separate payment for an advice service rather than a detrimental feature of collective investment vehicles. Indeed, it is often possible to purchase units or shares directly from the providers without bearing this cost.

Lack of Choice

Although the investor can choose the type of fund to invest in, they have no control over the choice of individual holdings that make up the fund.

Loss of Owner's Rights

If the investor holds shares directly, he has the right to attend the company's annual general meeting and vote on important matters. Investors in a collective investment vehicle often have none of the rights connected with individual investments within the fund.

Style

Investment Aims and Benchmarking

Each fund has a defined investment goal to describe the remit of the investment manager and to help investors decide if the fund is right for them. The investment aims will typically fall into the broad categories of Income (value) investment or Growth investment. Income or value based investment tends to select stocks with strong income streams, often more established businesses. Growth investment selects stocks that tend to reinvest their income to generate growth. Each strategy has its critics and proponents; some prefer a *blend* approach using aspects of each.

Funds are often distinguished by asset-based categories such as *equity, bonds, property*, etc. Also, perhaps most commonly funds are divided by their *geographic markets* or *themes*.

Examples:
- The largest markets—U.S., Japan, Europe, UK and Far East are often divided into smaller funds e.g. US large caps, Japanese smaller companies, European Growth, UK mid caps etc.
- Themed funds—Technology, Healthcare, Socially responsible funds.

In most instances whatever the investment aim the fund manager will select an appropriate index or combination of indices to measure its performance against; e.g. FTSE 100. This becomes the benchmark to measure success or failure against.

Active or Passive Management

The aim of most funds is to make money by investing in assets to obtain a real return (i.e. better than inflation). The philosophy used to manage the fund's investment vary and two opposing views exist.
- Active management: Active managers seek to outperform the market as a whole, by selectively holding securities according to an investment strategy. Therefore, they employ dynamic portfolio strategies, buying and selling investments with changing market conditions, based on their belief that particular individual holdings or sections of the market will perform better than others.

- Passive management—Passive managers stick to a portfolio strategy determined at outset of the fund and not varied thereafter, aiming to minimize the ongoing costs of maintaining the portfolio. Many passive funds are index funds, which attempt to replicate the performance of a market index by holding securities proportionally to their value in the market as a whole. Another example of passive management is the "buy and hold" method used by many traditional unit investment trusts where the portfolio is fixed from outset.

Additionally, some funds use a hybrid management strategy of enhanced indexing, in which the manager minimizes costs by broadly following a passive indexing strategy, but has the discretion to actively deviate from the index in the hopes of earning modestly higher returns.

An example of active management success:

In 1998 Richard Branson (head of Virgin) publicly bet Nicola Horlick (head of SG Asset Management) that her SG UK Growth fund would not beat the FTSE 100 index, nor his Virgin Index Tracker fund over three years, nor achieve its stated aim to beat the index by 2% each year. He lost and paid £6,000 to charity.

Alpha, Beta, R-squared and Standard Deviation

When analysing investment performance, statistical measures are often used to compare 'funds'. These statistical measures are often reduced to a single figure representing an aspect of past performance:

- Alpha represents the fund's return when the benchmark's return is 0. This shows the fund's performance relative to the benchmark and can demonstrate the value added by the fund manager. The higher the 'alpha' the better the manager. Alpha investment strategies tend to favour *stock selection* methods to achieve growth.

- Beta represents an estimate of how much the fund will move if its benchmark moves by 1 unit. This shows the fund's sensitivity to changes in the market. Beta investment strategies tend to favour asset allocation models to achieve *outperformance*.

- R-squared is a measure of the association between a fund and its benchmark. Values are between 0 and 1. Perfect correlation is indicated by 1, and 0 indicates no correlation. This measure is useful in determining if the fund manager is adding value in their investment choices or acting as a *closet tracker* mirroring the market and making little difference. For example, an index fund will have an R-squared with its benchmark index very close to 1, indicating close to perfect correlation (the index fund's fees and tracking error prevent the correlation from ever equalling 1).

- Standard deviation is a measure of volatility of the fund's performance over a period of time. The higher the figure the greater the variability of the fund's performance. High historical volatility may indicate high future volatility, and therefore increased investment risk in a fund.

Types of Risk

Depending on the nature of the investment, the type of 'investment' risk will vary.

A common concern with any investment is that you may lose the money you invest—your capital. This risk is therefore often referred to as capital risk.

If the assets you invest in are held in another currency there is a risk that currency movements alone may affect the value. This is referred to as currency risk.

Many forms of investment may not be readily salable on the open market (e.g. commercial property) or the market has a small capacity and investments may take time to sell. Assets that are easily sold are termed *liquid* therefore this type of risk is termed liquidity risk.

Charging Structures and Fees

Fee Types

For an open-end fund, there may be an initial charge levied on the purchase of units or shares this covers dealing costs, and commissions paid to intermediaries or salespeople. Typically this fee is a percentage of the investment. Some vehicles waive the initial charge and apply an exit charge instead. This may be gradually disappearing after a number of years. Closed-end funds traded on an exchange are subject to brokerage commissions, in the same manner as a stock trade.

The vehicle will charge an annual management charge or AMC to cover the cost of administering the vehicle and remunerating the investment manager. This may be a flat rate based on the value of the assets or a performance related fee based on a predefined target being achieved.

Different unit/share classes may have different combinations of fees/charges.

Pricing Models

Open-ended vehicles are either *dual priced* or *single priced*.

Dual priced vehicles have a buying (offer) price and selling or (bid) price. The buying price is higher than the selling price, this difference is known as the *spread* or *bid-offer spread*. The difference is typically 5% and may be varied by the vehicle's manager to reflect changes in the market; the amount of variation may be limited by the vehicles rules or regulatory rules. The difference between the buying and selling price includes initial charge for entering the fund.

The internal workings of a fund are more complicated than this description suggests. The manager sets a price for creation of units/shares and for cancellation. There is a differential between the cancellation and bid prices, and the creation and offer prices. The additional units are created are place in the managers box for future purchasers. When heavy selling occurs units are liquidated from the managers box to protect the existing investors from the increased dealing costs. Adjusting the bid/offer prices closer to the cancellation/creation prices allows the manager to protect the interest of the existing investors in changing market conditions. Most unit trusts are dual priced.

Single priced vehicles notionally have a single price for units/shares and this price is the same if buying or selling. As single prices vehicle can't adjust the difference between the buying and selling price to adjust for market conditions, another mechanism, the *dilution levy* exists. SICAVs, OEICs and U.S. mutual funds are single priced.

A dilution levy can be charged at the discretion of the fund manager, to offset the cost of market transactions resulting from large un-matched buy or sell orders. For example, if the volume of purchases outweigh the volume of sales in a particular trading period the fund manager will have to go to the market to buy more of the assets underlying the fund, incurring a brokerage fee in the process and having an adverse effect on the fund as a whole ("diluting" the fund). The same is the case with large sell orders. A dilution levy is therefore applied where appropriate and paid for by the investor in order that large single transactions do not reduce the value of the fund as a whole.

Hedge Fund

A hedge fund is an investment fund that pools capital from accredited investors or institutional investors and invests in a variety of assets, often with complicated portfolio-construction and risk management techniques. It is administered by a professional investment management firm, and often structured as a limited partnership, limited liability company, or similar vehicle. Hedge funds are generally distinct from mutual funds and regarded as alternative investments, as their use of leverage is not capped by regulators, and distinct from private equity funds, as the majority of hedge funds invest in relatively liquid assets. However, funds which operate similarly to hedge funds but are regulated similarly to mutual funds are available and known as liquid alternative investments.

The term "hedge fund" originated from the paired long and short positions that the first of these funds used to hedge market risk. Over time, the types and nature of the hedging concepts expanded, as did the different types of investment vehicles. Today, hedge funds engage in a diverse range of markets and strategies and employ a wide variety of financial instruments and risk management techniques.

Hedge funds are made available only to certain sophisticated or accredited investors, and cannot be offered or sold to the general public. As such, they generally avoid direct regulatory oversight, bypass licensing requirements applicable to investment companies, and operate with greater flexibility than mutual funds and other investment funds. However, following the financial crisis of 2007–2008, regulations were passed in the United States and Europe with the intention of increasing government oversight of hedge funds and eliminating certain regulatory gaps.

Hedge funds have existed for many decades and have become increasingly popular. They have now grown to be a substantial fraction of asset management, with assets totaling around $3.235 trillion in 2018.

Hedge funds are almost always open-end funds, and allow additions or withdrawals by their investors (generally on a monthly or quarterly basis). The value of an investor's holding is directly related to the fund net asset value.

Many hedge fund investment strategies aim to achieve a positive return on investment regardless of whether markets are rising or falling ("absolute return"). Hedge fund managers often invest money of their own in the fund they manage. A hedge fund typically pays its investment manager an annual management fee (for example, 2% of the assets of the fund), and a performance fee (for example, 20% of the increase in the fund's net asset value during the year). Both co-investment and performance fees serve to align the interests of managers with those of the investors in the fund. Some hedge funds have several billion dollars of assets under management (AUM).

The word "hedge", meaning a line of bushes around the perimeter of a field, has long been used as a metaphor for placing limits on risk. Early hedge funds sought to hedge specific investments against general market fluctuations by shorting the market, hence the name.[4] Nowadays, however, many different investment strategies are used, many of which do not "hedge risk".

Strategies

A prospectus from the US.

Hedge fund strategies are generally classified among four major categories: global macro, directional, event-driven, and relative value (arbitrage). Strategies within these categories each entail characteristic risk and return profiles. A fund may employ a single strategy or multiple strategies for flexibility, risk management, or diversification. The hedge fund's prospectus, also known as an offering memorandum, offers potential investors information about key aspects of the fund, including the fund's investment strategy, investment type, and leverage limit.

The elements contributing to a hedge fund strategy include: the hedge fund's approach to the market; the particular instrument used; the market sector the fund specializes in (e.g., healthcare); the method used to select investments; and the amount of diversification within the fund. There are a variety of market approaches to different asset classes, including equity, fixed income, commodity, and currency. Instruments used include: equities, fixed income, futures, options, and swaps. Strategies can be divided into those in which investments can be selected by managers, known as "discretionary/qualitative", or those in which investments are selected using a computerized system, known as "systematic/quantitative". The amount of diversification within the fund can vary; funds may be multi-strategy, multi-fund, multi-market, multi-manager, or a combination.

Sometimes hedge fund strategies are described as "absolute return" and are classified as either "market neutral" or "directional". Market neutral funds have less correlation to overall market performance by "neutralizing" the effect of market swings, whereas directional funds utilize trends and inconsistencies in the market and have greater exposure to the market's fluctuations.

Global Macro

Hedge funds using a global macro investing strategy take sizable positions in share, bond, or currency markets in anticipation of global macroeconomic events in order to generate a risk-adjusted return. Global macro fund managers use macroeconomic ("big picture") analysis based on global market events and trends to identify opportunities for investment that would profit from anticipated price movements. While global macro strategies have a large amount of flexibility (due to their ability to use leverage to take large positions in diverse investments in multiple markets), the timing of the implementation of the strategies is important in order to generate attractive, risk-adjusted returns. Global macro is often categorized as a directional investment strategy.

Global macro strategies can be divided into discretionary and systematic approaches. Discretionary trading is carried out by investment managers who identify and select investments, whereas systematic trading is based on mathematical models and executed by software with limited human involvement beyond the programming and updating of the software. These strategies can also be divided into trend or counter-trend approaches depending on whether the fund attempts to profit from following market trend (long or short-term) or attempts to anticipate and profit from reversals in trends.

Within global macro strategies, there are further sub-strategies including "systematic diversified", in which the fund trades in diversified markets, or sector specialists cush as "systematic currency", in which the fund trades in currency markets or any other sector specialisition.[348] Other sub-strategies include those employed by commodity trading advisors (CTAs), where the fund trades in futures (or options) in commodity markets or in swaps. This is also known as a "managed future fund". CTAs trade in commodities (such as gold) and financial instruments, including stock indices. They also take both long and short positions, allowing them to make profit in both market upswings and downswings. Most Global Macro managers tends to be a CTA from a regulatory perspective and the main divide is between systematic and discretionary strategies. A classification framework for CTA/Macro Strategies can be found in the reference.

Directional

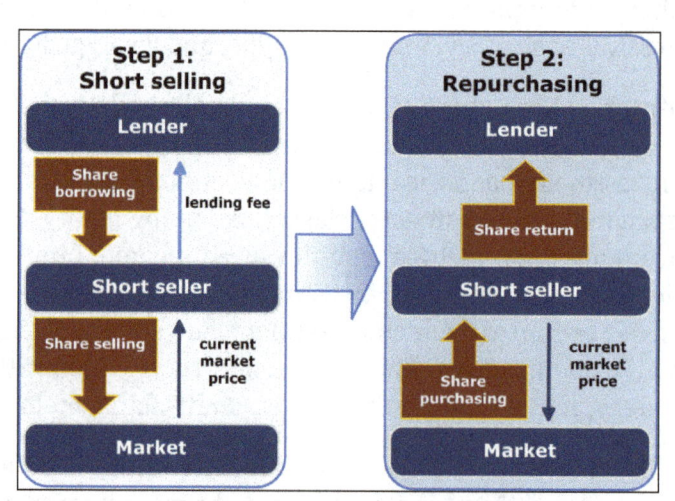

Schematic representation of short selling in two steps. The short seller borrows shares and immediately sells them. The short seller then expects the price to decrease, when the seller can profit by purchasing the shares to return to the lender.

Directional investment strategies use market movements, trends, or inconsistencies when picking stocks across a variety of markets. Computer models can be used, or fund managers will identify and select investments. These types of strategies have a greater exposure to the fluctuations of the overall market than do market neutral strategies. Directional hedge fund strategies include US and international long/short equity hedge funds, where long equity positions are hedged with short sales of equities or equity index options.

Within directional strategies, there are a number of sub-strategies. "Emerging markets" funds focus on emerging markets such as China and India, whereas "sector funds" specialize in specific areas including technology, healthcare, biotechnology, pharmaceuticals, energy, and basic materials. Funds using a "fundamental growth" strategy invest in companies with more earnings growth than the overall stock market or relevant sector, while funds using a "fundamental value" strategy invest in undervalued companies. Funds that use quantitative and financial signal processing techniques for equity trading are described as using a "quantitative directional" strategy.[345] Funds using a "short bias" strategy take advantage of declining equity prices using short positions.

Event-Driven

Event-driven strategies concern situations in which the underlying investment opportunity and risk are associated with an event. An event-driven investment strategy finds investment opportunities in corporate transactional events such as consolidations, acquisitions, recapitalizations, bankruptcies, and liquidations. Managers employing such a strategy capitalize on valuation inconsistencies in the market before or after such events, and take a position based on the predicted movement of the security or securities in question. Large institutional investors such as hedge funds are more likely to pursue event-driven investing strategies than traditional equity investors because they have the expertise and resources to analyze corporate transactional events for investment opportunities.

Corporate transactional events generally fit into three categories: distressed securities, risk arbitrage, and special situations. Distressed securities include such events as restructurings, recapitalizations, and bankruptcies. A distressed securities investment strategy involves investing in the bonds or loans of companies facing bankruptcy or severe financial distress, when these bonds or loans are being traded at a discount to their value. Hedge fund managers pursuing the distressed debt investment strategy aim to capitalize on depressed bond prices. Hedge funds purchasing distressed debt may prevent those companies from going bankrupt, as such an acquisition deters foreclosure by banks. While event-driven investing in general tends to thrive during a bull market, distressed investing works best during a bear market.

Risk arbitrage or merger arbitrage includes such events as mergers, acquisitions, liquidations, and hostile takeovers. Risk arbitrage typically involves buying and selling the stocks of two or more merging companies to take advantage of market discrepancies between acquisition price and stock price. The risk element arises from the possibility that the merger or acquisition will not go ahead as planned; hedge fund managers will use research and analysis to determine if the event will take place.

Special situations are events that impact the value of a company's stock, including the restructuring of a company or corporate transactions including spin-offs, share buy backs, security issuance/repurchase, asset sales, or other catalyst-oriented situations. To take advantage of special situations the hedge fund manager must identify an upcoming event that will increase or decrease the value of the company's equity and equity-related instruments.

Other event-driven strategies include: credit arbitrage strategies, which focus on corporate fixed income securities; an activist strategy, where the fund takes large positions in companies and uses the ownership to participate in the management; a strategy based on predicting the final approval of new pharmaceutical drugs; and legal catalyst strategy, which specializes in companies involved in major lawsuits.

Relative Value

Relative value arbitrage strategies take advantage of relative discrepancies in price between securities. The price discrepancy can occur due to mispricing of securities compared to related securities, the underlying security or the market overall. Hedge fund managers can use various types of analysis to identify price discrepancies in securities, including mathematical, technical, or fundamental techniques. Relative value is often used as a synonym for market neutral, as strategies in this category typically have very little or no directional market exposure to the market as a whole. Other relative value sub-strategies include:

- Fixed income arbitrage: Exploit pricing inefficiencies between related fixed income securities.

- Equity market neutral: Exploit differences in stock prices by being long and short in stocks within the same sector, industry, market capitalization, country, which also creates a hedge against broader market factors.

- Convertible arbitrage: Exploit pricing inefficiencies between convertible securities and the corresponding stocks.

- Asset-backed securities (fixed-income asset-backed): Fixed income arbitrage strategy using asset-backed securities.

- Credit long / short: The same as long / short equity, but in credit markets instead of equity markets.

- Statistical arbitrage: Identifying pricing inefficiencies between securities through mathematical modeling techniques

- Volatility arbitrage: Exploit the change in volatility, instead of the change in price.

- Yield alternatives: Non-fixed income arbitrage strategies based on the yield, instead of the price.

- Regulatory arbitrage: Exploit regulatory differences between two or more markets.

- Risk arbitrage: Exploit market discrepancies between acquisition price and stock price.

Risk

For an investor who already holds large quantities of equities and bonds, investment in hedge funds may provide diversification and reduce the overall portfolio risk. Managers of hedge funds use particular trading strategies and instruments with the specific aim of reducing market risks to produce risk-adjusted returns that are consistent with investors' desired level of risk. Hedge funds ideally produce returns relatively uncorrelated with market indices. While "hedging" can be a way of reducing the risk of an investment, hedge funds, like all other investment types, are not immune to risk. hedge funds were approximately one-third less volatile than the S&P 500 between 1993 and 2010.

Risk Management

Investors in hedge funds are, in most countries, required to be qualified investors who are assumed to be aware of the investment risks, and accept these risks because of the potential returns relative to those risks. Fund managers may employ extensive risk management strategies in order to protect the fund and investors. "Big hedge funds have some of the most sophisticated and exacting risk management practices anywhere in asset management." Hedge fund managers that hold a large number of investment positions for short durations are likely to have a particularly comprehensive risk management system in place, and it has become usual for funds to have independent risk officers who assess and manage risks but are not otherwise involved in trading. A variety of different measurement techniques and models are used to estimate risk according to the fund's leverage, liquidity, and investment strategy. Non-normality of returns, volatility clustering and trends are not always accounted for by conventional risk measurement methodologies and so in addition to value at risk and similar measurements, funds may use integrated measures such as drawdowns.

In addition to assessing the market-related risks that may arise from an investment, investors commonly employ operational due diligence to assess the risk that error or fraud at a hedge fund might result in loss to the investor. Considerations will include the organization and management of operations at the hedge fund manager, whether the investment strategy is likely to be sustainable, and the fund's ability to develop as a company.

Transparency and Regulatory Considerations

Since hedge funds are private entities and have few public disclosure requirements, this is sometimes perceived as a lack of transparency. Another common perception of hedge funds is that their managers are not subject to as much regulatory oversight and/or registration requirements as other financial investment managers, and more prone to manager-specific idiosyncratic risks such as style drifts, faulty operations, or fraud. New regulations introduced in the US and the EU as of 2010 required hedge fund managers to report more information, leading to greater transparency. In addition, investors, particularly institutional investors, are encouraging further developments in hedge fund risk management, both through internal practices and external regulatory requirements. The increasing influence of institutional investors has led to greater transparency: hedge funds increasingly provide information to investors including valuation methodology, positions, and leverage exposure.

Risks Shared with Other Investment Types

Hedge funds share many of the same types of risk as other investment classes, including liquidity risk and manager risk. Liquidity refers to the degree to which an asset can be bought and sold or converted to cash; similar to private equity funds, hedge funds employ a lock-up period during which an investor cannot remove money. Manager risk refers to those risks which arise from the management of funds. As well as specific risks such as style drift, which refers to a fund manager "drifting" away from an area of specific expertise, manager risk factors include valuation risk, capacity risk, concentration risk, and leverage risk. Valuation risk refers to the concern that the net asset value (NAV) of investments may be inaccurate; capacity risk can arise from placing too much money into one particular strategy, which may lead to fund performance deterioration; and concentration risk may arise if a fund has too much exposure to a particular investment, sector, trading strategy, or group of correlated funds. These risks may be managed through defined controls over conflict of interest, restrictions on allocation of funds, and set exposure limits for strategies.

Many investment funds use leverage, the practice of borrowing money, trading on margin, or using derivatives to obtain market exposure in excess of that provided by investors' capital. Although leverage can increase potential returns, the opportunity for larger gains is weighed against the possibility of greater losses. Hedge funds employing leverage are likely to engage in extensive risk management practices. In comparison with investment banks, hedge fund leverage is relatively low; according to a National Bureau of Economic Research working paper, the average leverage for investment banks is 14.2, compared to between 1.5 and 2.5 for hedge funds.

Some types of funds, including hedge funds, are perceived as having a greater appetite for risk, with the intention of maximizing returns, subject to the risk tolerance of investors and the fund manager. Managers will have an additional incentive to increase risk oversight when their own capital is invested in the fund.

Fees and Remuneration

Fees Paid to Hedge Funds

Hedge fund management firms typically charge their funds both a management fee and a performance fee.

Management fees are calculated as a percentage of the fund's net asset value and typically range from 1% to 4% per annum, with 2% being standard. They are usually expressed as an annual percentage, but calculated and paid monthly or quarterly. Management fees for hedge funds are designed to cover the operating costs of the manager, whereas the performance fee provides the manager's profits. However, due to economies of scale the management fee from larger funds can generate a significant part of a manager's profits, and as a result some fees have been criticized by some public pension funds, such as CalPERS, for being too high.

The performance fee is typically 20% of the fund's profits during any year, though performance fees range between 10% and 50%. Performance fees are intended to provide an incentive for a manager to generate profits. Performance fees have been criticized by Warren Buffett, who believes that because hedge funds share only the profits and not the losses, such fees create an incentive for high-risk investment management. Performance fee rates have fallen since the start of the credit crunch.

Almost all hedge fund performance fees include a "high water mark" (or "loss carryforward provision"), which means that the performance fee only applies to net profits (*i.e.*, profits after losses in previous years have been recovered). This prevents managers from receiving fees for volatile performance, though a manager will sometimes close a fund that has suffered serious losses and start a new fund, rather than attempt to recover the losses over a number of years without a performance fee.

Some performance fees include a "hurdle", so that a fee is only paid on the fund's performance in excess of a benchmark rate (*e.g.*, LIBOR) or a fixed percentage. A "soft" hurdle means the performance fee is calculated on all the fund's returns if the hurdle rate is cleared. A "hard" hurdle is calculated only on returns above the hurdle rate. A hurdle is intended to ensure that a manager is only rewarded if the fund generates returns in excess of the returns that the investor would have received if they had invested their money elsewhere.

Some hedge funds charge a redemption fee (or withdrawal fee) for early withdrawals during a specified period of time (typically a year), or when withdrawals exceed a predetermined percentage of the original investment. The purpose of the fee is to discourage short-term investing, reduce turnover, and deter withdrawals after periods of poor performance. Unlike management fees and performance fees, redemption fees are usually kept by the fund.

Remuneration of Portfolio Managers

Hedge fund management firms are often owned by their portfolio managers, who are therefore entitled to any profits that the business makes. As management fees are intended to cover the firm's operating costs, performance fees (and any excess management fees) are generally distributed to the firm's owners as profits. Funds do not tend to report compensation, and so published lists of the amounts earned by top managers tend to be estimates based on factors such as the fees charged by their funds and the capital they are thought to have invested in them. Many managers have accumulated large stakes in their own funds and so top hedge fund managers can earn extraordinary amounts of money, perhaps up to $4 billion in a good year.

Earnings at the very top are higher than in any other sector of the financial industry, and collectively the top 25 hedge fund managers regularly earn more than all 500 of the chief executives in the S&P 500. Most hedge fund managers are remunerated much less, however, and if performance fees are not earned then small managers at least are unlikely to be paid significant amounts.

In 2011, the top manager earned $3,000m, the tenth earned $210m, and the 30th earned $80m. In 2011, the average earnings for the 25 highest-compensated hedge fund managers in the United States was $576 million. while the mean total compensation for all hedge fund investment professionals was $690,786 and the median was $312,329. The same figures for hedge fund CEOs were $1,037,151 and $600,000, and for chief investment officers were $1,039,974 and $300,000, respectively.

Of the 1,226 people on the Forbes World's Billionaires List for 2012, 36 of the financiers listed "derived significant chunks" of their wealth from hedge fund management. Among the richest 1,000 people in the United Kingdom, 54 were hedge fund managers.

A porfolio manager risks losing his past compensation if he engages in insider trading. In Morgan Stanley v. Skowron, 989 F. Supp. 2d 356 (S.D.N.Y. 2013), applying New York's faithless servant doctrine, the court held that a hedge fund's portfolio manager engaging in insider trading in violation of his company's code of conduct, which also required him to report his misconduct, must repay his employer the full $31 million his employer paid him as compensation during his period of faithlessness.

The court called the insider trading the "ultimate abuse of a portfolio manager's position." The judge also wrote: "In addition to exposing Morgan Stanley to government investigations and direct financial losses, Skowron's behavior damaged the firm's reputation, a valuable corporate asset."

Structure

A hedge fund is an investment vehicle that is most often structured as an offshore corporation, limited partnership, or limited liability company. The fund is managed by an investment manager in the form of an organization or company that is legally and financially distinct from the hedge fund and its portfolio of assets. Many investment managers utilize service providers for operational support. Service providers include prime brokers, banks, administrators, distributors, and accounting firms.

Prime Broker

Prime brokers clear trades, and provide leverage and short-term financing. They are usually divisions of large investment banks. The prime broker acts as a counterparty to derivative contracts, and lends securities for particular investment strategies, such as long/short equities and convertible bond arbitrage. It can provide custodial services for the fund's assets, and execution and clearing services for the hedge fund manager.

Administrator

Hedge fund administrators are typically responsible for valuation services, and often operations and accounting.

Calculation of the net asset value ("NAV") by the administrator, including the pricing of securities at current market value and calculation of the fund's income and expense accruals, is a core administrator task, because it is the price at which investors buy and sell shares in the fund. The accurate and timely calculation of NAV by the administrator is vital. The case of *Anwar v. Fairfield Greenwich* (SDNY 2015) is the major case relating to fund administrator liability for failure to handle its NAV-related obligations properly. There, the hedge fund administrator and other defendants settled in 2016 by paying the *Anwar* investor plaintiffs $235 million.

Administrator back office support allows fund managers to concentrate on trades. Administrators also process subscriptions and redemptions, and perform various shareholder services. Hedge funds in the United States are not required to appoint an administrator, and all of these functions can be performed by an investment manager. A number of conflict of interest situations may arise in this arrangement, particularly in the calculation of a fund's net asset value. Some funds employ external auditors, thereby arguably offering a greater degree of transparency.

Distributor

A distributor is an underwriter, broker, dealer, or other person who participates in the distribution of securities. The distributor is also responsible for marketing the fund to potential investors. Many hedge funds do not have distributors, and in such cases the investment manager will be responsible for distribution of securities and marketing, though many funds also use placement agents and broker-dealers for distribution.

Auditor

Most funds use an independent accounting firm to audit the assets of the fund, provide tax services, and perform a complete audit of the fund's financial statements. The year-end audit is often performed in accordance with the standard accounting practices enforced within the country in which the fund it established, US GAAP or the International Financial Reporting Standards (IFRS). The auditor may verify the fund's NAV and assets under management (AUM). Some auditors only provide "NAV lite" services, meaning that the valuation is based on prices received from the manager rather than independent assessment.

Domicile and Taxation

The legal structure of a specific hedge fund, in particular its domicile and the type of legal entity in use, is usually determined by the tax expectations of the fund's investors. Regulatory considerations will also play a role. Many hedge funds are established in offshore financial centers to avoid adverse tax consequences for its foreign and tax-exempt investors. Offshore funds that invest in the US typically pay withholding taxes on certain types of investment income, but not US capital gains tax. However, the fund's investors are subject to tax in their own jurisdictions on any increase in the value of their investments. This tax treatment promotes cross-border investments by limiting the potential for multiple jurisdictions to layer taxes on investors.

US tax-exempt investors (such as pension plans and endowments) invest primarily in offshore hedge funds to preserve their tax exempt status and avoid unrelated business taxable income. The investment manager, usually based in a major financial center, pays tax on its management fees per the tax laws of the state and country where it is located. In 2011, half of the existing hedge funds were registered offshore and half onshore. The Cayman Islands was the leading location for offshore funds, accounting for 34% of the total number of global hedge funds. The US had 24%, Luxembourg 10%, Ireland 7%, the British Virgin Islands 6%, and Bermuda had 3%.

Basket Options

Deutsche Bank and Barclays created special options accounts for hedge fund clients in the banks' names and claimed to own the assets, when in fact the hedge fund clients had full control of the assets and reaped the profits. The hedge funds would then execute trades — many of them a few seconds in duration — but wait until just after a year had passed to exercise the options, allowing them to report the profits at a lower long-term capital gains tax rate.

The US Senate Permanent Subcommittee on Investigations chaired by Carl Levin issued a 2014 report that found that from 1998 and 2013, hedge funds avoided billions of dollars in taxes by using basket options. The Internal Revenue Service began investigating Renaissance Technologies in 2009, and Levin criticized the IRS for taking six years to investigate the company. Using basket options Renaissance avoided "more than $6 billion in taxes over more than a decade".

These banks and hedge funds involved in this case used dubious structured financial products in a giant game of 'let's pretend,' costing the Treasury billions and bypassing safeguards that protect the economy from excessive bank lending for stock speculation.

A dozen other hedge funds along with Renaissance Technologies used Deutsche Bank's and Barclays' basket options. Renaissance argued that basket options were "extremely important because they gave the hedge fund the ability to increase its returns by borrowing more and to protect against model and programming failures". In July 2015 the United States Internal Revenue claimed hedge funds used basket options "to bypass taxes on short-term trades". These basket options will now be labeled as listed transactions that must be declared on tax returns, and a failure to do would result in a penalty.

Investment Manager Locations

In contrast to the funds themselves, investment managers are primarily located onshore. The United States remains the largest center of investment, with US-based funds managing around 70% of global assets at the end of 2011. As of April 2012, there were approximately 3,990 investment advisers managing one or more private hedge funds registered with the Securities and Exchange Commission. New York City and the Gold Coast area of Connecticut are the leading locations for US hedge fund managers.

London was Europe's leading center for hedge fund managers, but since the Brexit referendum some formerly London-based hedge funds have relocated to other European financial centers such as Frankfurt, Luxembourg, Paris, and Dublin, while some other hedge funds have moved their European head offices back to New York City. Before Brexit, according to EuroHedge data, around 800 funds located in the UK had managed 85% of European-based hedge fund assets in 2011. Interest in hedge funds in Asia has increased significantly since 2003, especially in Japan, Hong Kong, and Singapore. After Brexit, Europe and the US remain the leading locations for the management of Asian hedge fund assets.

Legal Entity

Hedge fund legal structures vary depending on location and the investor(s). US hedge funds aimed at US-based, taxable investors are generally structured as limited partnerships or limited liability companies. Limited partnerships and other flow-through taxation structures assure that investors in hedge funds are not subject to both entity-level and personal-level taxation. A hedge fund structured as a limited partnership must have a general partner. The general partner may be an individual or a corporation. The general partner serves as the manager of the limited partnership, and has unlimited liability. The limited partners serve as the fund's investors, and have no responsibility for management or investment decisions. Their liability is limited to the amount of money they invest for partnership interests. As an alternative to a limited partnership arrangement, U.S. domestic hedge funds may be structured as limited liability companies, with members acting as corporate shareholders and enjoying protection from individual liability.

By contrast, offshore corporate funds are usually used for non-US investors, and when they are domiciled in an applicable offshore tax haven, no entity-level tax is imposed. Many managers of offshore funds permit the participation of tax-exempt US investors, such as pensions funds, institutional endowments, and charitable trusts. As an alternative legal structure, offshore funds may be formed as an open-ended unit trust using an unincorporated mutual fund structure. Japanese investors prefer to invest in unit trusts, such as those available in the Cayman Islands.

The investment manager who organizes the hedge fund may retain an interest in the fund, either as the general partner of a limited partnership or as the holder of "founder shares" in a corporate fund. For offshore funds structured as corporate entities, the fund may appoint a board of directors. The board's primary role is to provide a layer of oversight while representing the interests of the shareholders. However, in practice board members may lack sufficient expertise to be effective in performing those duties. The board may include both affiliated directors who are employees of the fund and independent directors whose relationship to the fund is limited.

Types of Funds

- Open-ended hedge funds continue to issue shares to new investors and allow periodic withdrawals at the net asset value ("NAV") for each share.
- Closed-ended hedge funds issue a limited number of tradeable shares at inception.
- Shares of Listed hedges funds are traded on stock exchanges, such as the Irish Stock Exchange, and may be purchased by non-accredited investors.

Side Pockets

A side pocket is a mechanism whereby a fund compartmentalizes assets that are relatively illiquid or difficult to value reliably. When an investment is side-pocketed, its value is calculated separately from the value of the fund's main portfolio. Because side pockets are used to hold illiquid investments, investors do not have the standard redemption rights with respect to the side pocket investment that they do with respect to the fund's main portfolio. Profits or losses from the investment are allocated on a *pro rata* basis only to those who are investors at the time the investment is placed into the side pocket and are not shared with new investors. Funds typically carry side pocket assets "at cost" for purposes of calculating management fees and reporting net asset values. This allows fund managers to avoid attempting a valuation of the underlying investments, which may not always have a readily available market value.

Side pockets were widely used by hedge funds during the financial crisis of 2007–2008 amidst a flood of withdrawal requests. Side pockets allowed fund managers to lay away illiquid securities until market liquidity improved, a move that could reduce losses. However, as the practice restricts investors' ability to redeem their investments it is often unpopular and many have alleged that it has been abused or applied unfairly. The SEC also has expressed concern about aggressive use of side pockets and has sanctioned certain fund managers for inappropriate use of them.

Performance

Measurement

Performance statistics for individual hedge funds are difficult to obtain, as the funds have historically not been required to report their performance to a central repository, and restrictions against public offerings and advertisement have led many managers to refuse to provide performance information publicly. However, summaries of individual hedge fund performance are occasionally available in industry journals and databases.

One estimate is that the average hedge fund returned 11.4% per year, representing a 6.7% return above overall market performance before fees, based on performance data from 8,400 hedge funds. Another estimate is that between January 2000 and December 2009 hedge funds outperformed other investments and were substantially less volatile, with stocks falling an average of 2.62% per year over the decade and hedge funds rising an average of 6.54% per year; this was an unusually volatile period with both the 2001-2002 dot-com bubble and a recession beginning mid 2007. However, more recent data show that hedge fund performance declined and underperformed the market from about 2009 to 2016.

Hedge funds performance is measured by comparing their returns to an estimate of their risk. Common measures are the Sharpe ratio, Treynor measure and Jensen's alpha. These measures work best when returns follow normal distributions without autocorrelation, and these assumptions are often not met in practice.

New performance measures have been introduced that attempt to address some of theoretical concerns with traditional indicators, including: modified Sharpe ratios; the Omega ratio introduced by Keating and Shadwick in 2002; Alternative Investments Risk Adjusted Performance (AIRAP) published by Sharma in 2004; and Kappa developed by Kaplan and Knowles in 2004.

Sector-size Effect

There is a debate over whether alpha (the manager's skill element in performance) has been diluted by the expansion of the hedge fund industry. Two reasons are given. First, the increase in traded volume may have been reducing the market anomalies that are a source of hedge fund performance. Second, the remuneration model is attracting more managers, which may dilute the talent available in the industry.

Hedge Fund Indices

Indices that track hedge fund returns are, in order of development, called Non-investable, Investable, and Clone. They play a central and unambiguous role in traditional asset markets, where they are widely accepted as representative of their underlying portfolios. Equity and debt index fund products provide investable access to most developed markets in these asset classes. Hedge funds, however, are actively managed, so that tracking is impossible. Non-investable hedge fund indices on the other hand may be more or less representative, but returns data on many of the reference group of funds is non-public. This may result in biased estimates of their returns. In an attempt to address this problem, clone indices have been created in an attempt to replicate the statistical properties of hedge funds without being directly based on their returns data. None of these approaches achieves the accuracy of indices in other asset classes for which there is more complete published data concerning the underlying returns.

Non-investable Indices

Non-investable indices are indicative in nature, and aim to represent the performance of some database of hedge funds using some measure such as mean, median, or weighted mean from a hedge fund database. The databases have diverse selection criteria and methods of construction, and no single database captures all funds. This leads to significant differences in reported performance between different indices.

Although they aim to be representative, non-investable indices suffer from a lengthy and largely unavoidable list of biases. Funds' participation in a database is voluntary, leading to self-selection bias because those funds that choose to report may not be typical of funds as a whole. For example, some do not report because of poor results or because they have already reached their target size and do not wish to raise further money.

The short lifetimes of many hedge funds means that there are many new entrants and many departures each year, which raises the problem of survivorship bias. If we examine only funds that have survived to the present, we will overestimate past returns because many of the worst-performing funds have not survived, and the observed association between fund youth and fund performance suggests that this bias may be substantial.

When a fund is added to a database for the first time, all or part of its historical data is recorded ex-post in the database. It is likely that funds only publish their results when they are favorable, so that the average performances displayed by the funds during their incubation period are inflated. This is known as "instant history bias" or "backfill bias".

Investable Indices

Investable indices are an attempt to reduce these problems by ensuring that the return of the index is available to shareholders. To create an investable index, the index provider selects funds and develops structured products or derivative instruments that deliver the performance of the index. When investors buy these products the index provider makes the investments in the underlying funds, making an investable index similar in some ways to a fund of hedge funds portfolio.

To make the index investable, hedge funds must agree to accept investments on the terms given by the constructor. To make the index liquid, these terms must include provisions for redemptions that some managers may consider too onerous to be acceptable. This means that investable indices do not represent the total universe of hedge funds. Most seriously, they under-represent more successful managers, who typically refuse to accept such investment protocols.

Hedge Fund Replication

The most recent addition to the field approach the problem in a different manner. Instead of reflecting the performance of actual hedge funds they take a statistical approach to the analysis of historic hedge fund returns, and use this to construct a model of how hedge fund returns respond to the movements of various investable financial assets. This model is then used to construct an investable portfolio of those assets. This makes the index investable, and in principle they can be as representative as the hedge fund database from which they were constructed. However, these clone indices rely on a statistical modelling process. Such indices have too short a history to state whether this approach will be considered successful.

Closures

In March 2017, HFR – a hedge fund research data and service provider – reported that there were more hedge-fund closures in 2016 than during the 2009 recession. According to the report, several large public pension funds pulled their investments in hedge funds, because the funds' subpar performance as a group did not merit the high fees they charged.

Despite the hedge fund industry topping $3 trillion for the first time ever in 2016, the number of new hedge funds launched fell short of levels before the financial crisis of 2007–2008. There were 729 hedge fund launches in 2016, fewer than the 784 opened in 2009, and dramatically fewer than the 968 launches in 2015.

Vulture Fund

A vulture fund is a hedge fund, private equity fund or distressed debt fund, that invests in debt considered to be very weak or in default, known as distressed securities. Investors in the fund profit by buying debt at a discounted price on a secondary market and then using numerous methods to gain a larger amount than the purchasing price. Debtors include companies, countries, and individuals.

Vulture funds have had success in bringing attachment and recovery actions against sovereign debtor governments, usually settling with them before realizing the attachments in forced sales. Settlements typically are made at a discount in hard or local currency or in the form of new debt issuance. In one instance involving Peru, such a seizure threatened payments to other creditors of the sovereign obliger.

Corporation Law and Theory of Finance

Businesses that need more capital than their founders can raise by personal contacts are enabled by this legal method of attracting investors to buy a portion of the business. Owners would invest capital and obtain common stock or equity in exchange for invested cash or other property like machines, factories, warehouses, patents or other interests. Then the owners would raise additional capital by borrowing from lenders in capital markets by selling bonds. In corporation law, the owners of these bonds come first in line for repayment so that if there is not sufficient funds to repay the bondholders, the stockholders get wiped out. The bondholders step into the shoes of the former shareholders. The shareholders own nothing because they, the owners, could not fully repay all the contractual promises, or loans. So like a bank (the mortgagee) that has lent money to a home buyer (the mortgagor) takes possession of the security (the home) when mortgage payments are not made (i.e. foreclosure), the bondholders of a corporation take possession of the business from the former owners (the shareholders) when the corporation falls into bankruptcy. Thus, when shareholders cannot repay bondholders, in principle, bondholders become the new shareholders. In practice, however, it is more complicated.

In the financial markets, the bonds of troubled public companies trade in a manner similar to common stock of solvent companies.

Investment Trust

An investment trust is a form of investment fund found mostly in the United Kingdom and Japan. Investment trusts are closed-end funds and are constituted as public limited companies. In many respects, the investment trust was the progenitor of the investment company in the U.S.

The name is somewhat misleading, given that (according to law) an investment "trust" is not in fact a "trust" in the legal sense at all, but a separate legal person or a company. This matters for the fiduciary duties owed by the board of directors and the equitable ownership of the fund's assets.

In the United Kingdom, the term "investment trust" has a strict meaning under tax law. However, the term is more commonly used within the UK to include any closed-ended investment company, including venture capital trusts (VCTs). The Association of Investment Companies is the trade association representing investment trusts and VCTs.

In Japan, investment trusts are called trust accounts; the largest stockholder of many public companies are usually trust banks handling the investment trusts, the largest being the Japan Trustee Services Bank, The Master Trust Bank of Japan and the Trust & Custody Services Bank.

Investors' money is pooled together from the sale of a fixed number of shares which a trust issues when it launches. The board will typically delegate responsibility to a professional fund manager to invest in the stocks and shares of a wide range of companies (more than most people could practically invest in themselves). The investment trust often has no employees, only a board of directors comprising only non-executive directors.

Investment trust shares are traded on stock exchanges, like those of other public companies. The share price does not always reflect the underlying value of the share portfolio held by the investment trust. In such cases, the investment trust is referred to as trading at a discount (or premium) to NAV (net asset value).

Unlike open-ended funds that are UCITS, investment trusts may borrow money in an attempt to enhance investment returns (known as gearing or leverage). UCITS funds are not permitted to gear for investment purposes.

The investment trust sector, in particular split capital investment trusts, suffered somewhat from around 2000 to 2003 after which creation of a compensation scheme resolved some problems. The sector has grown in recent years particularly through the launch of investment trusts investing in more illiquid assets such as property, private equity and infrastructure. Assets managed by investment trusts reached £174.4 billion at the end of December 2017.

Classification of Investment Trusts

Investment trusts can hold a variety of assets: listed equities, government/corporate bonds, real estate, private companies and so on. These assets may be listed/incorporated/domiciled in any region. Moreover the investment objectives (growth, income, capital preservation...), risk profile (level of gearing, level of diversification via assets and risk factors) varies. According to such factors, investment trusts are classified into sectors by the industry body, the Association of Investment Companies. The largest sectors by assets under management in December 2017 were Global (£27.1 billion), Private Equity (£14.7 billion), UK Equity Income (£12.0 billion), Infrastructure (£10.0 billion) and Specialist Debt (£7.8 billion).

These sector classifications were revamped in spring 2019. The new list of sectors and constituents comprised 13 new sectors, 15 renamed sectors and 31 sectors that were unchanged. The new sectors were added to reflect the greater numbers of investment companies investing in alternative assets. The amount of money invested by investment companies in alternative assets grew from £39.5bn in 2014 to £75.9bn in 2019. The growing debt sector was separated into three new sectors, Debt – Direct Lending, Debt – Loans & Bonds, and Debt – Structured Finance. Similarly, there were more specialist property sectors: Property – UK Commercial, Property – UK Healthcare, Property – UK Residential, and Property – Debt. Most of the equity sectors were unchanged, but Asia was split into three new sectors, Asia Pacific, Asia Pacific Income, and Asia Pacific Smaller Companies. There were new sectors for Growth Capital and for Royalties.

Split Capital Investment Trusts

Most investment trusts issue only one type of share (ordinary shares) and have an unlimited life. Split capital investment trusts are investment trusts with more than one type of share, such as zero dividend preference shares, income shares and capital shares. However, the number of split capital trusts has fallen dramatically since the split capital investment trust crisis and there were only 12 split capital investment trusts left in existence by 2018. Each of these 12 has only two classes of share: zero dividend preference shares and ordinary shares.

Some split capital trusts have a limited life determined at launch known as the wind-up date. Typically the life of a split capital trust is five to ten years. However, this life can be extended by shareholder vote.

In the heyday of split capital trusts, splits were more complicated and could have share classes such as the following (in order of typical priority and increasing risk):

- Zero Dividend Preference shares: No dividends, only capital growth at a pre-established redemption price (assuming sufficient assets).

- Income shares: Entitled to most (or all) of the income generated from the assets of a trust until the wind-up date, with some capital protection.

- Annuity Income shares: Very high and rising yield, but virtually no capital protection.

- Ordinary Income shares (AKA Income & Residual Capital shares): A high income and a share of the remaining assets of the trust after prior ranking shares.

- Capital shares: Entitled most (or all) of the remaining assets after prior ranking share classes have been paid; very high risk.

The type of share invested in is ranked in a predetermined order of priority, which becomes important when the trust reaches its wind-up date. If the Split has acquired any debt, debentures or loan stock, then this is paid out first, before any shareholders. Next in line to be repaid are Zero Dividend Preference shares, followed by any Income shares and then Capital. Although this order of priority is the most common way shares are paid out at the wind-up date, it may alter slightly from trust to trust.

Splits may also issue *Packaged Units* combining certain classes of share, usually reflecting the share classes in the trust usually in the same ratio. This makes them essentially the same investment as an ordinary share in a conventional Investment Trust.

Real Estate Investment Trusts

In the United Kingdom, REITs are constituted as investment trusts. They must be UK resident and publicly listed on a stock exchange recognised by the Financial Conduct Authority. They must distribute at least 90% of their income.

Taxation

Provided that it is approved by HM Revenue & Customs, an investment trust's investment income and capital gains are generally not taxed within the investment trust. This avoids the double taxation which would otherwise arise when shareholders receive income, or sell their shares in the investment trust and are taxed on their gains.

An approved investment trust must:

- Be resident in the United Kingdom.
- Derive most of its income from investments.
- Distribute at least 85% of its investment income as dividends (unless prohibited by company law).

The company must not hold more than 15% of its investments in any single company (except another investment trust) and must not be a close company. Investment trusts were in 2012 given the ability to distribute capital profits to shareholders. Investment trusts that wished to take advantage of this had to change their Articles of Association, with shareholders' approval, to allow such distributions. However, only a small minority of investment trusts distribute their capital profits.

Performance

Not helped by a weak finish to the year, investment trusts suffered a modestly negative 2018, but outperformed against other UK indices. The FTSE 350 Equity Investment Instruments Index, mainly comprising investment trusts, fell by 3.8%, outperforming the FTSE 100 Index (-10.9%) and the MSCI World Index, down by 10.3% over the same period. The growing importance of alternative assets in the industry, and also a significant international exposure that benefited from the weakness of sterling, helped the sector to record a relatively resilient performance.

Feeder Fund

A feeder fund is one of a number of funds that put all investment capital into an overarching umbrella fund that is called the master fund, for which one investment advisor handles all portfolio investments and trading. The two-tiered investment structure of a feeder fund and a master fund is commonly used by hedge funds as a means of assembling a larger portfolio account by pooling investment capital. Profits from the master fund are then split, or distributed, proportionately to the feeder funds based on the percentage of investment capital they have contributed to the master fund.

In a feeder fund arrangement, all management fees and any performance fees due are paid by investors at the feeder fund level.

The primary purpose served by the feeder fund-master fund structure is the reduction of trading costs and overall operating costs. The master fund effectively achieves economies of scale through having access to the large pool of investment capital provided by a number of feeder funds, which enables it to operate less expensively than would be possible for any of the feeder funds investing on their own.

The use of this two-tiered fund structure can be very advantageous when the feeder funds share common investment goals and strategies but are not appropriate for a feeder fund with a unique investment strategy or aim since those unique characteristics would be lost in the combination with other funds within a master fund.

Structure of Feeder Funds and Master Funds

The feeder funds that invest capital in a master fund operate as separate legal entities from the master fund and may be invested in more than one master fund. Various feeder funds invested in a master fund often differ substantially from one another in terms of things such as expense fees or investment minimums and do not usually have identical net asset values (NAV). In the same way that a feeder fund is free to invest in more than one master fund, a master fund is likewise free to accept investments from a number of feeder funds.

In regard to feeder funds operating in the United States, it is common for the master fund to be established as an offshore entity. This frees up the master fund to accept investment capital from both tax-exempt and U.S.-taxable investors. If, however, an offshore master fund elects to be taxed as a partnership or limited liability company (LLC) for U.S. tax purposes, then onshore feeder funds receive pass-through treatment of their share of the master fund's gains or losses, thus avoiding double taxation.

New Rules on International Feeder Funds

In March 2017, the Securities and Exchange Commission (SEC) ruled to allow foreign-regulated companies (foreign feeder funds) to invest in open-end master funds (U.S. Master Fund), making it easier for global managers to market their investment products in different foreign jurisdictions employing a master fund.

The letter modified parts 12(d)(1)(A) and (B) of the 1940 Act, which previously limited the use of foreign feeder funds into U.S.-registered funds. The SEC regulated the practice for several reasons. First, it wanted to prevent master funds from exerting too much influence over an acquired fund. It also aimed to protect investors in the funds from layered fees and the possibility of fund structures becoming so complex that they became difficult to understand.

References

- Investment-management, encyclopedias-almanacs-transcripts-and-maps: encyclopedia.com, Retrieved 05 January, 2019
- Investment-risks: wellington.com, Retrieved 25 June, 2019
- Managing-investment-risk, tools-and-resources: moneysmart.gov.au, Retrieved 28 April, 2019
- Portfoliomanagement: investopedia.com, Retrieved 16 May, 2019
- "The end of active investing?". Financial Times. Retrieved 2017-02-28

Valuation

CHAPTER 5

Valuation refers to the process of estimating the present value of an asset. A few of the common business valuation methods include relative valuation, absolute valuation, discounted cash flow, bond valuation, stock valuation etc. This chapter discusses in detail these different business valuation methods.

Valuation is the analytical process of determining the current (or projected) worth of an asset or a company. There are many techniques used for doing a valuation. An analyst placing a value on a company looks at the business's management, the composition of its capital structure, the prospect of future earnings, and the market value of its assets, among other metrics.

Fundamental analysis is often employed in valuation, although several other methods may be employed such as the capital asset pricing model (CAPM) or the dividend discount model (DDM).

A valuation can be useful when trying to determine the fair value of a security, which is determined by what a buyer is willing to pay a seller, assuming both parties enter the transaction willingly. When a security trades on an exchange, buyers and sellers determine the market value of a stock or bond.

The concept of intrinsic value, however, refers to the perceived value of a security based on future earnings or some other company attribute unrelated to the market price of a security. That's where valuation comes into play. Analysts do a valuation to determine whether a company or asset is overvalued or undervalued by the market.

Effects of Earnings on Valuation

The earnings per share (EPS) formula is stated as earnings available to common shareholders divided by the number of common stock shares outstanding. EPS is an indicator of company profit because the more earnings a company can generate per share, the more valuable each share is to investors.

Analysts also use the price-to-earnings (P/E) ratio for stock valuation, which is calculated as market price per share divided by EPS. The P/E ratio calculates how expensive a stock price is relative to the earnings produced per share.

For example, if the P/E ratio of a stock is 20 times earnings, an analyst compares that P/E ratio with other companies in the same industry and with the ratio for the broader market. In equity analysis, using ratios like the P/E to value a company is called a multiples-based, or multiples approach, valuation. Other multiples, such as EV/EBITDA, are compared with similar companies and historical multiples to calculate intrinsic value.

Valuation of financial assets is done using one or more of these types of models:

- Absolute value models that determine the present value of an asset's expected future cash flows. These kinds of models take two general forms: multi-period models such as discounted cash flow models or single-period models such as the Gordon model. These models rely on mathematics rather than price observation.
- Relative value models determine value based on the observation of market prices of similar assets.
- Option pricing models are used for certain types of financial assets (e.g., warrants, put/call options, employee stock options, investments with embedded options such as a callable bond) and are a complex present value model. The most common option pricing models are the Black–Scholes-Merton models and lattice models.
- Fair value is used in accordance with US GAAP (FAS 157), where fair value is the amount at which the asset could be bought or sold in a current transaction between willing parties, or transferred to an equivalent party, other than in a liquidation sale. This is used for assets whose carrying value is based on mark-to-market valuations; for fixed assets carried at historical cost (less accumulated depreciation), the fair value of the asset is not used.

Common terms for the value of an asset or liability are fair market value, fair value, and intrinsic value. The meanings of these terms differ. For instance, when an analyst believes a stock's intrinsic value is greater (less) than its market price, an analyst makes a "buy" ("sell") recommendation. Moreover, an asset's intrinsic value may be subject to personal opinion and vary among analysts.

When a plant asset is purchased for cash, its acquisition cost is simply the agreed on cash price. However, when a business acquires plant assets in exchange for other non-cash assets (shares of stock, a customer's note, or a tract of land) or as gifts, it is more difficult to establish a cash price.

Emerging Values: Environmentalism and Green Energy.

The general rule on non-cash exchanges is to value the non-cash asset received at its fair market value or the fair market value of what was given up, whichever is more clearly evident. The reason for not using the book value of the old asset to value the new asset is that the asset being given up is often carried in the accounting records at historical cost. In the case of a fixed asset, its value on the balance sheet is historical cost less accumulated depreciation, or book value. Neither amount may adequately represent the actual fair market value of either asset. Therefore, if the fair market value of one asset is clearly evident, a firm should record this amount for the new asset at the time of the exchange.

Appraised Value

Sometimes, neither of the items exchanged has a clearly determinable fair market value. Then, accountants record exchanges of items at their appraised values as determined by a professional appraiser. An appraised value is an expert's opinion of an item's fair market price if the item were sold. Appraisals are used often to value works of art, rare books, antiques, and real estate.

Book Value

The book value of a fixed asset asset is its recorded cost less accumulated depreciation. An old asset's book value is usually not a valid indication of the new asset's fair market value. However, if a better basis is not available, a firm could use the book value of the old asset.

Occasionally, a company receives an asset without giving up anything for it. For example, to attract industry to an area and provide jobs for local residents, a city may give a company a tract of land on which to build a factory. Although such a gift costs the recipient company nothing, it usually records the asset (land) at its fair market value. Accountants record gifts of plant assets at fair market value to provide information on all assets owned by the company. Omitting some assets may make information provided misleading. They would credit assets received as gifts to a stockholders' equity account titled Paid-in Capital—Donations.

Additional Factors to Consider

There are additional factors to consider when valuing a business including competition, management stability, etc.

Competition

An important aspect of company valuation is determined when examining it in comparison to competitors. The company's relative size compared with other businesses in its industry, relative product or service quality, product or service differentiation from others in the industry, market strengths, market size and share, competitiveness within its industry in terms of price and reputation, and copyright or patent protection of its products are all important in this examination.

- The most narrow form is direct competition (also called "category competition" or "brand competition"), where products which perform the same function compete against each other. For example, one brand of pick-up trucks competes with several other brands of pick-up trucks. Sometimes, two companies are rivals, and one adds new products to their line, which leads to the other company distributing the same new things, and in this manner they compete.

- The next form is substitute or indirect competition, where products which are close substitutes for one another compete. For example, butter competes with margarine, mayonnaise, and other various sauces and spreads.
- The broadest form of competition is typically called "budget competition." Included in this category is anything on which the consumer might want to spend their available money. For example, a family which has $20,000 available may choose to spend it on many different items, which can all be seen as competing with each other for the family's expenditure. This form of competition is also sometimes described as a competition of "share of wallet."

Management Ability

When examining this factor as a part of business valuation, one must consider if the management is skilled and experienced enough to maintain the company's position, and potentially improve it in the future. Several factors can indicate management ability: accounts receivable, inventory, fixed assets, and total asset turnover; employee turnover; condition of the facilities; family involvement, if any; quality of books and records; and sales, as well as gross and operating profit.

Financial Strength

Consideration of financial strength entails a number of ratios, including a company's total debt to assets, long-term debt to equity, current and quick ratios, interest coverage, and operating cycle.

- Total debt to assets: total debt/total assets or total liability /total assets.
- Long term debt to equity: long term debt(liabilities)/equity.
- Current ratio: current assets/current liabilities.

Profitability and Stability of Earnings

In accounting, profit is the difference between the purchase and the component costs of delivered goods and/or services and any operating or other expenses. This can help determine the financial stability of a company when viewing its profitability during its operating history, including the number of years the company has been in business, its sales and earnings trends, the life cycle of the industry as a whole, and returns on sales, assets and equity.

Other Factors

Along with the aforementioned considerations, a valuator must also keep in mind the economic conditions in which the company is operating, including the broad industry outlook and the impact of various IRS rulings and court cases that may affect the company's value.

In addition, the valuator must analyze the values of comparable companies to determine their relationship to the company's value. Intangible factors such as goodwill and non-compete agreements are important as well.

Finally, the valuator needs to consider the discount or capitalization rate of the company, specify what percentage of the company is being valued, and take into account any marketability or minority interest discounts.

CHAPTER 5 Valuation

Perhaps the most difficult part of the entire process is knowing how to combine all of these factors in a meaningful way to reach a value that will withstand any challenges by potential buyers, the IRS, dissatisfied partners or others.

Fair value should also be a consideration when valuing certain assets. Under US GAAP (FAS 157), fair value is the amount at which the asset could be bought or sold in a current transaction between willing parties, or transferred to an equivalent party, other than in a liquidation sale. This is used for assets whose carrying value is based on mark-to-market valuations; for fixed assets carried at historical cost (less accumulated depreciation), the fair value of the asset is not used.

Apple is a successful company with considerable goodwill.: This is an example of an additional factor beyond book value that contributes to the overall valuation of a company.

Valuing Repairs, Maintenance and Additions

Improvements to existing plant assets are capital expenditures because they increase the quality of services obtained from the asset.

Betterments or improvements to existing plant assets are capital expenditures because they increase the quality of services obtained from the asset. Because these add to the service-rendering ability of assets, firms charge them to the asset accounts.

For example, installing an air conditioner in an automobile that did not previously have one is a betterment. The debit for such an expenditure is to the asset account, Automobiles.

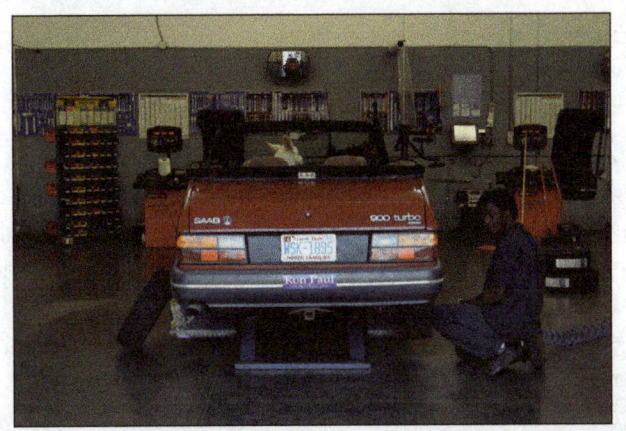

Car Repairs: Cars require regular maintenance. Such contingent liabilities can be estimated reliably based on historical cost and readily available information.

Occasionally, expenditures made on plant assets extend the quantity of services beyond the original estimate but do not improve the quality of the services. Since these expenditures benefit an increased number of future periods, accountants capitalize rather than expense them. However, since there is no visible, tangible addition to, or improvement in, the quality of services, they charge the expenditures to the accumulated depreciation account, thus reducing the credit balance in that account. Such expenditures cancel a part of the existing accumulated depreciation; firms often call them extraordinary repairs.

If an expenditure that should be expensed is capitalized, the effects are more significant. Assume now that USD 6,000 in repairs expense is incurred for a plant asset that originally cost USD 40,000 and had a useful life of four years and no estimated salvage value. This asset had been depreciated using the straight-line method for one year and had a book value of USD 30,000 (USD 40,000 cost—USD 10,000 first-year depreciation) at the beginning of 2010. The company capitalized the USD 6,000 that should have been charged to repairs expense in 2010. The charge for depreciation should have remained at USD 10,000 for each of the next three years. With the incorrect entry, however, depreciation increases.

Deferred maintenance is the practice of postponing maintenance activities such as repairs on both real property (i.e. infrastructure) and personal property (i.e. machinery) in order to save costs, meet budget-funding levels, or realign available budget monies. The failure to perform needed repairs could lead to asset deterioration and, ultimately, asset impairment. Generally, a policy of continued deferred maintenance may result in higher costs, asset failure, and in some cases, health and safety implications.

Valuing Asset-related Costs

Under US GAAP (FAS 157), fair value is the amount at which an asset and its related costs could be bought or sold in a current market transaction between willing parties or transferred to an equivalent party other than in a liquidation sale. Therefore, asset repairs and maintenance are expensed on the income statement at the market value paid for the services rendered. Asset additions/improvements are capitalized to their respective asset accounts on the balance sheet at the market value of the addition.

BUSINESS VALUATION

Business valuation is a process and a set of procedures used to estimate the economic value of an owner's interest in a business. Valuation is used by financial market participants to determine the price they are willing to pay or receive to effect a sale of a business. In addition to estimating the selling price of a business, the same valuation tools are often used by business appraisers to resolve disputes related to estate and gift taxation, divorce litigation, allocate business purchase price among business assets, establish a formula for estimating the value of partners' ownership interest for buy-sell agreements, and many other business and legal purposes such as in shareholders deadlock, divorce litigation and estate contest. In some cases, the court would appoint a forensic accountant as the joint expert doing the business valuation.

Standard and Premise of Value

Before the value of a business can be measured, the valuation assignment must specify the reason for and circumstances surrounding the business valuation. These are formally known as the business value standard and premise of value.

The standard of value is the hypothetical conditions under which the business will be valued. The premise of value relates to the assumptions, such as assuming that the business will continue forever in its current form (going concern), or that the value of the business lies in the proceeds from the sale of all of its assets minus the related debt (sum of the parts or assemblage of business assets).

Standards of Value

- Fair market value: A value of a business enterprise determined between a willing buyer and a willing seller both in full knowledge of all the relevant facts and neither compelled to conclude a transaction.
- Investment value: A value the company has to a particular investor. Note that the effect of synergy is included in valuation under the investment standard of value.
- Intrinsic value: The measure of business value that reflects the investor's in-depth understanding of the company's economic potential.

Premises of Value

- Going Concern: Value in continued use as an ongoing operating business enterprise.
- Assemblage of assets: Value of assets in place but not used to conduct business operations.
- Orderly disposition: Value of business assets in exchange, where the assets are to be disposed of individually and not used for business operations.
- Liquidation: Value in exchange when business assets are to be disposed of in a forced liquidation.

Premise of value for fair value Calculation:

- In use: If the asset would provide maximum value to the market participants principally through its use in combination with other assets as a group.
- In Exchange: If the asset would provide maximum value to the market participants principally on a stand-alone basis.

Business valuation results can vary considerably depending upon the choice of both the standard and premise of value. In an actual business sale, it would be expected that the buyer and seller, each with an incentive to achieve an optimal outcome, would determine the fair market value of a business asset that would compete in the market for such an acquisition. If the synergies are specific to the company being valued, they may not be considered. Fair value also does not incorporate discounts for lack of control or marketability.

Note, however, that it is possible to achieve the fair market value for a business asset that is being liquidated in its secondary market. This underscores the difference between the standard and premise of value.

These assumptions might not, and probably do not, reflect the actual conditions of the market in which the subject business might be sold. However, these conditions are assumed because they yield a uniform standard of value, after applying generally accepted valuation techniques, which allows meaningful comparison between businesses which are similarly situated.

Elements of Business Valuation

Economic Conditions

A business valuation report generally begins with a summary of the purpose and scope of business appraisal as well as its date and stated audience. What follows is a description of national, regional and local economic conditions existing as of the valuation date, as well as the conditions of the industry in which the subject business operates. A common source of economic information for the first section of the business valuation report is the Federal Reserve Board's Beige Book, published eight times a year by the Federal Reserve Bank. State governments and industry associations also publish useful statistics describing regional and industry conditions.

Financial Analysis

The financial statement analysis generally involves common size analysis, ratio analysis (liquidity, turnover, profitability, etc.), trend analysis and industry comparative analysis. This permits the valuation analyst to compare the subject company to other businesses in the same or similar industry, and to discover trends affecting the company and/or the industry over time. By comparing a company's financial statements in different time periods, the valuation expert can view growth or decline in revenues or expenses, changes in capital structure, or other financial trends. How the subject company compares to the industry will help with the risk assessment and ultimately help determine the discount rate and the selection of market multiples.

It is important to mention that among the financial statements, the primary statement to show the liquidity of the company is cash flow. Cash flow shows the company's cash in and out flow.

Normalization of Financial Statements

The key objective of normalization is to identify the ability of the business to generate income for its owners. A measure of the income is the amount of cash flow that the owners can remove from the business without adversely affecting its operations. The most common normalization adjustments fall into the following four categories:

- Comparability Adjustments: The valuer may adjust the subject company's financial statements to facilitate a comparison between the subject company and other businesses in the same industry or geographic location. These adjustments are intended to eliminate differences between the way that published industry data is presented and the way that the subject company's data is presented in its financial statements.

- Non-operating Adjustments: It is reasonable to assume that if a business were sold in a hypothetical sales transaction (which is the underlying premise of the fair market value standard), the seller would retain any assets which were not related to the production of earnings or price those non-operating assets separately. For this reason, non-operating assets (such as excess cash) are usually eliminated from the balance sheet.

- Non-recurring Adjustments: The subject company's financial statements may be affected by events that are not expected to recur, such as the purchase or sale of assets, a lawsuit, or an unusually large revenue or expense. These non-recurring items are adjusted so that the financial statements will better reflect the management's expectations of future performance.

- Discretionary Adjustments: The owners of private companies may be paid at variance from the market level of compensation that similar executives in the industry might command. In order to determine fair market value, the owner's compensation, benefits, perquisites and distributions must be adjusted to industry standards. Similarly, the rent paid by the subject business for the use of property owned by the company's owners individually may be scrutinized.

Income, Asset and Market Approaches

Three different approaches are commonly used in business valuation: the income approach, the asset-based approach, and the market approach. Within each of these approaches, there are various techniques for determining the value of a business using the definition of value appropriate for the appraisal assignment. Generally, the income approaches determine value by calculating the net present value of the benefit stream generated by the business (discounted cash flow); the asset-based approaches determine value by adding the sum of the parts of the business (net asset value); and the market approaches determine value by comparing the subject company to other companies in the same industry, of the same size, and/or within the same region. A number of business valuation models can be constructed that utilize various methods under the three business valuation approaches. Venture Capitalists and Private Equity professionals have long used the First chicago method which essentially combines the income approach with the market approach.

In certain cases equity may also be valued by applying the techniques and frameworks developed for financial options, via a real options framework.

In determining which of these approaches to use, the valuation professional must exercise discretion. Each technique has advantages and drawbacks, which must be considered when applying those techniques to a particular subject company. Most treatises and court decisions encourage the valuator to consider more than one technique, which must be reconciled with each other to arrive at a value conclusion. A measure of common sense and a good grasp of mathematics is helpful.

Income Approach

The income approach relies upon the economic principle of expectation: the value of business is based on the expected economic benefit and level of risk associated with the investment. Income based valuation methods determine fair market value by dividing the benefit stream generated by the subject or target company times a discount or capitalization rate. The discount or capitalization rate converts the stream of benefits into present value. There are several different income methods, including capitalization of earnings or cash flows, discounted future cash flows ("DCF"), and the excess earnings method (which is a hybrid of asset and income approaches). The result of a value calculation under the income approach is generally the fair market value of a controlling, marketable interest in the subject company, since the entire benefit stream of the subject company is most often valued, and the capitalization and discount rates are derived from statistics concerning public companies. IRS Revenue Ruling 59-60 states that earnings are preeminent for the valuation of closely held operating companies.

However, income valuation methods can also be used to establish the value of a severable business asset as long as an income stream can be attributed to it. An example is licensable intellectual property whose value needs to be established to arrive at a supportable royalty structure.

Discount or Capitalization Rates

A discount rate or capitalization rate is used to determine the present value of the expected returns of a business. The discount rate and capitalization rate are closely related to each other, but distinguishable. Generally speaking, the discount rate or capitalization rate may be defined as the yield necessary to attract investors to a particular investment, given the risks associated with that investment.

- In DCF valuations, the discount rate, often an estimate of the cost of capital for the business, is used to calculate the net present value of a series of projected cash flows. The discount rate can also be viewed as the required rate of return the investors expect to receive from the business enterprise, given the level of risk they undertake.

- On the other hand, a capitalization rate is applied in methods of business valuation that are based on business data for a single period of time. For example, in real estate valuations for properties that generate cash flows, a capitalization rate may be applied to the net operating income (NOI) (i.e., income before depreciation and interest expenses) of the property for the trailing twelve months.

There are several different methods of determining the appropriate discount rates. The discount rate is composed of two elements: (1) the risk-free rate, which is the return that an investor would expect from a secure, practically risk-free investment, such as a high quality government bond; plus (2) a risk premium that compensates an investor for the relative level of risk associated with a particular investment in excess of the risk-free rate. Most importantly, the selected discount or capitalization rate must be consistent with stream of benefits to which it is to be applied.

Capitalization and discounting valuation calculations become mathematically equivalent under the assumption that the business income grows at a constant rate.

Capital Asset Pricing Model (CAPM)

The capital asset pricing model (CAPM) provides one method of determining a discount rate in business valuation. The CAPM originated from the Nobel Prize-winning studies of Harry Markowitz, James Tobin, and William Sharpe. The method derives the discount rate by adding risk premium to the risk-free rate. The risk premium is derived by multiplying the equity risk premium with "beta", a measure of stock price volatility. Beta is compiled by various researchers for particular industries and companies, and measures systematic risks of investment.

One of the criticisms of the CAPM is that beta is derived from volatility of prices of publicly traded companies, which differ from non-publicly companies in liquidity, marketability, capital structures and control. Other aspects such as access to credit markets, size, and management depth are generally different, too. The rate build-up method also requires an assessment of the subject company's risk, which provides valuation of itself. Where a privately held company can be shown to be sufficiently similar to a public company, the CAPM may be suitable. However, it requires the knowledge of market stock prices for calculation. For private companies that do not sell stock on the public capital markets, this information is not readily available. Therefore, calculation of beta for private firms is problematic. The build-up cost of capital model is the typical choice in such cases.

Alternative Valuation Approaches and Factor Models

With regard to capital market-oriented valuation approaches there are numerous valuation approaches besides the traditional CAPM model. They include, for example, the Arbitrage pricing theory (APT) as well as the Consumption-based Capital Asset Pricing Model (CCAPM). Furthermore, alternative capital market models were developed, having in common that expected return hinge on *multiple* risk sources and thus being less restrictive:

- Models of the Q theory.
- Fama–French three-factor model.
- Carhart four-factor model.
- Fama-French five-factor model.

Nevertheless, even these models are not wholly consistent, as they also show market anomalies. However, the method of incomplete replication and risk covering come along without the need of capital market data and thus being more solid. Equally notable is the existence of investment based approaches, considering different investment opportunities and determining an investment program by means of linear optimization. Among them the approximative decomposition valuation approach can be found.

Modified Capital Asset Pricing Model

The Cost of Equity (Ke) is computed by using the Modified Capital Asset Pricing Model (Mod. CAPM),

$$k_e = R_f + \beta(R_m - R_f) + SCRP + CSRP$$

Where:

R_f = Risk free rate of return (Generally taken as 10-year Government Bond Yield).

β = Beta Value (Sensitivity of the stock returns to market returns).

k_e = Cost of Equity.

R_m = Market Rate of Return.

SCRP = Small Company Risk Premium.

CSRP= Company specific Risk premium.

Weighted Average Cost of Capital ("WACC")

The weighted average cost of capital is an approach to determining a discount rate. The WACC method determines the subject company's actual cost of capital by calculating the weighted average of the company's cost of debt and cost of equity. The WACC must be applied to the subject company's net cash flow to total invested capital.

One of the problems with this method is that the valuator may elect to calculate WACC according to the subject company's existing capital structure, the average industry capital structure, or the optimal capital structure. Such discretion detracts from the objectivity of this approach, in the minds of some critics.

Indeed, since the WACC captures the risk of the subject business itself, the existing or contemplated capital structures, rather than industry averages, are the appropriate choices for business valuation.

Once the capitalization rate or discount rate is determined, it must be applied to an appropriate economic income stream: pretax cash flow, aftertax cash flow, pretax net income, after tax net income, excess earnings, projected cash flow, etc. The result of this formula is the indicated value before discounts. Before moving on to calculate discounts, however, the valuation professional must consider the indicated value under the asset and market approaches.

Careful matching of the discount rate to the appropriate measure of economic income is critical to the accuracy of the business valuation results. Net cash flow is a frequent choice in professionally conducted business appraisals. The rationale behind this choice is that this earnings basis corresponds to the equity discount rate derived from the Build-Up or CAPM models: the returns obtained from investments in publicly traded companies can easily be represented in terms of net cash flows. At the same time, the discount rates are generally also derived from the public capital markets data.

Build-Up Method

The Build-Up Method is a widely recognized method of determining the after-tax net cash flow discount rate, which in turn yields the capitalization rate. The figures used in the Build-Up Method are derived from various sources. This method is called a "build-up" method because it is the sum of risks associated with various classes of assets. It is based on the principle that investors would require a greater return on classes of assets that are more risky.

- The first element of a Build-Up capitalization rate is the risk-free rate, which is the rate of return for long-term government bonds.

- Investors who buy large-cap equity stocks, which are inherently more risky than long-term government bonds, require a greater return, so the next element of the Build-Up method is the equity risk premium. In determining a company's value, the long-horizon equity risk premium is used because the Company's life is assumed to be infinite. The sum of the risk-free rate and the equity risk premium yields the long-term average market rate of return on large public company stocks.

- Similarly, investors who invest in small cap stocks, which are riskier than blue-chip stocks, require a greater return, called the "size premium." Size premium data is generally available from two sources: Morningstar's (formerly Ibbotson & Associates') Stocks, Bonds, Bills & Inflation and Duff & Phelps' Risk Premium Report.

By adding the first three elements of a Build-Up discount rate, we can determine the rate of return that investors would require on their investments in small public company stocks. These three elements of the Build-Up discount rate are known collectively as the "systematic risks." This type of investment risk cannot be avoided through portfolio diversification. It arises from external factors and affect every type of investment in the economy. As a result, investors taking systematic risk are rewarded by an additional premium.

In addition to systematic risks, the discount rate must include "unsystematic risk" representing that portion of total investment risk that can be avoided through diversification. Public capital markets do not provide evidence of unsystematic risk since investors that fail to diversify cannot expect additional returns. Unsystematic risk falls into two categories.

- One of those categories is the "industry risk premium". It is also known as idiosyncratic risk and can be observed by studying the returns of a group of companies operating in the same industry sector. Morningstar's yearbooks contain empirical data to quantify the risks associated with various industries, grouped by SIC industry code.

- The other category of unsystematic risk is referred to as "company specific risk."

Historically, no published data has been available to quantify specific company risks. However, as of late 2006, new research has been able to quantify, or isolate, this risk for publicly traded stocks through the use of Total Beta calculations. P. Butler and K. Pinkerton have outlined a procedure which sets the following two equations together:

Total Cost of Equity (TCOE) = risk-free rate + total beta * equity risk premium

= risk-free rate + beta * equity risk premium + size premium + company-specific risk premium

The only unknown in the two equations is the company specific risk premium. While it is possible to isolate the company-specific risk premium as shown above, many appraisers just key in on the total cost of equity (TCOE) provided by the first equation.

It is similar to using the market approach in the income approach instead of adding separate (and potentially redundant) measures of risk in the build-up approach. The use of total beta (developed by Aswath Damodaran) is a relatively new concept. It is, however, gaining acceptance in the business valuation Consultancy community since it is based on modern portfolio theory. Total beta can help appraisers develop a cost of capital who were content to use their intuition alone when previously adding a purely subjective company-specific risk premium in the build-up approach.

It is important to understand why this capitalization rate for small, privately held companies is significantly higher than the return that an investor might expect to receive from other common types of investments, such as money market accounts, mutual funds, or even real estate. Those investments involve substantially lower levels of risk than an investment in a closely held company. Depository accounts are insured by the federal government (up to certain limits); mutual funds are composed of publicly traded stocks, for which risk can be substantially minimized through portfolio diversification.

Closely held companies, on the other hand, frequently fail for a variety of reasons too numerous to name. Examples of the risk can be witnessed in the storefronts on every Main Street in America. There are no federal guarantees. The risk of investing in a private company cannot be reduced through diversification, and most businesses do not own the type of hard assets that can ensure capital appreciation over time. This is why investors demand a much higher return on their investment in closely held businesses; such investments are inherently much more risky. (This paragraph is biased, presuming that by the mere fact that a company is closely held, it is prone towards failure.)

Asset-based Approaches

In asset-based analysis the value of a business is equal to the sum of its parts. That is the theory underlying the asset-based approaches to business valuation. The asset approach to business valuation reported on the books of the subject company at their acquisition value, net of depreciation where applicable. These values must be adjusted to fair market value wherever possible. The value of a company's intangible assets, such as goodwill, is generally impossible to determine apart from the company's overall enterprise value. For this reason, the asset-based approach is not the most probative method of determining the value of going business concerns. In these cases, the asset-based approach yields a result that is probably lesser than the fair market value of the business. In considering an asset-based approach, the valuation professional must consider whether the shareholder whose interest is being valued would have any authority to access the value of the assets directly. Shareholders own shares in a corporation, but not its assets, which are owned by the corporation. A controlling shareholder may have the authority to direct the corporation to sell all or part of the assets it owns and to distribute the proceeds to the shareholder(s). The non-controlling shareholder, however, lacks this authority and cannot access the value of the assets. As a result, the value of a corporation's assets is not the true indicator of value to a shareholder who cannot avail himself of that value. The asset based approach is the entry barrier value and should preferably to be used in businesses having mature or declining growth cycle and is more suitable for capital intensive industry.

Adjusted net book value may be the most relevant standard of value where liquidation is imminent or ongoing; where a company earnings or cash flow are nominal, negative or worth less than its assets; or where net book value is standard in the industry in which the company operates. The adjusted net book value may also be used as a "sanity check" when compared to other methods of valuation, such as the income and market approaches.

Market Approaches

The market approach to business valuation is rooted in the economic principle of competition: that in a free market the supply and demand forces will drive the price of business assets to a certain equilibrium. Buyers would not pay more for the business, and the sellers will not accept less, than the price of a comparable business enterprise. The buyers and sellers are assumed to be equally well informed and acting in their own interests to conclude a transaction. It is similar in many respects to the "comparable sales" method that is commonly used in real estate appraisal. The market price of the stocks of publicly traded companies engaged in the same or a similar line of business, whose shares are actively traded in a free and open market, can be a valid indicator of value when the transactions in which stocks are traded are sufficiently similar to permit meaningful comparison.

The difficulty lies in identifying public companies that are sufficiently comparable to the subject company for this purpose. Also, as for a private company, the equity is less liquid (in other words its stocks are less easy to buy or sell) than for a public company, its value is considered to be slightly lower than such a market-based valuation would give.

When there is a lack of comparison with direct competition, a meaningful alternative could be a vertical value-chain approach where the subject company is compared with, for example, a known downstream industry to have a good feel of its value by building useful correlations with its downstream companies. Such comparison often reveals useful insights which help business analysts better understand performance relationship between the subject company and its downstream industry. For example, if a growing subject company is in an industry more concentrated than its downstream industry with a high degree of interdependence, one should logically expect the subject company performs better than the downstream industry in terms of growth, margins and risk.

Guideline Public Company Method

Guideline Public Company method entails a comparison of the subject company to publicly traded companies. The comparison is generally based on published data regarding the public companies' stock price and earnings, sales, or revenues, which is expressed as a fraction known as a "multiple." If the guideline public companies are sufficiently similar to each other and the subject company to permit a meaningful comparison, then their multiples should be similar. The public companies identified for comparison purposes should be similar to the subject company in terms of industry, product lines, market, growth, margins and risk.

However, if the subject company is privately owned, its value must be adjusted for lack of marketability. This is usually represented by a discount, or a percentage reduction in the value of the company when compared to its publicly traded counterparts. This reflects the higher risk associated with holding stock in a private company. The difference in value can be quantified by applying a discount for lack of marketability. This discount is determined by studying prices paid for shares of ownership in private companies that eventually offer their stock in a public offering. Alternatively, the lack of marketability can be assessed by comparing the prices paid for restricted shares to fully marketable shares of stock of public companies.

Option Pricing Approaches

In certain cases equity may be valued by applying the techniques and frameworks developed for financial options, via a real options framework.

In general, equity may be viewed as a call option on the firm, and this allows for the valuation of troubled firms which may otherwise be difficult to analyse. The classic application of this approach is to the valuation of distressed securities. Here, since the principle of limited liability protects equity investors, shareholders would choose not to repay the firm's debt where the value of the firm (as perceived) is less than the value of the outstanding debt. Of course, where firm value is greater than debt value, the shareholders would choose to repay (i.e. exercise their option) and not to liquidate. Thus analogous to out the money options which nevertheless have value, equity will (may) have value even if the value of the firm falls (well) below the face value of the outstanding debt—and this value can (should) be determined using the appropriate option valuation technique.

Certain business situations, and the parent firms in those cases, are also logically analysed under an options framework. Just as a financial option gives its owner the right, but not the obligation, to buy or sell a security at a given price, companies that make strategic investments have the right, but not the obligation, to exploit opportunities in the future; management will of course only exercise where this makes economic sense. Thus, for companies facing uncertainty of this type, the stock price may (should) be seen as the sum of the value of existing businesses (i.e., the discounted cash flow value) plus any real option value. Equity valuations here, may (should) thus proceed likewise. Compare PVGO.

A common application is to natural resource investments. Here, the underlying asset is the resource itself; the value of the asset is a function of both quantity of resource available and the price of the commodity in question. The value of the resource is then the difference between the value of the asset and the cost associated with developing the resource. Where positive ("in the money") management will undertake the development, and will not do so otherwise, and a resource project is thus effectively a call option. A resource firm may (should) therefore also be analysed using the options approach. Specifically, the value of the firm comprises the value of already active projects determined via DCF valuation (or other standard techniques) and undeveloped reserves as analysed using the real options framework.

Product patents may also be valued as options, and the value of firms holding these patents — typically firms in the bio-science, technology, and pharmaceutical sectors — can (should) similarly be viewed as the sum of the value of products in place and the portfolio of patents yet to be deployed. As regards the option analysis, since the patent provides the firm with the right to develop the product, it will do so only if the present value of the expected cash flows from the product exceeds the cost of development, and the patent rights thus correspond to a call option. Similar analysis may be applied to options on films (or other works of intellectual property) and the valuation of film studios.

Cultural Valuation Method

Besides mathematical approaches for the valuation of companies a rather unknown method includes also the cultural aspect. The so-called Cultural valuation method (Cultural Due Diligence) seeks to combine existing knowledge, motivation and internal culture with the results of a net-asset-value method. Especially during a company takeover uncovering hidden problems is of high importance for a later success of the business venture.

Discounts and Premiums

The valuation approaches yield the fair market value of the Company as a whole. In valuing a minority, non-controlling interest in a business, however, the valuation professional must consider the applicability of discounts that affect such interests. Discussions of discounts and premiums frequently begin with a review of the "levels of value". There are three common levels of value: controlling interest, marketable minority, and non-marketable minority. The intermediate level, marketable minority interest, is less than the controlling interest level and higher than the non-marketable minority interest level. The marketable minority interest level represents the perceived value of equity interests that are freely traded without any restrictions. These interests are generally traded on the New York Stock Exchange, AMEX, NASDAQ, and other exchanges where there is a ready market for equity securities. These values represent a minority interest in the subject companies – small blocks of stock that represent less than 50% of the company's equity, and usually much less than 50%. Controlling interest level is the value that an investor would be willing to pay to acquire more than 50% of a company's stock, thereby gaining the attendant prerogatives of control. Some of the prerogatives of control include: electing directors, hiring and firing the company's management and determining their compensation; declaring dividends and distributions, determining the company's strategy and line of business, and acquiring, selling or liquidating the business. This level of value generally contains a control premium over the intermediate level of value, which typically ranges from 25% to 50%. An additional premium may be paid by strategic investors who are motivated by synergistic motives. Non-marketable, minority level is the lowest level on the chart, representing the level at which non-controlling equity interests in private companies are generally valued or traded. This level of value is discounted because no ready market exists in which to purchase or sell interests. Private companies are less "liquid" than publicly traded companies, and transactions in private companies take longer and are more uncertain. Between the intermediate and lowest levels of the chart, there are restricted shares of publicly traded companies. Despite a growing inclination of the IRS and Tax Courts to challenge valuation discounts, Shannon Pratt suggested in a scholarly presentation recently that valuation discounts are actually increasing as the differences between public and private companies is widening . Publicly traded stocks have grown more liquid in the past decade due to rapid electronic trading, reduced commissions, and governmental deregulation. These developments have not improved the liquidity of interests in private companies, however. Valuation discounts are multiplicative, so they must be considered in order. Control premiums and their inverse, minority interest discounts, are considered before marketability discounts are applied.

Discount for Lack of Control

The first discount that must be considered is the discount for lack of control, which in this instance is also a minority interest discount. Minority interest discounts are the inverse of control premiums, to which the following mathematical relationship exists: $MID = 1 - [1 / (1 + CP)]$. The most common source of data regarding control premiums is the Control Premium Study, published annually by Mergerstat since 1972. Mergerstat compiles data regarding publicly announced mergers, acquisitions and divestitures involving 10% or more of the equity interests in public companies, where the purchase price is $1 million or more and at least one of the parties to the transaction is a U.S. entity. Mergerstat defines the "control premium" as the percentage difference between the acquisition price and the share price of the freely traded public shares five days prior to the announcement of the M&A transaction. While it is not without valid criticism, Mergerstat control premium data (and the minority interest discount derived therefrom) is widely accepted within the valuation profession.

Discount for Lack of Marketability

A "discount for lack of marketability" (DLOM) may be applied to a minority block of stock to alter the valuation of that block.

Another factor to be considered in valuing closely held companies is the marketability of an interest in such businesses. Marketability is defined as the ability to convert the business interest into cash quickly, with minimum transaction and administrative costs, and with a high degree of certainty as to the amount of net proceeds. There is usually a cost and a time lag associated with locating interested and capable buyers of interests in privately held companies, because there is no established market of readily available buyers and sellers.

All other factors being equal, an interest in a publicly traded company is worth more because it is readily marketable. Conversely, an interest in a private-held company is worth less because no established market exists. "The IRS Valuation Guide for Income, Estate and Gift Taxes, Valuation Training for Appeals Officers" acknowledges the relationship between value and marketability, stating: "Investors prefer an asset which is easy to sell, that is, liquid."

The discount for lack of control is separate and distinguishable from the discount for lack of marketability. It is the valuation professional's task to quantify the lack of marketability of an interest in a privately held company. Because, in this case, the subject interest is not a controlling interest in the Company, and the owner of that interest cannot compel liquidation to convert the subject interest to cash quickly, and no established market exists on which that interest could be sold, the discount for lack of marketability is appropriate.

Several empirical studies have been published that attempt to quantify the discount for lack of marketability. These studies include the restricted stock studies and the pre-IPO studies. The aggregate of these studies indicate average discounts of 35% and 50%, respectively. Some experts believe the Lack of Control and Marketability discounts can aggregate discounts for as much as ninety percent of a Company's fair market value, specifically with family-owned companies.

Restricted Stock Studies

Restricted stocks are equity securities of public companies that are similar in all respects to the freely traded stocks of those companies except that they carry a restriction that prevents them from being traded on the open market for a certain period of time, which is usually one year (two years prior to 1990). This restriction from active trading, which amounts to a lack of marketability, is the only distinction between the restricted stock and its freely traded counterpart. Restricted stock can be traded in private transactions and usually do so at a discount. The restricted stock studies attempt to verify the difference in price at which the restricted shares trade versus the price at which the same unrestricted securities trade in the open market as of the same date. The underlying data by which these studies arrived at their conclusions has not been made public. Consequently, it is not possible when valuing a particular company to compare the characteristics of that company to the study data. Still, the existence of a marketability discount has been recognized by valuation professionals and the Courts, and the restricted stock studies are frequently cited as empirical evidence. Notably, the lowest average discount reported by these studies was 26% and the highest average discount was 40%.

Option Pricing

In addition to the restricted stock studies, U.S. publicly traded companies are able to sell stock to offshore investors (SEC Regulation S, enacted in 1990) without registering the shares with the

Securities and Exchange Commission. The offshore buyers may resell these shares in the United States, still without having to register the shares, after holding them for just 40 days. Typically, these shares are sold for 20% to 30% below the publicly traded share price. Some of these transactions have been reported with discounts of more than 30%, resulting from the lack of marketability. These discounts are similar to the marketability discounts inferred from the restricted and pre-IPO studies, despite the holding period being just 40 days. Studies based on the prices paid for options have also confirmed similar discounts. If one holds restricted stock and purchases an option to sell that stock at the market price (a put), the holder has, in effect, purchased marketability for the shares. The price of the put is equal to the marketability discount. The range of marketability discounts derived by this study was 32% to 49%. However, ascribing the entire value of a put option to marketability is misleading, because the primary source of put value comes from the downside price protection. A correct economic analysis would use deeply in-the-money puts or Single-stock futures, demonstrating that marketability of restricted stock is of low value because it is easy to hedge using unrestricted stock or futures trades.

Pre-IPO Studies

Another approach to measure the marketability discount is to compare the prices of stock offered in initial public offerings (IPOs) to transactions in the same company's stocks prior to the IPO. Companies that are going public are required to disclose all transactions in their stocks for a period of three years prior to the IPO. The pre-IPO studies are the leading alternative to the restricted stock stocks in quantifying the marketability discount.

The pre-IPO studies are sometimes criticized because the sample size is relatively small, the pre-IPO transactions may not be arm's length, and the financial structure and product lines of the studied companies may have changed during the three year pre-IPO window.

Applying the Studies

The studies confirm what the marketplace knows intuitively: Investors covet liquidity and loathe obstacles that impair liquidity. Prudent investors buy illiquid investments only when there is a sufficient discount in the price to increase the rate of return to a level which brings risk-reward back into balance. The referenced studies establish a reasonable range of valuation discounts from the mid-30%s to the low 50%s. The more recent studies appeared to yield a more conservative range of discounts than older studies, which may have suffered from smaller sample sizes. Another method of quantifying the lack of marketability discount is the Quantifying Marketability Discounts Model (QMDM).

Estimates of Business Value

The evidence on the market value of specific businesses varies widely, largely depending on reported market transactions in the equity of the firm. A fraction of businesses are "publicly traded," meaning that their equity can be purchased and sold by investors in stock markets available to the general public. Publicly traded companies on major stock markets have an easily calculated "market capitalization" that is a direct estimate of the market value of the firm's equity. Some publicly traded firms have relatively few recorded trades (including many firms traded "over the counter" or in "pink sheets"). A far larger number of firms are privately held. Normally, equity interests in these firms (which include corporations, partnerships, limited-liability companies, and some other organizational forms) are traded privately, and often irregularly. As a result, previous transactions provide limited evidence as to the current value of a private company primarily because business value changes over time, and the share price is associated with considerable uncertainty due to limited market exposure and high transaction costs.

A number of stock market indicators in the United States and other countries provide an indication of the market value of publicly traded firms. The Survey of Consumer Finance in the US also includes an estimate of household ownership of stocks, including indirect ownership through mutual funds. The 2004 and 2007 SCF indicate a growing trend in stock ownership, with 51% of households indicating a direct or indirect ownership of stocks, with the majority of those respondents indicating indirect ownership through mutual funds. Few indications are available on the value of privately held firms. Anderson (2009) recently estimated the market value of U.S. privately held and publicly traded firms, using Internal Revenue Service and SCF data. He estimates that privately held firms produced more income for investors, and had more value than publicly held firms, in 2004.

Business Valuation Methods

Three Business Valuation Methods

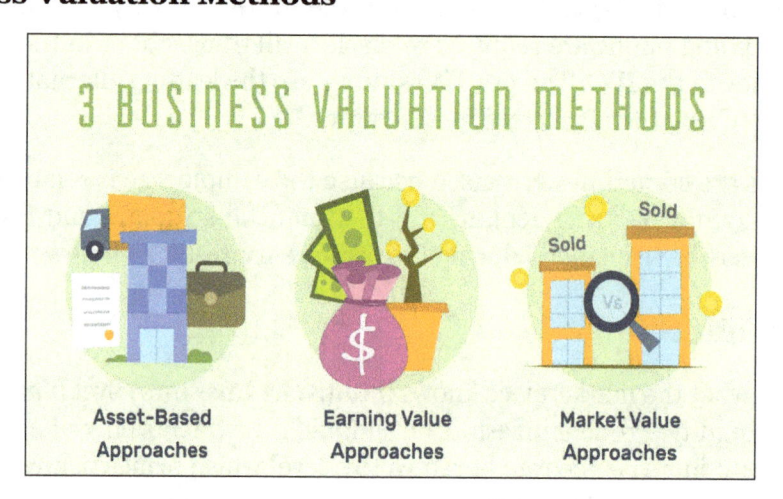

Asset-based Approaches

Basically, these business valuation methods total up all the investments in the business. Asset-based business valuations can be done on a going concern or on a liquidation basis.

- A going concern asset-based approach lists the business's net balance sheet value of its assets and subtracts the value of its liabilities.

- A liquidation asset-based approach determines the net cash that would be received if all assets were sold and liabilities paid off.

Using the asset-based approach to value a sole proprietorship is more difficult. In a corporation, all assets are owned by the company and would normally be included in a sale of the business. Assets in a sole proprietorship exist in the name of the owner and separating assets from business and personal use can be difficult.

For instance, a sole proprietor in a lawn care business may use various pieces of lawn care equipment for both business and personal use. A potential purchaser of the business would need to sort out which assets the owner intends to sell as part of the business.

Earning Value Approaches

These business valuation methods are predicated on the idea that a business's true value lies in its ability to produce wealth in the future. The most common earning value approach is Capitalizing Past Earning.

With this approach, a valuator determines an expected level of cash flow for the company using a company's record of past earnings, normalizes them for unusual revenue or expenses, and multiplies the expected normalized cash flows by a capitalization factor. The capitalization factor is a reflection of what rate of return a reasonable purchaser would expect on the investment, as well as a measure of the risk that the expected earnings will not be achieved.

Discounted Future Earnings is another earning value approach to business valuation where instead of an average of past earnings, an average of the trend of predicted future earnings is used and divided by the capitalization factor.

Valuation of a sole proprietorship in terms of past earnings can be tricky, as customer loyalty is directly tied to the identity of the business owner. Whether the business involves plumbing or management consulting, will existing customers automatically expect that a new owner delivers the same degree of service and professionalism?

Any valuation of a service-oriented sole proprietorship needs to involve an estimate of the percentage of business that might be lost under a change of ownership.

Valuation of a sole proprietorship in terms of past earnings can be tricky, as customer loyalty is directly tied to the identity of the business owner. Whether the business involves plumbing or management consulting, will existing customers automatically expect that a new owner delivers the same degree of service and professionalism?

Any valuation of a service-oriented sole proprietorship needs to involve an estimate of the percentage of business that might be lost under a change of ownership.

Market Value Approaches

Market value approaches to business valuation attempt to establish the value of your business by comparing your business to similar businesses that have recently sold. Obviously, this method is only going to work well if there are a sufficient number of similar businesses to compare.

Assigning a value to a sole proprietorship based on market value is particularly difficult. By definition, sole proprietorships are individually owned so attempting to find public information on prior sales of like businesses is not an easy task.

Although the Earning Value Approach is the most popular business valuation method, for most businesses, some combination of business valuation methods will be the fairest way to set a selling price.

Business Valuation Standard

Business Valuation Standards (BVS) are codes of practice that are used in business valuation. The major business appraisal standards are these:

- CICBV Practice Standards. Published by the CBV Institute.
- Uniform Standards of Professional Appraisal Practice (USPAP). Standards 9 and 10 cover business valuation and reporting standards. Published by the Appraisal Foundation.
- International Valuation Standards. Published by the International Valuation Standards Council.
- Statement on Standards for Valuation Services (SSVS No 1). Published by the American Institute of CPAs.

In addition, each of the three major United States valuation societies — the American Society of Appraisers (ASA), American Institute of Certified Public Accountants (CPA/ABV), and the National Association of Certified Valuation Analysts (NACVA) — has its own set of Business Valuation Guidelines, which it requires all of its accredited members to adhere to. The AICPA's standards are published as Statement on Standards for Valuation Services No.1 and the ASA's guidelines are published as the ASA Business Valuation Guidelines, which largely follow the USPAP Standard requirements. All AICPA members are required to follow SSVS1. Additionally, the majority of the State Accountancy Boards have adopted SSVS1 for CPAs licensed in their state.

Features

All of the standards have the following in common:

A Requirement of Independence

The appraiser must not act in favor of the client or any other party.

A Requirement that Fees be not Contingent on Appraised Value

Fees based upon, for example, a percentage of the valuation are unethical and are not allowed.

A Requirement that all Limiting Conditions be Explicitly Stated

The reader must be informed of all assumptions made as part of the valuation. For example, if a lawsuit is pending against a business, the valuation must explicitly state that the impact of the outcome of the lawsuit will have an unknown effect on the value, and what assumptions about the outcome have or have not been made.

A Requirement that all People Participating in the Valuation be Disclosed

All professionals participating in a valuation report must sign it, and must have certification of their independence, fee arrangements, and other factors.

A Requirement that all Information Sources be Stated

Readers must be able to replicate valuation reports for themselves. Therefore, all sources used in compiling the report must be stated.

Minimum Requirements for Contents of Reports

The precise minimum requirements vary from society to society, but roughly they include the purpose and scope of the assignment, the standard of value and specific valuation date being employed, an identification of the specific interest being evaluated, the relevant state and federal laws that govern the entity being valued, the scope of the procedures employed during valuation, the nature and history of the business, the historical financial information on the business, a thorough financial analysis of the business comparing the business' performance with industry trends, an overview of the industry in which the business operates and the impact of market conditions on the business, and the current investment climate.

ABSOLUTE VALUATION MODEL

Absolute value, also known as an intrinsic value, refers to a business valuation method that uses discounted cash flow (DCF) analysis to determine a company's financial worth. The absolute value method differs from the relative value models that examine what a company is worth compared to its competitors. Absolute value models try to determine a company's intrinsic worth based on its projected cash flows.

Finding out whether a stock is under or overvalued is a primary play of value investors. Value investors use popular metrics like the price-to-earnings ratio (P/E) and the price-to-book ratio (P/B) to determine whether to buy or sell a stock based on its estimated worth. In addition to using these ratios as a valuation guide, another way to determine absolute value is the discounted cash flow (DCF) valuation analysis.

Some form of a company's future cash flows (CF) is estimated with a DCF model and is then discounted to the present value in order to determine an absolute value for the company. The present value is regarded as the true worth or intrinsic value of the firm. By comparing what a company's share price should be given its absolute value to the price that the stock is actually trading at, investors can determine if a stock is currently under or overvalued.

Examples of methods used under the DCF model include the following models:

- Dividend discount model.
- Discounted asset model.
- Discounted residual income method.
- Discounted FCF method.

All of these models require a rate of return or discount rate which is used to discount a firm's cash flows—dividends, earnings, operating cash flow (OCF), or free cash flow (FCF)—to get the absolute value of the firm. Depending on the method employed to run a valuation analysis, the investor or analyst could use either the cost of equity or the weighted average cost of capital (WACC) as a discount rate.

Absolute Value vs. Relative Value

Relative value is the opposite of absolute value. While absolute value examines the intrinsic value of an asset or company without comparing it to any others, relative value is based on the value of similar assets or companies. Analysts and investors who use relative value analysis for stocks look at financial statements and other multiples of the companies they're interested in and compare it to other, similar firms to determine if those potential companies are over or undervalued. For instance, an investor will look at the variables—market capitalization, revenues, sales figures, P/E ratios, etc.—for companies like Amazon, Target, and/or Costco if they want to know the relative value of Walmart.

Challenges of using Absolute Value

Estimating a company's absolute value does not come without its setbacks. Forecasting the cash flows with complete certainty and projecting how long the cash flows will remain on a growth trajectory is challenging. In addition to predicting an accurate growth rate, evaluating an appropriate discount rate to calculate the present value can be difficult.

Since the absolute valuation approach to determining the worth of a stock is strictly based on the characteristics and fundamentals of the company under analysis, there is no comparison made to other companies in the same sector or industry. But companies within the same sector should be considered when analyzing a firm since a market-moving activity—a bankruptcy, government regulatory changes, disruptive innovation, employee layoffs, mergers and acquisitions, etc.—in any one of these companies can affect how the entire sector moves. Therefore, the best way to evaluate a stock's real value is to incorporate a mix of both the absolute and relative value methods.

Example of Absolute Value

Consider Company X, which currently trades on the market for $370.50. After running a DCF analysis on its estimated future cash flows, an analyst determines that the absolute value of the firm is $450.30. This presents a buying opportunity for an investor who is led to believe, based on the numbers, that Company X is undervalued.

Absolute Valuation Formula

This equation and the stock is represented as follows –

Absolute Valuation Formula of Business

Mathematically, the Absolute Valuation Equation can be represented as,

$$\text{Absolute value} = \frac{CF_1}{(1+r)^1} + \frac{CF_2}{(1+r)^2} + \ldots + \frac{CF_n}{(1+r)^n} + \frac{Terminal\ value}{(1+r)^n}$$

$$\text{Absolute value} = \sum_{i=1}^{n} \frac{CF_i}{(1+r)^i} + \frac{\text{Terminal value}}{(1+r)^n}$$

where,

- CF_i = Cash flow in the ith year
- n = Last year of the projection
- r = Discount rate

Absolute Valuation Formula of Stock

Finally, the absolute value of a stock equation is calculated by dividing the absolute value of the business by the number of outstanding shares of the company in the market and the absolute value of a stock is represented as,

$$\text{Absolute value}_{\text{Stock}} = \text{Absolute value}_{\text{Business}} / \text{Number of outstanding shares}$$

Explanation of the Absolute Valuation Formula

The formula for absolute valuation can be calculated by using the following steps:

Step 1: Firstly, the projected cash flow during a year is noted from the company's financial projections. The cash flow can be in the form of dividend income, earnings, free cash flow, operating cash flow etc. The cash flow for the ith year is denoted by CF_i.

Step 2: Next, the weighted average cost of capital (WACC) of a company is usually taken as the discount rate because it denotes an investor's expected required rate of return from investment in that company and it is denoted by r.

Step 3: Next, the determine the terminal value by multiplying the cash flow of the last projected year by a factor which is usually the reciprocal of the required rate of return. The terminal value denotes the value of the on the assumption that the business will continue after the projected periods.

Terminal Value = CFn * Factor

Step 4: Next, calculate the present values of all the cash flows by discounting them using the discount rate.

Step 5: Next, the equation of absolute valuation calculation for the particular company is done by adding up all the present values of the cash flows and the terminal value calculated in step 4.

$$\text{Absolute value} = \frac{CF_1}{(1+r)^1} + \frac{CF_2}{(1+r)^2} + \ldots + \frac{CF_n}{(1+r)^n} + \frac{\text{Terminal value}}{(1+r)^n}$$

Step 6: Finally, the absolute valuation of a stock can be calculated by dividing the value in step 5 by the number of shares outstanding of the company.

$$\text{Absolute valuation}_{\text{Stock}} = \text{Absolute valuation}_{\text{Business}} / \text{Number of outstanding shares}$$

Example of Absolute Valuation Formula (with Excel Template)

Let us take an example of a company ABC Ltd and a particular analyst is interested in predicting the fair value of the company based on the available financial information. The investor's expected required rate of return in the market is 6%. On the other hand, the company has projected that the free cash flow of the company will grow at 7%. Determine the absolute valuation of the stock on the basis of the following financial estimates for CY19:

	A	B
1	All amount in Millions	CY19 (E)
2	NOPAT	$150.00
3	Depreciation & Amortisation Expense	$18.00
4	Increase in Working Capital	$17.00
5	Capital Expenditure during the Year	$200.00
6	Debt Repayment	$35.00
7	Fresh Debt Raised during the Year	$150.00
8	Investor's Expected Rate of Return	6.00%
9	Cash Flow Growth Rate	7.00%
10		

So, from the above-given data, we will first calculate the CF for CY19.

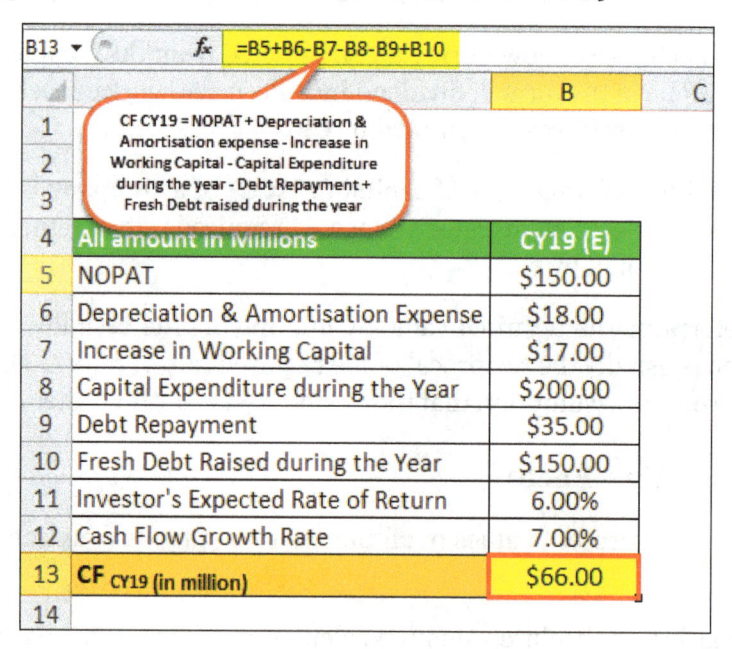

B13 fx =B5+B6-B7-B8-B9+B10

CF CY19 = NOPAT + Depreciation & Amortisation expense - Increase in Working Capital - Capital Expenditure during the year - Debt Repayment + Fresh Debt raised during the year

		B
4	All amount in Millions	CY19 (E)
5	NOPAT	$150.00
6	Depreciation & Amortisation Expense	$18.00
7	Increase in Working Capital	$17.00
8	Capital Expenditure during the Year	$200.00
9	Debt Repayment	$35.00
10	Fresh Debt Raised during the Year	$150.00
11	Investor's Expected Rate of Return	6.00%
12	Cash Flow Growth Rate	7.00%
13	CF CY19 (in million)	$66.00
14		

CF_{CY19} = NOPAT + Depreciation & Amortisation expense – Increase in Working Capital – Capital Expenditure during the year – Debt Repayment + Fresh Debt raised during the year

- $150.00 Mn + $18.00 Mn – $17.00 Mn – $200.00 Mn – $35.00 Mn + $150.00 Mn
- $66.00 Mn

Now, using this CF of CY19 and CF growth rate we will calculate the Projected CF for CY20 TO CY23.

Projected CF of CY20

	A	B	C
1			
2	CF Growth Rate	7%	
3	CF of CY19 (in millions)	$66.00	
4	**Projected CF for CY20**	$70.62	
5			

B4 fx =B3*(1+B2)

- Projected CF $_{CY20}$ = $66.00 Mn * (1 + 7%) = $70.62 Mn

Projected CF of CY21

	A	B	C
1			
2	CF Growth Rate	7%	
3	CF of CY19 (in millions)	$66.00	
4	**Projected CF for CY21**	$75.56	
5			

C21 fx =B18*(1+B17)^2

- Projected CF $_{CY21}$ = $66.00 Mn * (1 + 7%)^2 = $75.56 Mn

Projected CF of CY22

	A	B	C
1			
2	CF Growth Rate	7%	
3	CF of CY19 (in millions)	$66.00	
4	**Projected CF for CY22**	$80.85	
5			

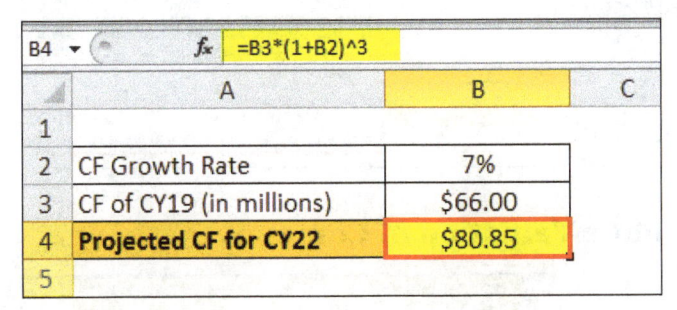

B4 fx =B3*(1+B2)^3

- Projected CF $_{CY22}$ = $66.00 Mn * (1 + 7%)^3 = $80.85 Mn

Projected CF of CY23

	A	B	C
1			
2	CF Growth Rate	7%	
3	CF of CY19 (in millions)	$66.00	
4	**Projected CF for CY23**	$86.51	
5			

B4 fx =B3*(1+B2)^4

- Projected CF $_{CY23}$ = $66.00 Mn * (1 + 7%)^4 = $86.51 Mn

Now we will calculate the Terminal value.

	A	B
	B4 fx =B2*(1/B3)	
1		
2	Projected CF for CY23	$86.51
3	Expected Rate of Return	6.00%
4	Terminal Value	$1,441.88
5		

Terminal value = CFn * Factor

- Terminal value = CF_{CY23} * (1 / Required rate of return)
- $86.51 Mn * (1 / 6%)
- $1,441.88 Mn

Therefore, the calculation of absolute valuation will be as follows –

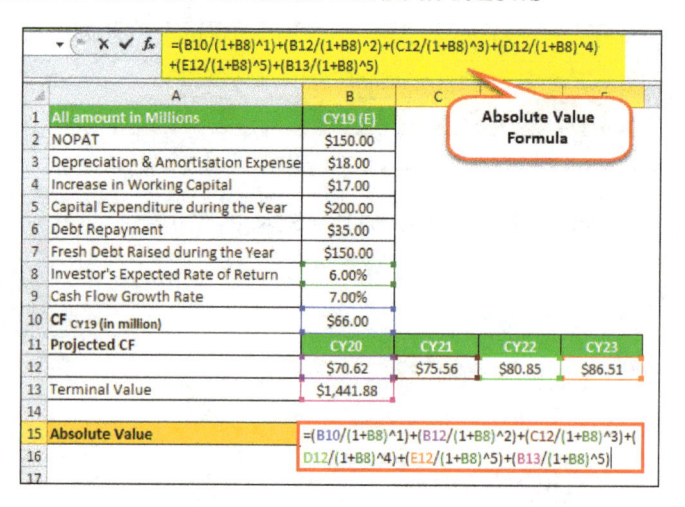

	A	B	C	D	E
	fx =(B10/(1+B8)^1)+(B12/(1+B8)^2)+(C12/(1+B8)^3)+(D12/(1+B8)^4)+(E12/(1+B8)^5)+(B13/(1+B8)^5)				
1	All amount in Millions	CY19 (E)			
2	NOPAT	$150.00			
3	Depreciation & Amortisation Expense	$18.00			
4	Increase in Working Capital	$17.00			
5	Capital Expenditure during the Year	$200.00			
6	Debt Repayment	$35.00			
7	Fresh Debt Raised during the Year	$150.00			
8	Investor's Expected Rate of Return	6.00%			
9	Cash Flow Growth Rate	7.00%			
10	CF_{CY19} (in million)	$66.00			
11	Projected CF	CY20	CY21	CY22	CY23
12		$70.62	$75.56	$80.85	$86.51
13	Terminal Value	$1,441.88			
14					
15	Absolute Value	=(B10/(1+B8)^1)+(B12/(1+B8)^2)+(C12/(1+B8)^3)+(D12/(1+B8)^4)+(E12/(1+B8)^5)+(B13/(1+B8)^5)			
16					

Absolute Value Formula

Calculation of Absolute Valuation of Company

	A	B	C	D	E
	B15 fx =(B10/(1+B8)^1)+(B12/(1+B8)^2)+(C12/(1+B8)^3)+(D12/(1+B8)^4)+(E12/(1+B8)^5)+(B13/(1+B8)^5)				
1	All amount in Millions	CY19 (E)			
2	NOPAT	$150.00			
3	Depreciation & Amortisation Expense	$18.00			
4	Increase in Working Capital	$17.00			
5	Capital Expenditure during the Year	$200.00			
6	Debt Repayment	$35.00			
7	Fresh Debt Raised during the Year	$150.00			
8	Investor's Expected Rate of Return	6.00%			
9	Cash Flow Growth Rate	7.00%			
10	CF_{CY19} (in million)	$66.00			
11	Projected CF	CY20	CY21	CY22	CY23
12		$70.62	$75.56	$80.85	$86.51
13	Terminal Value	$1,441.88			
14					
15	Absolute Value	$1,394.70			
16					

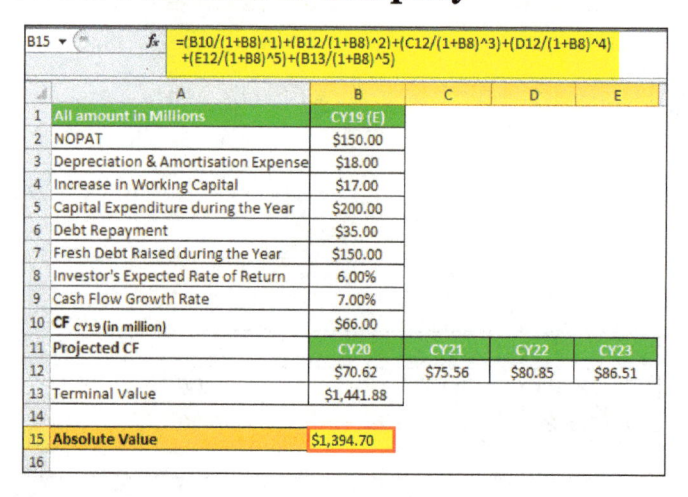

- Absolute Value = $1,394.70 Mn

CHAPTER 5 Valuation

Now, we will calculate the fair value of the stock which is as follows –

- The absolute valuation of the stock = Absolute valuation of company / Number of outstanding shares
- $1,394.70 Mn / 60,000,000

	A	B	C	D	E
1	All amount in Millions				
2	NOPAT				
3	Depreciation & Amortisation Expense	$18.00			
4	Increase in Working Capital	$17.00			
5	Capital Expenditure during the Year	$200.00			
6	Debt Repayment	$35.00			
7	Fresh Debt Raised during the Year	$150.00			
8	Investor's Expected Rate of Return	6.00%			
9	Cash Flow Growth Rate	7.00%			
10	CF $_{CY19}$ (in million)	$66.00			
11	Projected CF	CY20	CY21	CY22	CY23
12		$70.62	$75.56	$80.85	$86.51
13	Terminal Value	$1,441.88			
14					
15	Absolute Value	$1,394.70			
16	No of Outstanding Shares	$60.00			
17	Absolute Value of Stock	=B15/B16			
18					

Formula bar: =B15/B16 — absolute value of the stock = Absolute value of company / Number of outstanding shares

Calculation of Absolute valuation of Stock

B17: =B15/B16

	A	B	C	D	E
1	All amount in Millions	CY19 (E)			
2	NOPAT	$150.00			
3	Depreciation & Amortisation Expense	$18.00			
4	Increase in Working Capital	$17.00			
5	Capital Expenditure during the Year	$200.00			
6	Debt Repayment	$35.00			
7	Fresh Debt Raised during the Year	$150.00			
8	Investor's Expected Rate of Return	6.00%			
9	Cash Flow Growth Rate	7.00%			
10	CF $_{CY19}$ (in million)	$66.00			
11	Projected CF	CY20	CY21	CY22	CY23
12		$70.62	$75.56	$80.85	$86.51
13	Terminal Value	$1,441.88			
14					
15	Absolute Value	$1,394.70			
16	No of Outstanding Shares	$60.00			
17	Absolute Value of Stock	$23.25			
18					

- $23.25

Relevance and Use

From the perspective of a value investor, it is very important to understand the concept of an absolute valuation equation because it is used to check whether a stock is over or undervalued. However, it is very challenging to forecast the cash flows with certainty, the growth rate and to assess how long the cash flows will continue to grow in the future.

RELATIVE VALUATION MODEL

A relative valuation model is a business valuation method that compares a company's value to that of its competitors or industry peers to assess the firm's financial worth. Relative valuation models are an alternative to absolute value models, which try to determine a company's intrinsic worth based on its estimated future free cash flows discounted to their present value, without any reference to another company or industry average. Like absolute value models, investors may use relative valuation models when determining whether a company's stock is a good buy.

Types of Relative Valuation Models

There are many different types of relative valuation ratios, such as price to free cash flow, enterprise value (EV), operating margin, price to cash flow for real estate and price-to-sales (P/S) for retail.

One of the most popular relative valuation multiples is the price-to-earnings (P/E) ratio. It is calculated by dividing stock price by earnings per share (EPS), and is expressed as a company's share price as a multiple of its earnings. A company with a high P/E ratio is trading at a higher price per dollar of earnings than its peers and is considered overvalued. Likewise, a company with a low P/E ratio is trading at a lower price per dollar of EPS and is considered undervalued. This framework can be carried out with any multiple of price to gauge relative market value. Therefore, if the average P/E for an industry is 10x and a particular company in that industry is trading at 5x earnings, it is relatively undervalued to its peers.

Relative Valuation Model vs. Absolute Valuation Model

Relative valuation uses multiples, averages, ratios, and benchmarks to determine a firm's value. A benchmark may be selected by finding an industry-wide average, and that average is then used to determine relative value. An absolute measure, on the other hand, makes no external reference to a benchmark or average. A company's market capitalization, which is the aggregate market value of all of its outstanding shares, is expressed as a plain dollar amount and tells you little about its relative value. Of course, with enough absolute valuation measures in hand across several firms, relative inferences can be drawn.

Estimating Relative Value of Stock

In addition to providing a gauge for relative value, the P/E ratio allows analysts to back into the price that a stock should be trading at based on its peers. For example, if the average P/E for the specialty retail industry is 20x, it means the average price of stock from a company in the industry trades at 20 times its EPS.

Assume Company A trades for $50 in the market and has an EPS of $2. The P/E ratio is calculated by dividing $50 by $2, which is 25x. This is higher than the industry average of 20x, which means Company A is overvalued. If Company A were trading at 20 times its EPS, the industry average, it would be trading at a price of $40, which is the relative value. In other words, based on the industry average, Company A is trading at a price that is $10 higher than it should be, representing an opportunity to sell.

Because of the importance of developing an accurate benchmark or industry average, it is important to only compare companies in the same industry and market capitalization when calculating relative values.

INVENTORY VALUATION METHOD

An inventory valuation allows a company to provide a monetary value for items that make up their inventory. Inventories are usually the largest current asset of a business, and proper measurement of them is necessary to assure accurate financial statements. If inventory is not properly measured, expenses and revenues cannot be properly matched and a company could make poor business decisions.

Inventory Accounting System

The two most widely used inventory accounting systems are the periodic and the perpetual.

- Perpetual: The perpetual inventory system requires accounting records to show the amount of inventory on hand at all times. It maintains a separate account in the subsidiary ledger for each good in stock, and the account is updated each time a quantity is added or taken out.
- Periodic: In the periodic inventory system, sales are recorded as they occur but the inventory is not updated. A physical inventory must be taken at the end of the year to determine the cost of goods.

Regardless of what inventory accounting system is used, it is good practice to perform a physical inventory at least once a year.

Inventory Valuation Methods - Perpetual

The perpetual system records revenue each time a sale is made. Determining the cost of goods sold requires taking inventory. The most commonly used inventory valuation methods under a perpetual system are:

- First-in first-out (FIFO).
- Last-in first-out (LIFO).
- Highest in, first out (HIFO).
- Average cost or weighted average cost.

These methods produce different results because their flow of costs are based upon different assumptions. The FIFO method bases its cost flow on the chronological order purchases are made, while the LIFO method bases it cost flow in a reverse chronological order. The average cost method produces a cost flow based on a weighted average of goods.

Periodic versus Perpetual Systems

There are fundamental differences for accounting and reporting merchandise inventory transactions under the periodic and perpetual inventory systems. To record purchases, the periodic system debits the Purchases account while the perpetual system debits the Merchandise Inventory account. To record sales, the perpetual system requires an extra entry to debit the Cost of goods sold and credit Merchandise Inventory. By recording the cost of goods sold for each sale, the perpetual inventory system alleviated the need for adjusting entries and calculation of the goods sold at the end of a financial period, both of which the periodic inventory system requires.

In Perpetual Inventory System there must be actual figures and facts.

Using Non-cost Methods to Value Inventory

Under certain circumstances, valuation of inventory based on cost is impractical. If the market price of a good drops below the purchase price, the lower of cost or market method of valuation is recommended. This method allows declines in inventory value to be offset against income of the period. When goods are damaged or obsolete, and can only be sold for below purchase prices, they should be recorded at net realizable value. The net realizable value is the estimated selling price less any expense incurred to dispose of the good.

Methods used to Estimate Inventory Cost

In certain business operations, taking a physical inventory is impossible or impractical. In such a situation, it is necessary to estimate the inventory cost.

Two very popular methods are 1)- retail inventory method, and 2)- gross profit (or gross margin) method. The retail inventory method uses a cost to retail price ratio. The physical inventory is valued at retail, and it is multiplied by the cost ratio (or percentage) to determine the estimated cost of the ending inventory.

The gross profit method uses the previous years average gross profit margin (i.e. sales minus cost of goods sold divided by sales). Current year gross profit is estimated by multiplying current year sales by that gross profit margin, the current year cost of goods sold is estimated by subtracting the gross profit from sales, and the ending inventory is estimated by adding cost of goods sold to goods available for sale.

VALUATION USING MULTIPLES

In economics, valuation using multiples, or "relative valuation", is a process that consists of:

- Identifying comparable assets (the peer group) and obtaining market values for these assets.

- Converting these market values into standardized values relative to a key statistic, since the absolute prices cannot be compared. This process of standardizing creates valuation multiples.

- Applying the valuation multiple to the key statistic of the asset being valued, controlling for any differences between asset and the peer group that might affect the multiple.

Multiples analysis is one of the oldest methods of analysis. It was well understood in the 1800s and widely used by U.S. courts during the 20th century, although it has recently declined as Discounted Cash Flow and more direct market-based methods have become more popular.

Valuation Multiples

A valuation multiple is simply an expression of market value of an asset relative to a key statistic that is assumed to relate to that value. To be useful, that statistic – whether earnings, cash flow or some other measure – must bear a logical relationship to the market value observed; to be seen, in fact, as the driver of that market value.

In stock trading, one of the most widely used multiples is the price-earnings ratio (P/E ratio or PER) which is popular in part due to its wide availability and to the importance ascribed to earnings per share as a value driver. However, the usefulness of P/E ratios is lessened by the fact that earnings per share is subject to distortions from differences in accounting rules and capital structures between companies.

Other commonly used multiples are based on the enterprise value of a company, such as (EV/EBITDA, EV/EBIT, EV/NOPAT). These multiples reveal the rating of a business independently of its capital structure, and are of particular interest in mergers, acquisitions and transactions on private companies.

Not all multiples are based on earnings or cash flow drivers. The price-to-book ratio (P/B) is a commonly used benchmark comparing market value to the accounting book value of the firm's assets. The price/sales ratio and EV/sales ratios measure value relative to sales. These multiples must be used with caution as both sales and book values are less likely to be value drivers than earnings.

Less commonly, valuation multiples may be based on non-financial industry-specific value drivers, such as enterprise value / number of subscribers for cable or telecoms businesses or enterprise value / audience numbers for a broadcasting company. In real estate valuations, the sales comparison approach often makes use of valuation multiples based on the surface areas of the properties being valued.

Peer Group

A peer group is a set of companies or assets which are selected as being sufficiently comparable to the company or assets being valued (usually by virtue of being in the same industry or by having similar characteristics in terms of earnings growth and/or return on investment).

In practice, no two businesses are alike, and analysts will often make adjustment to the observed multiples in order to attempt to harmonize the data into more comparable format. These adjustments may be based on a number of factors, including:

- Industrial / business environment factors: Business model, industry, geography, seasonality, inflation.
- Accounting factors: Accounting policies, financial year end.

- Financial: Capital structure.
- Empirical factors: Size.

These adjustments can involve the use of regression analysis against different potential value drivers and are used to test correlations between the different value drivers.

When the peer group consists of public quoted companies, this type of valuation is also often described as comparable company analysis (or "comps", "peer group analysis", "equity comps", "trading comps", or "public market multiples"). When the peer group consists of companies or assets that have been acquired in mergers or acquisitions, this type of valuation is described as precedent transaction analysis (or "transaction comps", "deal comps", or "private market multiples").

Advantages/Disadvantages of Multiples

Disadvantages

There are a number of criticisms levied against multiples, but in the main these can be summarised as:

- Simplistic: A multiple is a distillation of a great deal of information into a single number or series of numbers. By combining many value drivers into a point estimate, multiples may make it difficult to disaggregate the effect of different drivers, such as growth, on value. The danger is that this encourages simplistic – and possibly erroneous – interpretation.
- Static: A multiple represents a snapshot of where a firm is at a point in time, but fails to capture the dynamic and ever-evolving nature of business and competition.
- Difficulties in comparisons: Multiples are primarily used to make comparisons of relative value. But comparing multiples is an exacting art form, because there are so many reasons that multiples can differ, not all of which relate to true differences in value. For example, different accounting policies can result in diverging multiples for otherwise identical operating businesses.
- Dependence on correctly valued peers: The use of multiples only reveals patterns in relative values, not absolute values such as those obtained from discounted cash flow valuations. If the peer group as a whole is incorrectly valued (such as may happen during a stock market "bubble") then the resulting multiples will also be misvalued.
- Short-term: Multiples are based on historic data or near-term forecasts. Valuations based on multiples will therefore fail to capture differences in projected performance over the longer term, and will have difficulty correctly valuing cyclical industries unless somewhat subjective normalization adjustments are made.

Advantages

Despite these disadvantages, multiples have several advantages.

- Usefulness: Valuation is about judgment, and multiples provide a framework for making value judgements. When used properly, multiples are robust tools that can provide useful information about relative value.

- Simplicity: Their very simplicity and ease of calculation makes multiples an appealing and user-friendly method of assessing value. Multiples can help the user avoid the potentially misleading precision of other, more 'precise' approaches such as discounted cash flow valuation or EVA, which can create a false sense of comfort.

- Relevance: Multiples focus on the key statistics that other investors use. Since investors in aggregate move markets, the most commonly used statistics and multiples will have the most impact.

These factors, and the existence of wide-ranging comparables, help explain the enduring use of multiples by investors despite the rise of other methods.

Comparison of Commonly used Valuation Multiples

Equity Price based Multiples

Equity price based multiples are most relevant where investors acquire minority positions in companies. Care should be used when comparing companies with very different capital structures. Different debt levels will affect equity multiples because of the gearing effect of debt. In addition, equity multiples will not explicitly take into account balance sheet risk.

Multiple	Definition	Advantages	Disadvantages
P/E ratio	Share price / Earnings per share (EPS). EPS is net income/weighted average no of shares in issue. EPS may be adjusted to eliminate exceptional items (core EPS) and/or outstanding dilutive elements (fully diluted EPS).	• Most commonly used equity multiple. • Data availability is high.	• EPS can be subject to differences in accounting policies and manipulation. • Unless adjusted, can be subject to one-off exceptional items. • Cannot be used if earnings are negative.
Price / cash earnings	Share price / earnings per share plus depreciation amortization and changes in non-cash provisions.	• Cash earnings are a rough measure of cash flow. • Unaffected by differences in accounting for depreciation.	• Incomplete treatment of cash flow. • Usually used as a supplement to other measures if accounting differences are material.
Price / book ratio	Share price / book value per share.	• Can be useful where assets are a core driver of earnings such as capital-intensive industries. • Most widely used in valuing financial companies, such as banks, because banks have to report accurate book values of their loans and deposits, and liquidation value is equal to book value since deposits and loans are liquidated at same value as reported book values.	• Book values for tangible assets are stated at historical cost, which is not a reliable indicator of economic value. • Book value for tangible assets can be significantly impacted by differences in accounting policies.

PEG ratio	Prospective PE ratio / prospective average earnings growth.	• Most suitable when valuing high growth companies.	• Requires credible forecasts of growth. • Can understate the higher risk associated with many high-growth stocks.
Dividend yield	Dividend per share / share price.	• Useful for comparing cash returns with types of investments. • Can be used to establish a floor price for a stock.	• Dependent on distribution policy of the company. • Yield to investor is subject to differences in taxation between jurisdictions. • Assumes the dividend is sustainable.
Price / Sales	Share price / sales per share.	• Easy to calculate. • Can be applied to loss making firms. • Less susceptible to accounting differences than other measures.	• Mismatch between nominator and denominator in formula (EV/Sales is a more appropriate measure). • Not used except in very broad, quick approximations.

Enterprise Value Based Multiples

Enterprise value based multiples are particularly relevant in mergers & acquisitions where the whole of the company's stock and liabilities are acquired. Certain multiples such as EV/EBITDA are also a useful complements to valuations of minority interests, especially when the P/E ratio is difficult to interpret because of significant differences in capital structures, in accounting policies or in cases where net earnings are negative or low.

Multiple	Definition	Advantages	Disadvantages
EV/Sales	Enterprise value / net sales.	• Least susceptible to accounting differences. • Remains applicable even when earnings are negative or highly cyclical.	• A crude measure as sales are rarely a direct value driver.
EV/EBITDAR	Enterprise value / Earnings before Interest, Tax, Depreciation & Amortization and Rental Costs.	• Proxy for operating free cash flows. • Attempts to normalize capital intensity between companies that choose to rent rather than own their core assets. • Most often used in the transport, hotel and retail industries.	• Rental costs may not be reported and need to be estimated. • Ignores variations in capital expenditure and depreciation. • Ignores value creation through tax management.
EV/EBITDA	Enterprise value / Earnings before Interest, Tax, Depreciation & Amortization. Also excludes movements in non-cash provisions and exceptional items.	• EBITDA is a proxy for free cash flows. • Probably the most popular of the EV based multiples. • Unaffected by depreciation policy.	• Ignores variations in capital expenditure and depreciation. • Ignores potential value creation through tax management.

EV/EBIT and EV/EBITA	Enterprise value / Earnings before interest and taxes (and Amortization).	• Better allows for differences in capital intensiveness compared to EBITDA by incorporating maintenance capital expenditure.	• Susceptible to differences in depreciation policy. • Ignores potential value creation through tax management.
EV/NOPLAT	Enterprise value / Net Operating Profit After Adjusted Tax.	• NOPLAT incorporates a number of adjustments to better reflect operating profitability.	• NOPLAT adjustments can be complicated and are not applied consistently by different analysts.
EV/opFCF	Enterprise value / Operating Free Cash Flow OpFCF is core EBITDA less estimated normative capital expenditure requirement and estimated normative variation in working capital requirement.	• Better allows for differences in capital intensiveness compared to EBITDA. • Less susceptible to accounting differences than EBIT. • Use of estimates allows for smoothing of irregular real capital expenditures.	• Introduces additional subjectivity in estimates of capital expenditure.
EV/ Enterprise FCF	Enterprise value / Free cash flow. Enterprise FCF is core EBITDA less actual capital expenditure requirement and actual increase in working capital requirement.	• Less subjective than opFCF • Better allows for differences in capital intensiveness compared to EBITDA. • Less susceptible to accounting differences than EBIT.	• Can be volatile and difficult to interpret as capital expenditure is often irregular and "lumpy".
EV/Invested Capital	Enterprise value / Invested capital.	• Can be useful where assets are a core driver of earnings, such as for capital-intensive industries.	• Book values for tangible assets are stated at historical cost, which is not a reliable indicator of economic value. • Book value for tangible assets can be significantly impacted by differences in accounting policies.
EV/Capacity Measure	Depends on industry (e.g. EV/subscribers, EV/production capacity, EV/audience).	• Not susceptible to accounting differences. • Remains applicable even when earnings are negative or highly cyclical.	• A crude measure as capacity measures are rarely a direct value driver.

Example (Discounted Forward PE Ratio Method)

Mathematics

$$C * \left(\text{Average} * \left(\frac{P}{NPP} * NPO * \frac{1}{(1+R_f)^{tf}} \right) \right) \left(\frac{}{S} \right)$$

Condition: Peer company is profitable.

Rf = discount rate during the last forecast year

tf = last year of the forecast period.

C = correction factor

P = current stock Price

NPP = net profit peer company

NPO = net profit of target company after forecast period

S = number of shares

Process Data Diagram

The following diagram shows an overview of the process of company valuation using multiples. Using the multiples method.

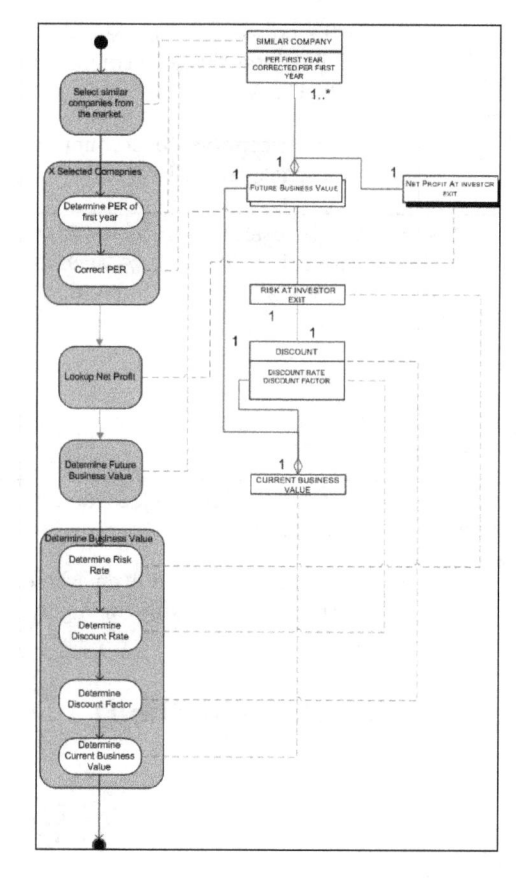

Using the Multiples Method

Determine Forecast Period

Determine the year after which the company value is to be known.

Example:

'VirusControl' is an ICT startup that has just finished their business plan. Their goal is to provide professionals with software for simulating virus outbreaks. Their only investor is required to wait for 5 years before making an exit. Therefore, VirusControl is using a forecast period of 5 years.

Identifying Peer Company

Search the (stock) market for companies most comparable to the target company. From the investor perspective, a peer universe can also contain companies that are not only direct product competitors but are subject to similar cycles, suppliers and other external factors (e.g. a door and a window manufacturer may be considered peers as well).

Important characteristics include: operating margin, company size, products, customer segmentation, growth rate, cash flow, number of employees, etc.

Example:

VirusControl has identified 4 other companies similar to itself.

- Medical Sim,
- Global Plan,
- Virus Solutions,
- PM Software.

Determining Correct Price Earning Ratio (P/E)

The price earnings ratio (P/E) of each identified peer company can be calculated as long as they are profitable. The P/E is calculated as:

P/E = Current stock price / (Net profit / Weighted average number of shares)

Particular attention is paid to companies with P/E ratios substantially higher or lower than the peer group. A P/E far below the average can mean (among other reasons) that the true value of a company has not been identified by the market, that the business model is flawed, or that the most recent profits include, for example, substantial one-off items. Companies with P/E ratios substantially different from the peers (the outliers) can be removed or other corrective measures used to avoid this problem.

Example:

P/E ratio of companies similar to Virus Control:

	Current Stock Price	Net profit	Number of Shares	P/E
Medical Sim	€'16.32	€'1.000.000	1.100.000	17.95
Global Plan	€'19.50	€'1.800.000	2.000.000	21.7
Virus Solutions	€'6.23	€'3.000.000	10.000.000	20.8
PM Software	€'12.97	€'4.000.000	2.000.000	6.5

One company, PM Software, has substantially lower P/E ratio than the others. Further market research shows that PM Software has recently acquired a government contract to supply the military with simulating software for the next three years. Therefore, VirusControl decides to discard this P/E ratio and only use the values of 17.95, 21.7 and 20.8.

Determining Future Company Value

The value of the target company after the forecast period can be calculated by:

Average corrected P/E ratio * net profit at the end of the forecast period.

Example:

VirusControl is expecting a net profit at the end of the fifth year of about €2.2 million. They use the following calculation to determine their future value:

((17.95 + 21.7 + 20.8) / 3) * 2.200.000 = €44.3 million

Determining Discount Rate/Factor

Determine the appropriate discount rate and factor for the last year of the forecast period based on the risk level associated with the target company.

Example:

VirusControl has chosen their discount rate very high as their company is potentially very profitable but also very risky. They calculate their discount factor based on five years.

Risk Rate	50%
Discount Rate	50%
Discount Factor	0.1316

Determining Current Company Value

Calculate the current value of the future company value by multiplying the future business value with the discount factor. This is known as the time value of money.

Example:

VirusControl multiplies their future company value with the discount factor:

44,300,000 * 0.1316 = 5,829,880

The company or equity value of VirusControl: €5.83 million.

EV/Ebitda

Enterprise value/EBITDA (more commonly referred to by the acronym EV/EBITDA) is a popular valuation multiple used in the finance industry to measure the value of a company. It is the most widely used valuation multiple based on enterprise value and is often used in conjunction with, or as an alternative to, the P/E ratio (Price/Earnings ratio) to determine the fair market value of a company.

Use

An advantage of this multiple is that it is capital structure-neutral, and, therefore, this multiple can be used to directly compare companies with different levels of debt.

The EV/EBITDA multiple requires prudent use for companies with low profit margins (i.e., for an EBITDA estimate to be reasonably accurate, the company under evaluation must have legitimate profitability).

Often, an industry average EV/EBITDA multiple is calculated on a sample of listed companies to use for comparison to the company of interest (i.e., as a benchmark). An example of such an index is one that provides an average EV/EBITDA multiple on a wide sample of transactions on private companies in the Eurozone.

The reciprocate multiple EBITDA/EV is used as a measure of cash return on investment.

BOND VALUATION

Bond valuation is the determination of the fair price of a bond. As with any security or capital investment, the theoretical fair value of a bond is the present value of the stream of cash flows it is expected to generate. Hence, the value of a bond is obtained by discounting the bond's expected cash flows to the present using an appropriate discount rate.

In practice, this discount rate is often determined by reference to similar instruments, provided that such instruments exist. Various related yield-measures are then calculated for the given price. Where the market price of bond is less than its face value (par value), the bond is selling at a discount. Conversely, if the market price of bond is greater than its face value, the bond is selling at a premium.

If the bond includes embedded options, the valuation is more difficult and combines option pricing with discounting. Depending on the type of option, the option price as calculated is either added to or subtracted from the price of the "straight" portion. This total is then the value of the bond.

As above, the fair price of a "straight bond" (a bond with no embedded options; is usually determined by discounting its expected cash flows at the appropriate discount rate. Although this present value relationship reflects the theoretical approach to determining the value of a bond, in practice its price is (usually) determined with reference to other, more liquid instruments. The two main approaches here, Relative pricing and Arbitrage-free pricing. Finally, where it is important to recognise that future interest rates are uncertain and that the discount rate is not adequately represented by a single fixed number—for example when an option is written on the bond in question—stochastic calculus may be employed.

Present Value Approach

Below is the formula for calculating a bond's price, which uses the basic present value (PV) formula for a given discount rate: (This formula assumes that a coupon payment has just been made):

$$P = \left(\frac{C}{1+i} + \frac{C}{(1+i)^2} + \ldots + \frac{C}{(1+i)^N} \right) + \frac{M}{(1+i)^N}$$

$$= \left(\sum_{n=1}^{N} \frac{C}{(1+i)^n} \right) + \frac{M}{(1+i)^N}$$

$$= C \left(\frac{1-(1+i)^{-N}}{i} \right) + M(1+i)^{-N}$$

where:

F = face values,

i_F = contractual interest rate,

C = F * i_F = coupon payment (periodic interest payment),

N = number of payments,

i = market interest rate, or required yield, or observed / appropriate yield to maturity,

M = value at maturity, usually equals face value,

P = market price of bond.

Relative Price Approach

Under this approach—an extension, or application, of the above—the bond will be priced relative to a benchmark, usually a government security. Here, the yield to maturity on the bond is determined based on the bond's Credit rating relative to a government security with similar maturity or duration). The better the quality of the bond, the smaller the spread between its required return and the YTM of the benchmark. This required return is then used to discount the bond cash flows, replacing *i* in the formula above, to obtain the price.

Arbitrage-free Pricing Approach

As distinct from the two related approaches above, a bond may be thought of as a "package of cash flows"—coupon or face—with each cash flow viewed as a zero-coupon instrument maturing on the date it will be received. Thus, rather than using a single discount rate, one should use multiple discount rates, discounting each cash flow at its own rate. Here, each cash flow is separately discounted at the same rate as a zero-coupon bond corresponding to the coupon date, and of equivalent credit worthiness (if possible, from the same issuer as the bond being valued, or if not, with the appropriate credit spread).

Under this approach, the bond price should reflect its "arbitrage-free" price, as any deviation from this price will be exploited and the bond will then quickly reprice to its correct level. Here, we apply the rational pricing logic relating to "Assets with identical cash flows". In detail: (1) the bond's coupon dates and coupon amounts are known with certainty. Therefore, (2) some multiple (or fraction) of zero-coupon bonds, each corresponding to the bond's coupon dates, can be specified so as to produce identical cash flows to the bond. Thus (3) the bond price today must be equal to the sum of each of its cash flows discounted at the discount rate implied by the value of the corresponding ZCB. Were this not the case, (4) the arbitrageur could finance his purchase of whichever of the bond or the sum of the various ZCBs was cheaper, by short selling the other, and meeting his cash flow commitments using the coupons or maturing zeroes as appropriate. Then (5) his "risk free", arbitrage profit would be the difference between the two values.

Stochastic Calculus Approach

When modelling a bond option, or other interest rate derivative (IRD), it is important to recognize that future interest rates are uncertain, and therefore, the discount rate(s) referred to above, under all three cases—i.e. whether for all coupons or for each individual coupon—is not adequately represented by a fixed (deterministic) number. In such cases, stochastic calculus is employed.

The following is a partial differential equation (PDE) in stochastic calculus, which, by arbitrage arguments, is satisfied by any zero-coupon bond P, over (instantaneous) time t, for corresponding changes in r, the short rate.

$$\frac{1}{2}\sigma(r)^2 \frac{\partial^2 P}{\partial r^2} + [a(r) + \sigma(r) + \varphi(r,t)]\frac{\partial P}{\partial r} + \frac{\partial P}{\partial t} - rP = 0$$

The solution to the PDE (i.e. the corresponding formula for bond value) — given in Cox et al. — is:

$$P[t,T,r(t)] = E_t^*[e^{-R(t,T)}]$$

where E_t^* is the expectation with respect to risk-neutral probabilities, and $R(t,T)$ is a random variable representing the discount rate.

To actually determine the bond price, the analyst must choose the specific short rate model to be employed. The approaches commonly used are:

- The CIR model.
- The Black-Derman-Toy model.
- The Hull-White model.
- The HJM framework.
- The Chen model.

Note that depending on the model selected, a closed-form ("Black like") solution may not be available, and a lattice- or simulation-based implementation of the model in question is then employed.

Clean and Dirty Price

When the bond is not valued precisely on a coupon date, the calculated price, using the methods above, will incorporate accrued interest: i.e. any interest due to the owner of the bond since the previous coupon date. The price of a bond which includes this accrued interest is known as the "dirty price" (or "full price" or "all in price" or "Cash price"). The "clean price" is the price excluding any interest that has accrued. Clean prices are generally more stable over time than dirty prices. This is because the dirty price will drop suddenly when the bond goes "ex interest" and the purchaser is no longer entitled to receive the next coupon payment. In many markets, it is market practice to quote bonds on a clean-price basis. When a purchase is settled, the accrued interest is added to the quoted clean price to arrive at the actual amount to be paid.

Yield and Price Relationships

Once the price or value has been calculated, various yields relating the price of the bond to its coupons can then be determined.

Yield to Maturity

The yield to maturity (YTM) is the discount rate which returns the market price of a bond without embedded optionality; it is identical to i (required return) in the above equation. YTM is thus the internal rate of return of an investment in the bond made at the observed price. Since YTM can be used to price a bond, bond prices are often quoted in terms of YTM.

To achieve a return equal to YTM, i.e. where it is the required return on the bond, the bond owner must:

- Buy the bond at price P_0,
- Hold the bond until maturity,
- Redeem the bond at par.

Coupon Rate

The coupon rate is simply the coupon payment C as a percentage of the face value F.

$$\text{Coupon rate} = \frac{C}{F}$$

Coupon yield is also called nominal yield.

Current Yield

The current yield is simply the coupon payment C as a percentage of the (*current*) bond price P.

$$\text{Current yield} = \frac{C}{P_0}.$$

Relationship

The concept of current yield is closely related to other bond concepts, including yield to maturity, and coupon yield. The relationship between yield to maturity and the coupon rate is as follows:

- When a bond sells at a discount, YTM > current yield > coupon yield.

- When a bond sells at a premium, coupon yield > current yield > YTM.
- When a bond sells at par, YTM = current yield = coupon yield.

Price Sensitivity

The sensitivity of a bond's market price to interest rate (i.e. yield) movements is measured by its duration, and, additionally, by its convexity.

Duration is a linear measure of how the price of a bond changes in response to interest rate changes. It is approximately equal to the percentage change in price for a given change in yield, and may be thought of as the elasticity of the bond's price with respect to discount rates. For example, for small interest rate changes, the duration is the approximate percentage by which the value of the bond will fall for a 1% per annum increase in market interest rate. So the market price of a 17-year bond with a duration of 7 would fall about 7% if the market interest rate (or more precisely the corresponding force of interest) increased by 1% per annum.

Convexity is a measure of the "curvature" of price changes. It is needed because the price is not a linear function of the discount rate, but rather a convex function of the discount rate. Specifically, duration can be formulated as the first derivative of the price with respect to the interest rate, and convexity as the second derivative. Continuing the above example, for a more accurate estimate of sensitivity, the convexity score would be multiplied by the square of the change in interest rate, and the result added to the value derived by the above linear formula.

Accounting Treatment

In accounting for liabilities, any bond discount or premium must be amortized over the life of the bond. A number of methods may be used for this depending on applicable accounting rules. One possibility is that amortization amount in each period is calculated from the following formula:

$$n \in \{0, 1, ..., N-1\}$$

a_{n+1} = amortization amount in period number "n+1"

$$a_{n+1} = |iP - C|(1+i)^n$$

Bond Discount or Bond Premium = $|F - P| = a_1 + a_2 + ... + a_N$

Bond Discount or Bond Premium = $F | i - i_F | (\frac{1-(1+i)^{-N}}{i})$

DISCOUNTED CASH FLOW

In finance, discounted cash flow (DCF) analysis is a method of valuing a project, company, or asset using the concepts of the time value of money. Discounted cash flow analysis is widely used in investment finance, real estate development, corporate financial management and patent valuation.

It was used in industry as early as the 1700s or 1800s, widely discussed in financial economics in the 1960s, and became widely used in U.S. courts in the 1980s and 1990s.

To apply the method, all future cash flows are estimated and discounted by using cost of capital to give their present values (PVs). The sum of all future cash flows, both incoming and outgoing, is the net present value (NPV), which is taken as the value of the cash flows in question.

Using DCF analysis to compute the NPV takes as input cash flows and a discount rate and gives as output a present value. The opposite process takes cash flows and a price (present value) as inputs, and provides as output the discount rate; this is used in bond markets to obtain the yield.

Discount Rate

The act of discounting future cash flows answers "how much money would have to be invested currently, at a given rate of return, to yield the forecast cash flow, at its future date?" In other words, discounting returns the present value of future cash flows, where the rate used is the cost of capital that *appropriately* reflects the risk, and timing, of the cash flows.

This "required return" thus incorporates:

- Time value of money (risk-free rate): According to the theory of time preference, investors would rather have cash immediately than having to wait and must therefore be compensated by paying for the delay.

- Risk premium: Reflects the extra return investors demand because they want to be compensated for the risk that the cash flow might not materialize after all.

For the latter, various models have been developed, where the premium is (typically) calculated as a function of the asset's performance with reference to some macroeconomic variable - for example, the CAPM compares the asset's historical returns to the "overall market's".

An alternate, although less common approach, is to apply a "fundamental valuation" method, such as the "T-model", which instead relies on accounting information. (Other methods of discounting, such as hyperbolic discounting, are studied in academia and said to reflect intuitive decision-making, but are not generally used in industry. In this context the above is referred to as "exponential discounting".)

Note that the terminology "expected return", although formally the mathematical expected value, is often used interchangeably with the above, where "expected" means "required" or "demanded" in the corresponding sense.

Mathematics

Discounted Cash Flows

The discounted cash flow formula is derived from the future value formula for calculating the time value of money and compounding returns.

$$DCF = \frac{CF_1}{(1+r)^1} + \frac{CF_2}{(1+r)^2} + \cdots + \frac{CF_n}{(1+r)^n}$$

$$FV = DCF \cdot (1+r)^n$$

Thus the discounted present value (for one cash flow in one future period) is expressed as:

$$PV = \frac{FV}{(1+r)^n}$$

where

- DPV is the discounted present value of the future cash flow (FV), or FV adjusted for the delay in receipt;
- FV is the nominal value of a cash flow amount in a future period;
- r is the interest rate or discount rate, which reflects the cost of tying up capital and may also allow for the risk that the payment may not be received in full;
- n is the time in years before the future cash flow occurs.

Where multiple cash flows in multiple time periods are discounted, it is necessary to sum them as follows:

$$DPV = \sum_{t=0}^{N} \frac{FV_t}{(1+r)^t}$$

for each future cash flow (FV) at any time period (t) in years from the present time, summed over all time periods. The sum can then be used as a net present value figure. If the amount to be paid at time 0 (now) for all the future cash flows is known, then that amount can be substituted for DPV and the equation can be solved for r, that is the internal rate of return.

All the above assumes that the interest rate remains constant throughout the whole period.

If the cash flow stream is assumed to continue indefinitely, the finite forecast is usually combined with the assumption of constant cash flow growth beyond the discrete projection period. The total value of such cash flow stream is the sum of the finite discounted cash flow forecast and the Terminal value (finance).

Continuous Cash Flows

For continuous cash flows, the summation in the above formula is replaced by an integration:

$$DPV = \int_0^T FV(t) e^{-\lambda t} dt = \int_0^T \frac{FV(t)}{(1+r)^t} dt,$$

where $FV(t)$ is now the *rate* of cash flow, and $\lambda = \ln(1+r)$.

Methods of Appraisal of a Company or Project

For these valuation purposes, a number of different DCF methods are distinguished today, some of which are outlined below. The details are likely to vary depending on the capital structure of the company. However the assumptions used in the appraisal (especially the equity discount rate and the projection of the cash flows to be achieved) are likely to be at least as important as the precise model used. Both the income stream selected and the associated cost of capital model determine the valuation result obtained with each method. (This is one reason these valuation methods are formally referred to as the Discounted Future Economic Income methods.) The below is offered as a simple treatment; for the components / steps of business modeling here.

EXAMPLE OF A FIRM

ATM – ASSOCIAÇÃO DE INVESTIDORES

	2007	2008	2009E	2010E	2011E	2012E	2013E	CAGR(Y07/Y13)
EBITA	$1,995	($1,571)	$941	$2,402	$3,472	$3,655	$3,633	10.51%
(+) Depreciation	$4,221	$4,647	$4,326	$4,145	$4,300	$4,244	$4,304	0.32%
(=) EBITDA	$6,216	$3,076	$5,267	$6,546	$7,771	$7,899	$7,937	4.16%
(+) (CapEx)	($3,976)	($3,356)	($2,163)	($2,072)	($2,150)	($2,122)	($2,152)	-9.73%
(+) CE+PF+CF	($11)	($71)	$19	($73)	($1)	$4	$7	N/A
(-) Δ Working Capital	$1,620	$1,223	$1,031	$53	$2,123	($124)	($526)	N/A
(+) Investment Subsidies	$208	$300	$269	$113	$106	$62	$61	-18.49%
Statutory Tax Rate	26.50%	26.50%	26.50%	26.50%	26.50%	26.50%	26.50%	0.00%
(-) EBITA*Statutory Tax	$409	($302)	$345	$660	$961	$996	$855	13.08%
(=) Free Cash Flow	408	-973	2,016	3,801	2,642	4,971	5,524	54.35%

Weight Average Cost of Capital %	8.73%	
Assumed Perpetual Growth %	2.96%	
Undiscounted Terminal Value	$95,737	
Net Present Value of Free Cash Flow to Enterprise	$77,315	
[Net Debt]	($15,628)	
[Minority Interests]	$0	
[Pensions and other financial liabilities]	$0	
Associate Investments	$0	
Tax Assets	$0	
Equity Value	$61,687	
Total Shares Outstanding	15,000	
FAIR VALUE per share	**$4.11**	
Margin of Safety and Risk-Averse	20.00%	
FAIR VALUE per Share (Ajusted)	$3.29	

DCF SENSITIVITY

WACC%	Assumed Perpetual Growth %		
	2.46%	2.96%	3.46%
7.73%	$4.76	$5.26	$5.89
8.73%	$3.78	**$4.11**	$4.51
9.73%	$3.07	$3.30	$3.58

STOCK OVERVIEW

Last Trade:	$1.70	to Fair Value:	141.91%
Prev Close:	$1.70	Bid	$1.69
52wk High:	$2.08	52wk Low:	$1.43
Volume:	15,000	Avg Vol (3n	3,000

MORE INFORMATION

Market Cap:	24.5M	Attributes:	
P/E (ttm):		ROI (ttm):	
P/S (ttm):		ROE (ttm):	
T. Revenue E:		Net Income E:	
EPS		EPS Est.	
Smallest FCF	2,016	Largest FCF	5,524
Range FCF E	3,508	Avg FCF E	3,791

OFFICERS AND COMPETITORS

Chairman Mr. Chistopher Anderson
CEO|CFO Mr. Matthew Wright   Mr. Sophia Sanchez
Key Competitors: XTPO   XTPE   XPTI

December 31st, 2008

Here, a spreadsheetvaluation, uses Free cash flows to estimate stock's Fair Value and measure the sensibility of WACC and Perpetual growth.

Equity-approach

- Flows to equity approach (FTE):

    ○ Discount the cash flows available to the holders of equity capital, after allowing for cost of servicing debt capital.

    ○ Advantages: Makes explicit allowance for the cost of debt capital.

    ○ Disadvantages: Requires judgement on choice of discount rate.

Entity-approach

- Adjusted present value approach (APV):

    ○ Discount the cash flows before allowing for the debt capital (but allowing for the tax relief obtained on the debt capital).

- Advantages: Simpler to apply if a specific project is being valued which does not have earmarked debt capital finance.
  - Disadvantages: Requires judgement on choice of discount rate; no explicit allowance for cost of debt capital, which may be much higher than a risk-free rate.
- Weighted average cost of capital approach (WACC):
  - Derive a weighted cost of the capital obtained from the various sources and use that discount rate to discount the cash flows from the project.
  - Advantages: Overcomes the requirement for debt capital finance to be earmarked to particular projects.
  - Disadvantages: Care must be exercised in the selection of the appropriate income stream. The net cash flow to total invested capital is the generally accepted choice.
- Total cash flow approach (TCF):
  - This distinction illustrates that the Discounted Cash Flow method can be used to determine the value of various business ownership interests. These can include equity or debt holders.
  - Alternatively, the method can be used to value the company based on the value of total invested capital. In each case, the differences lie in the choice of the income stream and discount rate. For example, the net cash flow to total invested capital and WACC are appropriate when valuing a company based on the market value of all invested capital.

Shortcomings

- Traditional DCF models assume we can accurately forecast revenue and earnings 3–5 years into the future. But studies have shown that growth is neither predictable nor persistent. In other terms, using DCF models is problematic due to the problem of induction, or presupposing that a sequence of events in the future will occur as it always has in the past. Colloquially, in the world of finance, the problem of induction is often simplified with the common phrase: past returns are not indicative of future results. In fact, the SEC demands that all mutual funds use this sentence to warn their investors. This observation has led some to conclude that DCF models should only be used to value companies with steady cash flows. For example, DCF models are widely used to value mature companies in stable industry sectors, such as utilities. For industries that are especially unpredictable and thus harder to forecast, DCF models can prove especially challenging.

- Industry Examples:
  - Real Estate- Investors use DCF models to value commercial real estate development projects. This practice has two main shortcomings. First, the discount rate assumption relies on the market for competing investments at the time of the analysis, which may not persist into the future. Second, assumptions about ten-year income increases are usually based on historic increases in the market rent. Yet the cyclical nature of most

real estate markets is not factored in. Most real estate loans are made during boom real estate markets and these markets usually last fewer than ten years. In this case, due to the problem of induction, using a DCF model to value commercial real estate during any but the early years of a boom market can lead to overvaluation.

  - Early-stage Technology Companies- In valuing startups, the DCF method can be applied a number of times, with differing assumptions, to assess a range of possible future outcomes—such as the best, worst and mostly likely case scenarios. Even so, the lack of historical company data and uncertainty about factors that can affect the company's development make DCF models especially difficult for valuing startups. There is a lack of credibility regarding future cash flows, future cost of capital, and the company's growth rate. By forecasting limited data into an unpredictable future, the problem of induction is especially pronounced.

- Traditional DCF models assume that the capital asset pricing model can be used to assess the riskiness of an investment and set an appropriate discount rate. But, according to some economists, the capital asset pricing model has been empirically invalidated.

- Input-output problem:
  - DCF is merely a mechanical valuation tool, which makes it subject to the principle "garbage in, garbage out." Small changes in inputs can result in large changes in the value of a company. This is especially the case with terminal values, which make up a large proportion of the Discounted Cash Flow's final value.

- Doesn't account for all variables:
  - Traditional DCF calculations only consider the financial costs and benefits of a decision. They do not include the environmental, social and governance performance of an organization.

Integrated Future Value (IntFV)

To address the lack of integration of the short and long term importance, value and risks associated with natural and social capital into the traditional DCF calculation, companies are valuing their environmental, social and governance (ESG) performance through an Integrated Management approach to reporting that expands DCF or Net Present Value to Integrated Future Value. This allows companies to value their investments not just for their financial return but also the long term environmental and social return of their investments. By highlighting environmental, social and governance performance in reporting, decision makers have the opportunity to identify new areas for value creation that are not revealed through traditional financial reporting. The social cost of carbon is one value that can be incorporated into Integrated Future Value calculations to encompass the damage to society from greenhouse gas emissions that result from an investment. This is an integrated approach to reporting that supports Integrated Bottom Line (IBL) decision making, which takes triple bottom line(TBL) a step further and combines financial, environmental and social performance reporting into one balance sheet. This approach provides decision makers with the insight to identify opportunities for value creation that promote growth and change within an organization.

Steps

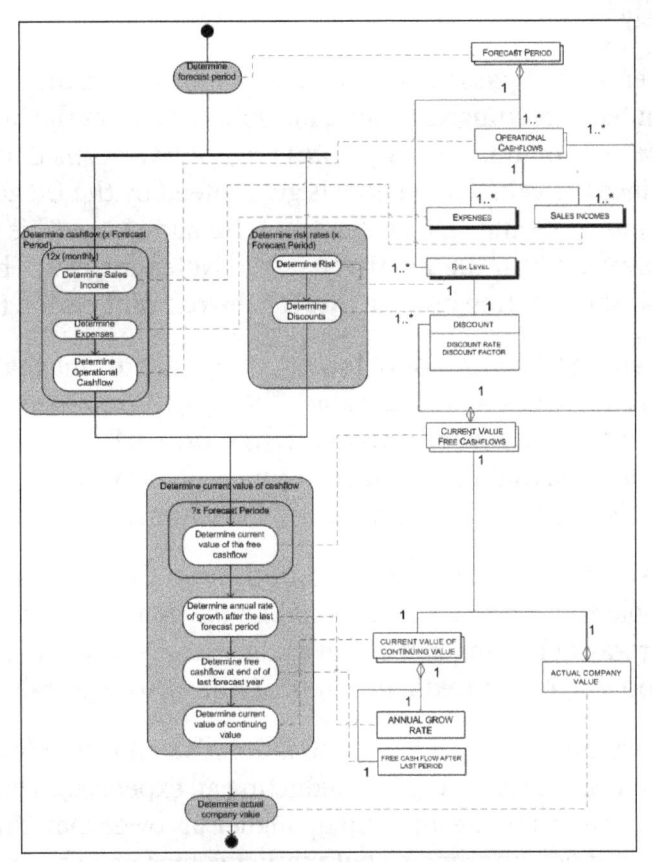

Flowchart for a typical DCF valuation, with each step detailed in the text.

On a very high level, the main steps are as follows:

- Free Cash Flow Projections: Projections of the amount of Cash produced by a company's business operations after paying for operating expenses and capital expenditures.
- Discount Rate: The cost of capital (Debt and Equity) for the business. This rate, which acts like an interest rate on future Cash inflows, is used to convert them into current dollar equivalents.
- Terminal Value: The value of a business at the end of the projection period (typical for a DCF analysis is either a 5-year projection period or, occasionally, a 10-year projection period).

Example DCF Calculation

To show how discounted cash flow analysis is performed, consider the following example.

John Doe buys a house for $100,000. Three years later, he expects to be able to sell this house for $150,000.

Simple subtraction suggests that the value of his profit on such a transaction would be $150,000 − $100,000 = $50,000, or 50%. If that $50,000 is amortized over the three years, his implied annual return (known as the internal rate of return) would be about 14.5%. Looking at those figures, he might be justified in thinking that the purchase looked like a good idea. 1.145³ x $100,000 = $150,000, approximately.

However, since three years have passed between the purchase and the sale, any cash flow from the sale must be discounted accordingly. At the time John Doe buys the house, the three-year US Treasury Note rate is 5% per annum. Treasury notes are generally considered to be inherently less risky than real estate, since the value of the note is guaranteed by the US government and there is a liquid market for the purchase and sale of T-notes. If he had not put his money into buying the house, he could have invested it in the relatively safe T-Notes instead. This 5% per annum can, therefore, be regarded as the risk-free interest rate for the relevant period (three years).

Using the DPV formula above (FV=$150,000, i=0.05, n=3), that means that the value of $150,000 received in three years actually has a present value of $129,576 (rounded off). In other words, we would need to invest $129,576 in a T-bond now to get $150,000 in three years almost risk-free. This is a quantitative way of showing that money in the future is not as valuable as money in the present ($150,000 in three years is not worth the same as $150,000 now; it is worth $129,576 now).

Subtracting the purchase price of the house ($100,000) from the present value results in the net present value of the whole transaction, which would be $29,576 or a little more than 29% of the purchase price. Another way of looking at the deal as the excess return achieved (over the risk-free rate) is (114.5 - 105)/(100 + 5) or approximately 9.0% (still very respectable).

But what about risk? We assume that the $150,000 is John's best estimate of the sale price that he will be able to achieve in three years time (after deducting all expenses). There is a lot of uncertainty about house prices, and the outcome may end up higher or lower than this estimate. (The house John is buying is in a "good neighborhood", but market values have been rising quite a lot lately and the real estate market analysts in the media are talking about a slow-down and higher interest rates. There is a probability that John might not be able to get the full $150,000 he is expecting in three years due to a slowing of price appreciation, or that loss of liquidity in the real estate market might make it very hard for him to sell at all.

Under normal circumstances, people entering into such transactions are risk-averse, that is to say that they are prepared to accept a lower expected return for the sake of avoiding risk. For the sake of the example (and this is a gross simplification), let us assume that he values this particular risk at 5% per annum. Therefore, allowing for this risk, his expected return is now 9.0% per annum (the arithmetic is the same as above). And the excess return over the risk-free rate is now (109 - 105)/(100 + 5) which comes to approximately 3.8% per annum.

That return rate may seem low, but it is still positive after all of our discounting, suggesting that the investment decision is probably a good one: it produces enough profit to compensate for tying up capital and incurring risk with a little extra left over. When investors and managers perform DCF analysis, the important thing is that the net present value of the decision after discounting all future cash flows at least be positive (more than zero). If it is negative, that means that the investment decision would actually *lose* money even if it appears to generate a nominal profit. For instance, if the expected sale price of John Doe's house in the example above was not $150,000 in three years, but *$130,000* in three years or $150,000 in *five* years, then on the above assumptions buying the house would actually cause John to *lose* money in present-value terms (about $3,000 in the first case, and about $8,000 in the second). Similarly, if the house was located in an undesirable neighborhood and the Federal Reserve Bank was about to raise interest rates by five percentage points, then the risk factor would be a lot higher than 5%: it might not be possible for him to predict a profit in discounted terms even if he thinks he could sell the house for $200,000 in three years.

In this example, only one future cash flow was considered. For a decision which generates multiple cash flows in multiple time periods, all the cash flows must be discounted and then summed into a single net present value.

VALUATION USING DISCOUNTED CASH FLOWS

Valuation using discounted cash flows (DCF valuation) is a method of estimating the current value of a company based on projected future cash flows adjusted for the time value of money. The cash flows are made up of the cash flows within the forecast period together with a continuing or terminal value that represents the cash flow stream after the forecast period. In several contexts, DCF valuation is referred to as the "income approach".

Discounted Cash Flow valuation was used in industry as early as the 1700s or 1800s; it was publicly explicated by John Burr Williams in his The Theory of Investment Value in 1938; it was widely discussed in financial economics in the 1960s; and became widely used in U.S. courts in the 1980s and 1990s.

Basic Formula for Firm Valuation using DCF Model

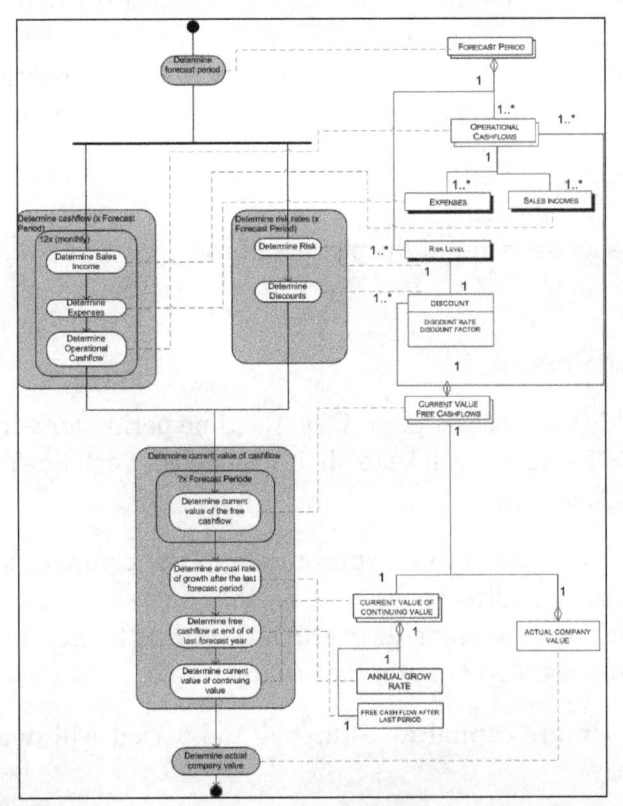

Flowchart for a typical DCF valuation, with each step detailed in the text.

$$\text{Value of firm} = \sum_{t=1}^{n} \frac{FCFF_t}{(1+WACC_t)^t} + \frac{\left[\dfrac{FCFF_{n+1}}{(WACC_{n+1} - g_{n+1})}\right]}{(1+WACC_n)^n}$$

where,

- *FCFF* is the Free Cash Flow to the Firm (essentially Operating cash flow minus capital expenditures) as reduced for tax.
- *WACC* is the Weighted Average Cost of Capital, combining the cost of equity and the after-tax cost of debt.
- *t* is the time period.
- *n* is the number of time periods to "maturity" or exit.
- *g* is the sustainable growth rate at that point.
- "Value of firm" represents the firm's enterprise value (i.e. its market value as distinct from market price); for corporate finance valuations, this represents the project's net present value or NPV.
- The second term represents the continuing value of future cash flows beyond the forecasting term; here applying a "perpetuity growth model".

Note that for valuing equity, as opposed to "the firm", free cash flow to equity (FCFE) or dividends are modeled, and these are discounted at the cost of equity instead of WACC which incorporates the cost of debt. Free cash flows to the firm are those distributed among - or at least due to - all securities holders of a corporate entity; to equity, are those distributed to shareholders only. Where the latter are dividends then the Dividend discount model can be applied, modifying the formula above.

Using the DCF Method

The diagram aside shows an overview of the process of company valuation. All steps are explained in detail below.

Determine Forecast Period

The initial step is to decide the forecast period, i.e. the time period for which the individual yearly cash flows input to the DCF formula will be explicitly modeled. Cash flows after the forecast period are represented by a single number.

The forecast period must be chosen to be appropriate to the company's strategy, its market, or industry; theoretically corresponding to the time for the company's (excess) return to "converge" to that of its industry, with constant, long term growth applying to the continuing value thereafter; although, regardless, 5–10 years is common in practice.

For private equity and venture capital investments, the period will depend on the investment timescale and exit strategy.

Determine Cash Flow for Each Forecast Period

As above, an explicit Cash flow forecast is required for each year during the forecast period. These must be "Free cash flow" or dividends.

Typically, this forecast will be constructed using historical internal accounting and sales data, in addition to external industry data and economic indicators (for these latter, typically relying on published surveys). The key aspect of the forecast is, arguably, predicting revenue, a function of the analyst's forecasts re market size, demand, inventory availability, and the firm's market share and market power; future costs, fixed and variable, as well as capital, can then be estimated as a function of sales via "common-sized analysis".

At the same time, the resultant line items must talk to the business' operations: In general, growth in revenue will require corresponding increases in working capital, fixed assets and associated financing; and in the long term, profitability (and other financial ratios) should tend to the industry average. Approaches to identifying which assumptions are most impactful on the value - and thus need the most attention - and to model "calibration" are discussed below (the process is then somewhat iterative).

There are several context dependent modifications:

- Importantly, in the case of a startup, substantial costs are often incurred at the start of the first year - and with certainty - and these should then be modelled separately from other cash flows, and not discounted at all. Ongoing costs, and capital requirements, can be proxied on a similar company, or industry averages; analogous to the "common-sized" approach mentioned.

- For corporate finance projects, cash flows should be estimated incrementally, i.e. the analysis should only consider cash flows that could change if the proposed investment is implemented. (This principle is generally correct, and applies to all (equity) investments, not just to corporate finance; in fact, the above formulae do reflect this, since, from the perspective of a listed or private equity investor *all* expected cash flows are incremental, and the full FCFF or dividend stream is then discounted.)

- For an M&A valuation the free cash flow is the amount of cash available to be paid out to all investors in the company after necessary investments for the business plan being valued. Synergies or strategic opportunities will often be dealt with either by probability weighting / haircutting these, or by separating these into their own DCF valuation where a higher discount rate reflects their uncertainty. Tax will receive very close attention. Often each business-line will be valued separately in a Sum-of-the-parts analysis.

- When valuing financial service firms, FCFE or dividends are typically modeled, as opposed to FCFF; this is because, often, capital expenditures, working capital and debt are not clearly defined for these corporates ("debt is more akin to raw material than to a source of capital"), and cash flows to the *firm*, and hence enterprise value, cannot then be easily estimated. Discounting is correspondingly at the cost of equity. Further, as these firms operate within a highly regulated environment, valuation assumptions must incorporate this reality, and outputs must similarly be "bound" by regulatory limits.

Alternate approaches within DCF valuation will more directly consider economic profit, and the definitions of "cashflow" will differ correspondingly; the best known is EVA. With the cost of capital correctly and correspondingly adjusted, the valuation should yield the same result. These approaches may be considered more appropriate for firms with negative free cash flow several years out, but which are expected to generate positive cash flow thereafter. Further, these may be less sensitive to terminal value.

Determine Discount Factor/Rate

A fundamental element of the valuation is to determine the *appropriate* required rate of return, as based on the risk level associated with the company and its market.

Typically, for an established (listed) company:

- For the cost of equity, the analyst will apply a model such as the CAPM most commonly An unlisted company's Beta can be based on that of a listed proxy as adjusted for gearing, ie debt, via Hamada's equation. (Other approaches, such as the "Build-Up method" or T-model are also applied.)

- The cost of debt may be calculated for each period as the scheduled after-tax interest payment as a percentage of outstanding debt.

- The value-weighted combination of these will then return the appropriate discount rate for each year of the forecast period. As the weight (and cost) of debt could vary over the period, each year's discount factor will be compounded over the rates to that date.

By contrast, for venture capital and private equity valuations - and particularly where the company is a startup, as in the example - the discount factor is often set by funding stage, as opposed to modeled ("Risk Group" in the example). In its early stages, where the business is more likely to fail, a higher return is demanded in compensation; when mature, an approach similar to the preceding may be applied. (Some analysts may instead account for this uncertainty by adjusting the cash flows directly: using certainty equivalents; or applying (subjective) "haircuts" to the forecast numbers, a "penalized present value"; or via probability-weighting these as in rNPV.)

Corporate finance analysts usually apply the first approach: here though it is the risk-characteristics of the project that must determine the cost of equity, and not those of the parent company. M&A analysts likewise apply the first approach, with risk as well as the target capital structure informing both the cost of equity and, naturally, WACC.

Determine Current Value

To determine current value, the analyst calculates the current value of the future cash flows simply by multiplying each period's cash flow by the discount factor for the period in question.

Where the forecast is yearly, an adjustment is sometimes made: although annual cash flows are discounted, it is not true that the entire cash flow comes in at the year end; rather, cash will flow in over the full year. To account for this, a "mid-year adjustment" is applied via the discount rate (and not to the forecast itself), affecting the required averaging.

Determine the Continuing Value

The continuing, or "terminal" value, is the estimated value of all cash flows after the forecast period.

- Typically the approach is to calculate this value using a "perpetuity growth model", essentially returning the value of the future cash flows via a geometric series. Key here is the treatment of the long term growth rate, and correspondingly, the forecast period number of years assumed for the company to arrive at this mature stage.

- The alternative, exit multiple approach, assumes that the business will be sold at the end of the projection period at some multiple of its final explicitly forecast cash flow. This is often the approach taken for venture capital valuations, where an exit transaction is explicitly planned.

Whichever approach, the terminal value is then discounted by the factor corresponding to the final explicit date.

Note that this step carries more risk than the previous: being more distant in time, and effectively summarizing the company's future, there is (significantly) more uncertainty as compared to the explicit forecast period; and yet, potentially, (often) this result contributes a significant proportion of the total value. Here, a very high proportion may suggest a flaw in the valuation (as commented in the example); but at the same time may, in fact, reflect how investors make money from equity investments – i.e. predominantly from capital gains or price appreciation. Its implied exit multiple can then act as a check, or "triangulation", on the perpetuity derived number.

Given this dependence on terminal value, analysts will often establish a "valuation range", or sensitivity table, corresponding to various appropriate - and internally consistent - discount rates, exit multiples and perpetuity growth rates.

For the valuation of mining projects (i.e. as to opposed to listed mining corporates) the forecast period is the same as the "life of mine" - i.e. the DCF model will explicitly forecast all cashflows due to mining the reserve (through mine closure) - and a continuing value is therefore not part of the valuation.

Determine Equity Value

The equity value is the sum of the present values of the explicitly forecast cash flows, and the continuing value. Where the forecast is of Free cash flow to firm, as above, the value of equity is calculated by subtracting any outstanding debts from the total of all discounted cash flows; where Free cash flow to equity (or dividends) has been modeled, this latter step is not required - and the discount rate would have been the cost of equity, as opposed to WACC.

The accuracy of the DCF valuation will be impacted by the accuracy of the various (numerous) inputs and assumptions. Addressing this, private equity and venture capital analysts, in particular, apply various of the following. With the first two, the output price is then market related, and the model will be driven by the relevant variables and assumptions. The latter two can be applied only at this stage.

- The DCF value is invariably "checked" by comparing its corresponding P/E or EV/EBITDA to the same of a relevant company or sector, based on share price or most recent transaction. This assessment is especially useful when the terminal value is estimated using the perpetuity approach; and can then also serve as a model "calibration". The use of traditional multiples may be limited in the case of startups - where profit and cash flows are often negative - and ratios such as Price/sales are then employed.

- Very commonly, analysts will produce a valuation range, especially based on different terminal value assumptions as mentioned. They may also carry out a sensitivity analysis - measuring the impact on value for a small change in the input - to demonstrate how "robust" the stated value is; and identify which model inputs are most critical to the value. This allows for focus on the inputs that "really drive value", reducing the need to estimate dozens of variables.

- Analysts often also generate scenario-based valuations, based on different assumptions on economy-wide, "global" factors as well as company-specific factors. In theory, an "unbiased" value is the probability-weighted average of the various scenarios (discounted using WACC from each). Note that in practice the required probability factors are usually too uncertain to do this.

- An extension of scenario-based valuations is to use Monte Carlo simulation, passing relevant model inputs through a spreadsheet risk-analysis add-in, such as @Risk or Crystal Ball. The output is a histogram of DCF values, which allows the analyst to read the expected (i.e. average) value over the inputs, or the probability that the investment will have at least a particular value, or will generate a specific return. The approach is sometimes applied to corporate finance projects,. But, again, in the venture capital context, it is not often applied, seen as adding "precision but not accuracy"; and the investment in time (and software) is then judged as unlikely to be warranted.

The DCF value may be applied differently depending on context. An investor in listed equity will compare the value per share to the share's traded price, amongst other stock selection criteria. To the extent that the price is lower than the DCF number, so she will be inclined to invest. The above calibration will be less relevant here; reasonable and robust assumptions more so. Corporations will often have several potential projects under consideration (or active). NPV is typically the primary selection criterion between these; although other investment measures considered, as visible from the DCF model itself, include ROI, IRR and payback period. Private equity and venture capital teams will similarly consider various measures and criteria, as well as recent comparable transactions, when selecting between potential investments; the valuation will typically be one step in, or following, a thorough due diligence. For an M&A valuation, the DCF will be one of several valuation results "combined" into a single number (and is usually not included in this for early stage companies); thereafter, other factors listed below, will then be considered in conjunction with this value.

DEPRIVAL VALUE

Deprival value is a concept used in accounting theory to determine the appropriate measurement basis for assets. It is an alternative to historical cost and fair value or mark to market accounting.

Some writers prefer terms such as 'value to the owner' or 'value to the firm'. Deprival value is also sometimes advocated for liabilities, in which case another term such as 'Relief value' may be used.

The deprival value of an asset is the extent to which the entity is "better off" because it holds the asset. This may be thought of as the answer to the following questions, all of which are equivalent: - What amount would just compensate the entity for the loss of the asset? - What loss would the entity sustain if deprived of the asset? - How much would the entity rationally pay to acquire the asset (if it did not already hold it)?

Deprival value is based on the premise that the value of an asset is equivalent to the loss that the owner of an asset would sustain if deprived of that asset. It builds on the insight that often the owner of an asset can use an asset to derive greater value than that which would be obtained from an immediate sale. For example, a machine may be profitably employed in a business but no more than scrap value could be obtained from its sale (net selling price).

Deprival value reasons that the maximum value at which an asset should be stated is its replacement cost as, by definition, the owner can make good the loss arising from deprival by incurring a cost equivalent to replacement cost. However, if that amount is greater than the amount that can be derived from ownership of the asset, it should be valued at no more than its recoverable amount. Recoverable amount is, in turn, defined as the higher of net selling price and value in use, which is the present value of the future returns that will be made by continuing to use the asset.

In summary:

- Deprival value equals the lower of replacement cost and recoverable amount; and
- Recoverable amount is the higher of net selling price and value in use.

An important practical implication of deprival value reasoning is that many assets will be stated at replacement cost, as entities tend to hold and use assets that they can employ profitably and dispose of those that they cannot.

Critics of deprival value assert that it is more complex than other measurement bases. Its use may also give rise to values that differ significantly from market values. Comparison between the values of assets owned by different entities may be difficult where deprival value is used because it reflects the position of the reporting entity. Critics also point out that the calculation of value in use is difficult and may be subjective.

MARKET VALUE

Market value or OMV (Open Market Valuation) is the price at which an asset would trade in a competitive auction setting. Market value is often used interchangeably with open market value, fair value or fair market value, although these terms have distinct definitions in different standards, and may or may not differ in some circumstances.

International Valuation Standards defines market value as "the estimated amount for which a property should exchange on the date of valuation between a willing buyer and a willing seller in an arm's-length transaction after proper marketing wherein the parties had each acted knowledgeably, prudently, and without compulsion".

Market value is a concept distinct from market price, which is "the price at which one can transact", while market value is "the true underlying value" according to theoretical standards. The concept is most commonly invoked in inefficient markets or disequilibrium situations where prevailing market prices are not reflective of true underlying market value. For market price to equal market value, the market must be informationally efficient and rational expectations must prevail.

Recently, Mocciaro Li Destri, Picone & Minà (2012) have underscored the subtle but important difference between the firms' capacity to create value through correct operational choices and valid strategies, on the one hand, and the epiphenomenal manifestation of variations in stockholder value on the financial markets (notably on stock markets). In this perspective, they suggest to implement new methodologies able to bring strategy back into financial performance measures.

Market value is also distinct from fair value in that fair value depends on the parties involved, while market value does not. For example, IVS currently notes fair value "requires the assessment of the price that is fair between two specific parties taking into account the respective advantages or disadvantages that each will gain from the transaction. Although market value may meet these criteria, this is not necessarily always the case. Fair value is frequently used when undertaking due diligence in corporate transactions, where particular synergies between the two parties may mean that the price that is fair between them is higher than the price that might be obtainable in the wider market. In other words "special value" may be generated. Market value requires this element of "special value" to be disregarded, but it forms part of the assessment of fair value.

Real Estate

The term is commonly used in real estate appraisal, since real estate markets are generally considered both informationally and transactionally inefficient. Also, real estate markets are subject to prolonged periods of disequilibrium, such as in contamination situations or other market disruptions.

Appraisals are usually performed under some set of assumptions about transactional markets, and those assumptions are captured in the definition of value used for the appraisal. Commonly, the definition set forth for U.S. federally regulated lending institutions is used, although other definitions may also be used under some circumstances:

"The most probable price (in terms of money) which a property should bring in a competitive and open market under all conditions requisite to a fair sale, the buyer and seller each acting prudently and knowledgeably, and assuming the price is not affected by undue stimulus. Implicit in this definition is the consummation of a sale as of a specified date and the passing of title from seller to buyer under conditions whereby: the buyer and seller are typically motivated; both parties are well informed or well advised, and acting in what they consider their best interests; a reasonable time is allowed for exposure in the open market; payment is made in terms of cash in United States dollars or in terms of financial arrangements comparable thereto; and the price represents the normal consideration for the property sold unaffected by special or creative financing or sales concessions granted by anyone associated with the sale."

In the US, Licensed or Certified Apppraisers may be required under state, federal, or local laws to develop appraisals subject to USPAP Uniform Standards of Professional Appraisal Practice. The Uniform Standards of Professional Appraisal Practice requires that when market value is the applicable definition, the appraisal must also contain an analysis of the highest and best use as well as an estimation of exposure time. All states require mandatory licensure of appraisers.

It is important to note that USPAP does not require that all real estate appraisals be performed based on a single definition of market value. Indeed, there are frequent situations when appraisers are called upon to appraise properties using other value definitions. If a value other than market value is appropriate, USPAP only requires that the appraiser provide both the definition of value being used and the citation for that definition.

Market value is the most commonly used type of value in real estate appraisal in the United States because it is required for all federally regulated mortgage transactions, and because it has been accepted by US courts as valid. However, real estate appraisers use many other definitions of value in other situations.

Liquidation Value

Liquidation value is the most probable price that a specified interest in real property is likely to bring under all of the following conditions:

- Consummation of a sale will occur within a severely limited future marketing period specified by the client.
- The actual market conditions currently prevailing are those to which the appraise property interest is subject.
- The buyer is acting prudently and knowledgeably.
- The seller is under extreme compulsion to sell.
- The buyer is typically motivated.
- The buyer is acting in what he or she considered his or her best interest.
- A limited marketing effort and time will be allowed for the completion of the sale.
- Payment will be made in cash in U.S. dollars or in terms of financial arrangements comparable thereto.
- The price represents the normal consideration for the property sold, unaffected by special or creative financing or sales concessions granted by anyone associated with the sale.

Orderly Liquidation Value

This value definition differs from the previous one in that it assumes an orderly transition, and not "extreme compulsion".

Federal Land Acquisition

For land acquisitions by or funded by U.S. federal agencies, a slightly different definition applies:

"Fair market value is defined as the amount in cash or terms reasonably equivalent to cash, for which in all probability the property would be sold by a knowledgeable owner willing but not obligated to sell to a knowledgeable purchaser who desired but is not obligated to buy. In ascertaining that figure, consideration should be given to all matters that might be brought forward and reasonably be given substantial weight in bargaining by persons of ordinary prudence, but no consideration whatever should be given to matters not affecting market value."

Going Concern Value

When a real estate appraiser works with a business valuation appraiser (and perhaps an equipment and machinery appraiser) to provide a value of the combination of a business and the real estate used for that business, the specific market value is called "going concern value". It recognizes that the combined market value may be different from the sum of the separate values: "The market value of all the tangible and intangible assets of an established operating business with an indefinite life, as if sold in aggregate."

Use Value

Use value takes into account a specific use for the subject property and does not attempt to ascertain the highest and best use of the real estate. For example, the appraisal may focus on the contributory value of the real estate to a business enterprise.

Some property tax jurisdictions allow agricultural use appraisals for farmland. Also, current IRS estate tax regulations allow land under an interim agricultural use to be valued according to its current use regardless of development potential.

Economic Value and Investor Confidence

Stability and economic growth are two factors that international investors are seeking when considering investment options. A country offering economic value amongst its other incentives attracts investment funds. A political unrest situation can be the cause of not only loss of confidence, but a reduced value in currency, creating transfer of capital to other and more stable sources.

In the event of a government printing currency to discharge a portion of a significant amount of debt, the supply of money is increased, with an ultimate reduction in its value, aggravated by inflation. Furthermore, should a government be unable to service its deficit by way of selling domestic bonds, thereby increasing the supply of money, it must increase the volume of saleable securities to foreigners, which in turn creates a decrease in their value.

A significant debt can prove a concern for foreign investors, should they believe there is a risk of the country defaulting on its obligations. They will be reluctant to purchase securities subject to that particular currency, if there is a perceived, significant risk of default. It is for this reason that the debt rating of a country; for example, as determined by Moody's or Standard & Poor's is a crucial indicator of its exchange rate.

Currency values and exchange rates play a crucial part in the rate of return on investments. Value for an investor, is the exchange rate of the currency which, contains the bulk of a portfolio, determining its real return. A declining value in the exchange rate has the effect of decreasing the purchasing power of income and capital gains, derived from any returns. In addition, other income factors such as interest rates, inflation and even capital gains from domestic securities, are influenced by the influential and complex factors, of the exchange rate.

INTRINSIC VALUE

In finance, intrinsic value or fundamental value is the "true, inherent, and essential value" of an asset independent of its market value.

Options

An option is said to have intrinsic value if the option is in-the-money. When out-of-the-money, its intrinsic value is *zero*.

The intrinsic value for an in-the-money option is calculated as the absolute value of the difference between the current price (S) of the underlying and the strike price (K) of the option.

$$IV_{\text{out-of-the-money}} = 0$$

$$IV_{\text{in-the-money}} = |S - K| = |K - S|$$

For example, if the strike price for a call option is USD $1 and the price of the underlying is USD 1.20, then the option has an intrinsic value of USD 0.20.

The value of an option is the sum of its intrinsic and its time value.

Equity

In valuing equity, securities analysts may use fundamental analysis—as opposed to technical analysis—to estimate the intrinsic value of a company. Here the "intrinsic" characteristic considered is the expected cash flow production of the company in question. Intrinsic value is therefore defined to be the present value of all expected future net cash flows to the company; i.e. it is calculated via discounted cash flow valuation.

An alternative, though related approach, is to view intrinsic value as the value of a business' ongoing operations, as opposed to its accounting based book value, or break-up value. Warren Buffett is known for his ability to calculate the intrinsic value of a business, and then buy that business when its price is at a discount to its intrinsic value.

Note that although stocks are assumed to be equity instruments - because they represent ownership interest in the company - the 'equity' label is somewhat questionable. Class C shares, for example, do not have any voting rights. The shares are considered equity instruments by finance professionals in that they are entitled to an equal share of the profits (dividends), even though shareholders lack the right to exercise control over the company.

Real Estate

In valuing real estate, a similar approach may be used. The "intrinsic value" of real estate is therefore defined as the net present value of all future net cash flows which are foregone by buying a piece of real estate instead of renting it in perpetuity. These cash flows would include rent, inflation, maintenance and property taxes. This calculation can be done using the Gordon model.

TERMINAL VALUE

In finance, the terminal value (continuing value or horizon value) of a security is the present value *at a future point in time* of all future cash flows when we expect stable growth rate forever. It is most often used in multi-stage discounted cash flow analysis, and allows for the limitation of cash flow projections to a several-year period. Forecasting results beyond such a period is impractical and exposes such projections to a variety of risks limiting their validity, primarily the great uncertainty involved in predicting industry and macroeconomic conditions beyond a few years.

Thus, the terminal value allows for the inclusion of the value of future cash flows occurring beyond a several-year projection period while satisfactorily mitigating many of the problems of valuing such cash flows. The terminal value is calculated in accordance with a stream of projected future free cash flows in discounted cash flow analysis. For whole-company valuation purposes, there are two methodologies used to calculate the Terminal Value.

Perpetuity Growth Model

The Perpetuity Growth Model accounts for the value of free cash flows that continue growing at an assumed constant rate in perpetuity; essentially, a geometric series which returns the value of a series of growing future cash flows. Here, the projected free cash flow in the first year beyond the projection horizon (N+1) is used. This value is then divided by the discount rate minus the assumed perpetuity growth rate:

$$T_0 = \frac{D_0(1+g)}{k-g}$$

- D_0 = Cash flows at a future point in time which is immediately prior to N+1, or at the end of period N, which is the final year in the projection period.
- k = Discount Rate.
- g = Growth Rate.

T_0 is the value of future cash flows; here dividends. When the valuation is based on free cash flow to firm then the formula becomes $\left[\dfrac{FCFF_{N+1}}{(WACC_N - g)}\right]$, where the discount rate is correspondingly the weighted average cost of capital.

To determine the present value of the terminal value, one must discount its value at T_0 by a factor equal to the number of years included in the initial projection period. If N is the 5th and final year in this period, then the Terminal Value is divided by $(1 + k)^5$ (or WACC). The Present Value of the Terminal Value is then added to the PV of the free cash flows in the projection period to arrive at an implied enterprise value.

If the growth rate in perpetuity is not constant, a multiple-stage terminal value is calculated. The terminal growth rate can be negative, if the company in question is assumed to disappear in the future.

Exit Multiple Approach

The Exit or Terminal Multiple Approach assumes a business will be sold at the end of the projection period. Valuation analytics are determined for various operating statistics using comparable acquisitions. A frequently used terminal multiple is Enterprise Value/EBITDA or EV/EBITDA. The analysis of comparable acquisitions will indicate an appropriate range of multiples to use. The multiple is then applied to the projected EBITDA in Year N, which is the final year in the projection period. This provides a future value at the end of Year N. The terminal value is then discounted using a factor equal to the number of years in the projection period. If N is the 5th and final year in this period, then the Terminal Value is divided by $(1+k)^5$. The Present Value of the Terminal Value is then added to the PV of the free cash flows in the projection period to arrive at an implied Enterprise Value. Note that if publicly traded comparable company multiples must be used, the resulting implied enterprise value will not reflect a control premium. Depending on the purposes of the valuation, this may not provide an appropriate reference range.

Comparison of Methodologies

There are several important differences between the two approaches.

The Perpetuity Growth Model has several inherent characteristics that make it intellectually challenging. Because both the discount rate and growth rate are assumptions, inaccuracies in one or both inputs can provide an improper value. The difference between the two values in the denominator determines the terminal value, and even with appropriate values for both, the denominator may result in a multiplying effect that does not estimate an accurate terminal value. Also, the perpetuity growth rate assumes that free cash flow will continue to grow at a constant rate into perpetuity. Consider that a perpetuity growth rate exceeding the annualized growth of the S&P 500 and/or the U.S. GDP implies that the company's cash flow will outpace and eventually absorb these rather large values. Perhaps the greatest disadvantage to the Perpetuity Growth Model is that it lacks the market-driven analytics employed in the Exit Multiple Approach. Such analytics result in a terminal value based on operating statistics present in a proven market for similar transactions. This provides a certain level of confidence that the valuation accurately depicts how the market would value the company in reality.

On the other hand, the Exit Multiple approach must be used carefully, because multiples change over time. Simply applying the current market multiple ignores the possibility that current multiples may be high or low by historical standards. In addition, it is important to note that at a given discount rate, any exit multiple implies a terminal growth rate and conversely any terminal growth rate implies an exit multiple. When using the Exit Multiple approach it is often helpful to calculate the implied terminal growth rate, because a multiple that may appear reasonable at first glance can actually imply a terminal growth rate that is unrealistic.

In practice, academics tend to use the Perpetuity Growth Model, while investment bankers favor the Exit Multiple approach. Ultimately, these methods are two different ways of saying the same thing. For both terminal value approaches, it is essential to use a range of appropriate discount rates, exit multiples and perpetuity growth rates in order to establish a functional valuation range.

LIQUIDATION VALUE

Liquidation value is the likely price of an asset when it is allowed insufficient time to sell on the open market, thereby reducing its exposure to potential buyers. Liquidation value is typically lower than fair market value. Unlike cash or securities, certain illiquid assets, like real estate, often require a period of several months in order to obtain their fair market value in a sale, and will generally sell for a significantly lower price if a sale is forced to occur in a shorter time period. Liquidation value may be either the result of a *forced liquidation* or an *orderly liquidation*. Either value assumes that the sale is consummated by a seller who is compelled to sell and assumes an exposure period which is less than market normal.

The most common definition used by real estate appraisers is as follows:

The most probable price that a specified interest in real property is likely to bring under all of the following conditions:

- Consummation of a sale will occur within a severely limited future marketing period specified by the client.
- The actual market conditions currently prevailing are those to which the appraised property interest is subject.
- The buyer is acting prudently and knowledgeably.
- The seller is under extreme compulsion to sell.
- The buyer is typically motivated.
- The buyer is acting in what he or she considers his or her best interest.
- A limited marketing effort and time will be allowed for the completion of a sale.
- Payment will be made in cash in U.S. dollars or in terms of financial arrangements comparable thereto.
- The price represents the normal consideration for the property sold, unaffected by special or creative financing or sales concessions granted by anyone associated with the sale.

BOOK VALUE

In accounting, book value is the value of an asset according to its balance sheet account balance. For assets, the value is based on the original cost of the asset less any depreciation, amortization or impairment costs made against the asset. Traditionally, a company's book value is its total assets minus intangible assets and liabilities. However, in practice, depending on the source of the calculation, book value may variably include goodwill, intangible assets, or both. The value inherent in its workforce, part of the intellectual capital of a company, is always ignored. When intangible assets and goodwill are explicitly excluded, the metric is often specified to be "tangible book value".

In the United Kingdom, the term net asset value may refer to the book value of a company.

Asset Book Value

An asset's initial book value is its actual cash value or its acquisition cost. Cash assets are recorded or "booked" at actual cash value. Assets such as buildings, land and equipment are valued based on their acquisition cost, which includes the actual cash cost of the asset plus certain costs tied to the purchase of the asset, such as broker fees. Not all purchased items are recorded as assets; incidental supplies are recorded as expenses. Some assets might be recorded as current expenses for tax purposes. An example of this is assets purchased and expensed under Section 179 of the US tax code.

1. [[{{}}]]===*Depreciable, amortizable and depletable assets*===

Monthly or annual depreciation, amortization and depletion are used to reduce the book value of assets over time as they are "consumed" or used up in the process of obtaining revenue. These non-cash expenses are recorded in the accounting books *after* a trial balance is calculated to ensure that cash transactions have been recorded accurately. Depreciation is used to record the declining value of buildings and equipment over time. Land is not depreciated. Amortization is used to record the declining value of intangible assets such as patents. Depletion is used to record the consumption of natural resources.

Depreciation, amortization and depletion are recorded as expenses against a contra account. Contra accounts are used in bookkeeping to record asset and liability valuation changes. "Accumulated depreciation" is a contra-asset account used to record asset depreciation.

Sample general journal entry for depreciation:

- Depreciation expenses: Building debit = $150, under expenses in retained earnings.
- Accumulated depreciation: Building credit = $150, under assets.

The balance sheet valuation for an asset is the asset's cost basis minus accumulated depreciation. Similar bookkeeping transactions are used to record amortization and depletion.

"Discount on notes payable" is a contra-liability account which decreases the balance sheet valuation of the liability.

When a company sells (issues) bonds, this debt is a long-term liability on the company's balance sheet, recorded in the account Bonds Payable based on the contract amount. After the bonds are sold, the book value of Bonds Payable is increased or decreased to reflect the actual amount received in payment for the bonds. If the bonds sell for less than face value, the contra account Discount on Bonds Payable is debited for the difference between the amount of cash received and the face value of the bonds.

Net Asset Value

In the United Kingdom, the term net asset value may refer to book value.

A mutual fund is an entity which primarily owns "financial assets" or capital assets such as bonds, stocks and commercial paper. The net asset value of a mutual fund is the market value of assets owned by the fund minus the fund's liabilities. This is similar to shareholders' equity, except the asset valuation is market-based rather than based on acquisition cost. In financial news reporting, the reported net asset value of a mutual fund is the net asset value of a single share in the fund. In the mutual fund's accounting records, the financial assets are recorded at acquisition cost. When assets are sold, the fund records a capital gain or capital loss.

Financial assets include stock shares and bonds owned by an individual or company. These may be reported on the individual or company balance sheet at cost or at market value.

Corporate Book Value

A company or corporation's book value, as an asset held by a separate economic entity, is the company or corporation's shareholders' equity, the acquisition cost of the shares, or the market value of the shares owned by the separate economic entity.

A corporation's book value is used in fundamental financial analysis to help determine whether the market value of corporate shares is above or below the book value of corporate shares. Neither market value nor book value is an unbiased estimate of a corporation's value. The corporation's bookkeeping or accounting records do not generally reflect the market value of assets and liabilities, and the market or trade value of the corporation's stock is subject to variations.

Tangible Common Equity

A variation of book value, tangible common equity, has recently come into use by the US Federal Government in the valuation of troubled banks. Tangible common equity is calculated as total book value minus intangible assets, goodwill, and preferred equity, and can thus be considered the most conservative valuation of a company and the best approximation of its value should it be forced to liquidate.

Since tangible common equity subtracts preferred equity from the tangible book value, it does a better job estimating what the value of the company is to holders of specifically *common* stock compared to standard calculations of book value.

Stock Pricing Book Value

To clearly distinguish the market price of shares from the core ownership equity or shareholders' equity, the term 'book value' is often used since it focuses on the values that have been added and subtracted in the accounting books of a business (assets – liabilities). The term is also used to distinguish between the market price of any asset and its accounting value which depends more on historical cost and depreciation. It may be used interchangeably with carrying value. While it can be used to refer to the business' total equity, it is most often used:

- As a 'per share value': The balance sheet Equity value is divided by the number of shares outstanding at the date of the balance sheet (not the average o/s in the period).

- As a 'diluted per share value': The Equity is bumped up by the exercise price of the options, warrants or preferred shares. Then it is divided by the number of shares that has been increased by those added.

Uses of Books

- Book value is used in the financial ratio price/book. It is a valuation metric that sets the floor for stock prices under a worst-case scenario. When a business is liquidated, the book value is what may be left over for the owners after all the debts are paid. Paying only a price/book = 1 means the investor will get all his investment back, assuming assets can be resold at their book value. Shares of capital intensive industries trade at lower price/book ratios because they generate lower earnings per dollar of assets. Business depending on human capital will generate higher earnings per dollar of assets, so will trade at higher price/book ratios.

- Book value per share can be used to generate a measure of comprehensive earnings, when the opening and closing values are reconciled. BookValuePerShare, beginning of year – Dividends + ShareIssuePremium + Comprehensive EPS = BookValuePerShare, end of year.

Changes are Caused by

- The sale of shares/units by the business increases the total book value. Book/sh will increase if the additional shares are issued at a price higher than the pre-existing book/sh.

- The purchase of its own shares by the business will decrease total book value. Book/shares will decrease if more is paid for them than was received when originally issued (pre-existing book/sh).

- Dividends paid out will decrease book value and book/sh.

- Comprehensive earnings/losses will increase/decrease book value and book/sh. Comprehensive earnings, in this case, includes net income from the Income Statement, foreign exchange translation changes to Balance Sheet items, accounting changes applied retroactively, and the opportunity cost of options exercised.

New Share Issues and Dilution

The issue of more shares does not necessarily decrease the value of the current owner. While it is correct that when the number of shares is doubled the EPS will be cut in half, it is too simple to be the full story. It all depends on how much was paid for the new shares and what return the new capital earns once invested.

Net Book Value of Long Term Assets

Book value is often used interchangeably with "net book value" or "carrying value," which is the original acquisition cost less accumulated depreciation, depletion or amortization. Book value is the term which means the value of the firm as per the books of the company. It is the value at which the assets are valued in the balance sheet of the company as on the given date.

Clean Surplus Accounting

The clean surplus accounting method provides elements of a forecasting model that yields price as a function of earnings, expected returns, and change in book value. The theory's primary use is to estimate the value of a company's shares (instead of discounted dividend/cash flow approaches). The secondary use is to estimate the cost of capital, as an alternative to e.g. the CAPM. The "clean surplus" is calculated by not including transactions with shareholders (such as dividends, share repurchases or share offerings) when calculating returns; whereas standard accounting for financial statements requires that the change in book value equal earnings minus dividends (net of capital changes).

Theory

The market value (MV) of the firm -- and hence security returns -- can be expressed in terms of balance sheet and income statement components, as below. This allows reading the firm's value directly from the balance sheet. The theory assumes ideal conditions. Here:

The market value of a firm = net book value of the firm's net assets + present value of future abnormal earnings (goodwill).

Logic:

- Goodwill is calculated as the difference between actual earnings and expected earnings ("abnormal earnings").
    - Actual earnings are the "clean surplus" - this ensures that all gains or losses go through the income statement. The impact of fair values is recognized in earnings.
    - Expected earnings = opening shareholders' equity X the firm's cost of capital (similar to accretion of discount.)
- Finally, convert book value to market value as above: firm value = net worth of the firm + calculated estimate of firm's goodwill.

Applicability

This approach provides a relatively "quick and dirty" method to calculate the market value of a firm - which should be (approximately) the same as a valuation based on discounted dividends or cash flows. The model provides one estimate of the firm's shares, useful for comparison to their market value. Research shows that this ratio provides a good predictor of share returns for 2–3 years into the future.

The model is applicable when abnormal earnings do not "persist" (i.e. no goodwill); in this case all gains and losses go through the income statement, and the firm's fair value appears on the balance sheet. The investor can then calculate expected earnings directly from the balance sheet, as above. However, if persistence is assumed, the income statement will have emerging "information content": this increases the impact of the income statement on firm value, and the method is less applicable. (Greater persistence similarly translates to a greater Earnings response coefficient.)

ADJUSTED PRESENT VALUE

Adjusted present value (APV) is a valuation method introduced in 1974 by Stewart Myers. The idea is to value the project as if it were all equity financed, and to then add the present value of the tax shield of debt and other side effects.

Technically, an APV valuation model looks similar to a standard DCF model. However, instead of WACC, cash flows would be discounted at the unlevered cost of equity, and tax shields at either the cost of debt (Myers) or following later academics also with the unlevered cost of equity. See Hamada's equation. APV and the standard DCF approaches should give the identical result if the capital structure remains stable.

According to Myers, the value of the levered firm (Value levered, Vl) is equal to the value of the firm with no debt (Value unlevered, Vu) plus the present value of the tax savings due to the tax deductability of interest payments, the so called value of the tax shield (VTS). Myers proposes calculating the VTS by discounting the tax savings at the cost of debt (Kd). The argument is that the risk of the tax saving arising from the use of debt is the same as the risk of the debt.

As mentioned, the method is to calculate the NPV of the project as if it is all-equity financed (so called "base case"). Then the base-case NPV is adjusted for the benefits of financing. Usually, the main benefit is a tax shield resulted from tax deductibility of interest payments. Another benefit can be a subsidized borrowing at sub-market rates. The APV method is especially effective when a leveraged buyout case is considered since the company is loaded with an extreme amount of debt, so the tax shield is substantial.

NET PRESENT VALUE

In finance, the net present value (NPV) or net present worth (NPW) applies to a series of cash flows occurring at different times. The present value of a cash flow depends on the interval of time between now and the cash flow. It also depends on the discount rate. NPV accounts for the time value of money. It provides a method for evaluating and comparing capital projects or financial products with cash flows spread over time, as in loans, investments, payouts from insurance contracts plus many other applications.

Time value of money dictates that time affects the value of cash flows. For example, a lender may offer 99 cents for the promise of receiving $1.00 a month from now, but the promise to receive that same dollar 20 years in the future would be worth much less today to that same person (lender), even if the payback in both cases was equally certain. This decrease in the current value of future cash flows is based on a chosen rate of return (or discount rate). If for example there exists a time series of identical cash flows, the cash flow in the present is the most valuable, with each future cash flow becoming less valuable than the previous cash flow. A cash flow today is more valuable than an identical cash flow in the future because a present flow can be invested immediately and begin earning returns, while a future flow cannot.

NPV is determined by calculating the costs (negative cash flows) and benefits (positive cash flows) for each period of an investment. The period is typically one year, but could be measured in quarter-years, half-years or months. After the cash flow for each period is calculated, the present value (PV) of each one is achieved by discounting its future value at a periodic rate of return (the rate of return dictated by the market). NPV is the sum of all the discounted future cash flows. Because of its simplicity, NPV is a useful tool to determine whether a project or investment will result in a net profit or a loss. A positive NPV results in profit, while a negative NPV results in a loss. The NPV measures the excess or shortfall of cash flows, in present value terms, above the cost of funds. In a theoretical situation of unlimited capital budgeting a company should pursue every investment with a positive NPV. However, in practical terms a company's capital constraints limit investments to projects with the highest NPV whose cost cash flows, or initial cash investment, do not exceed the company's capital. NPV is a central tool in discounted cash flow (DCF) analysis and is a standard method for using the time value of money to appraise long-term projects. It is widely used throughout economics, finance, and accounting.

In the case when all future cash flows are positive, or incoming (such as the principal and coupon payment of a bond) the only outflow of cash is the purchase price, the NPV is simply the PV of future cash flows minus the purchase price (which is its own PV). NPV can be described as the "difference amount" between the sums of discounted cash inflows and cash outflows. It compares the present value of money today to the present value of money in the future, taking inflation and returns into account.

The NPV of a sequence of cash flows takes as input the cash flows and a discount rate or discount curve and outputs a present value, which is the current fair price. The converse process in discounted cash flow (DCF) analysis takes a sequence of cash flows and a price as input and as output the discount rate, or internal rate of return (IRR) which would yield the given price as NPV. This rate, called the yield, is widely used in bond trading.

Many computer-based spreadsheet programs have built-in formulae for PV and NPV.

Formula

Each cash inflow/outflow is discounted back to its present value (PV). Then all are summed. Therefore, NPV is the sum of all terms,

$$\frac{R_t}{(1+i)^t}$$

where:

t is the time of the cash flow.

i is the discount rate, i.e. the return that could be earned per unit of time on an investment with similar risk.

R_t is the net cash flow i.e. cash inflow – cash outflow, at time t. For educational purposes, R_0 is commonly placed to the left of the sum to emphasize its role as (minus) the investment.

The result of this formula is multiplied with the Annual Net cash in-flows and reduced by Initial Cash outlay the present value but in cases where the cash flows are not equal in amount, then the previous formula will be used to determine the present value of each cash flow separately. Any cash flow within 12 months will not be discounted for NPV purpose, nevertheless the usual initial investments during the first year R_0 are summed up a negative cash flow.

Given the (period, cash flow) pairs (t, R_t) where N is the total number of periods, the net present value NPV is given by:

$$NPV(i,N) = \sum_{t=1}^{N} \frac{R_t}{(1+i)^t}$$

For constant cash flow R, the net present value NPV is a finite geometric series and is given by:

$$NPV(i,N,R) = R \left(\frac{1 - \left(\frac{1}{1+i}\right)^{N+1}}{1 - \left(\frac{1}{1+i}\right)} \right), \quad i \neq 0$$

The Discount Rate

The rate used to discount future cash flows to the present value is a key variable of this process.

A firm's weighted average cost of capital (after tax) is often used, but many people believe that it is appropriate to use higher discount rates to adjust for risk, opportunity cost, or other factors. A variable discount rate with higher rates applied to cash flows occurring further along the time span might be used to reflect the yield curve premium for long-term debt.

Another approach to choosing the discount rate factor is to decide the rate which the capital needed for the project could return if invested in an alternative venture. If, for example, the capital required for Project A can earn 5% elsewhere, use this discount rate in the NPV calculation to allow a direct comparison to be made between Project A and the alternative. Related to this concept is to use the firm's reinvestment rate. Re-investment rate can be defined as the rate of return for the firm's investments on average. When analyzing projects in a capital constrained environment, it may be appropriate to use the reinvestment rate rather than the firm's weighted average cost of capital as the discount factor. It reflects opportunity cost of investment, rather than the possibly lower cost of capital.

An NPV calculated using variable discount rates (if they are known for the duration of the investment) may better reflect the situation than one calculated from a constant discount rate for the entire investment duration.

For some professional investors, their investment funds are committed to target a specified rate of return. In such cases, that rate of return should be selected as the discount rate for the NPV calculation. In this way, a direct comparison can be made between the profitability of the project and the desired rate of return.

To some extent, the selection of the discount rate is dependent on the use to which it will be put. If the intent is simply to determine whether a project will add value to the company, using the firm's weighted average cost of capital may be appropriate. If trying to decide between alternative investments in order to maximize the value of the firm, the corporate reinvestment rate would probably be a better choice.

Using variable rates over time, or discounting "guaranteed" cash flows differently from "at risk" cash flows, may be a superior methodology but is seldom used in practice. Using the discount rate to adjust for risk is often difficult to do in practice (especially internationally) and is difficult to do well. An alternative to using discount factor to adjust for risk is to explicitly correct the cash flows for the risk elements using rNPV or a similar method, then discount at the firm's rate.

Use in Decision Making

NPV is an indicator of how much value an investment or project adds to the firm. With a particular project, if R_t is a positive value, the project is in the status of positive cash inflow in the time of t. If R_t is a negative value, the project is in the status of discounted cash outflow in the time o t. Appropriately risked projects with a positive NPV could be accepted. This does not necessarily mean that they should be undertaken since NPV at the cost of capital may not account for opportunity cost, i.e., comparison with other available investments. In financial theory, if there is a choice between two mutually exclusive alternatives, the one yielding the higher NPV should be selected. A positive net present value indicates that the projected earnings generated by a project or investment (in present dollars) exceeds the anticipated costs (also in present dollars). Generally, an investment with a positive NPV will be a profitable one and one with a negative NPV will result in a net loss. This concept is the basis for the Net Present Value Rule, which dictates that the only investments that should be made are those with positive NPVs.

If	It means	Then
NPV > 0	The investment would add value to the firm.	The project may be accepted.
NPV < 0	The investment would subtract value from the firm.	The project may be rejected.
NPV = 0	The investment would neither gain nor lose value for the firm.	We should be indifferent in the decision whether to accept or reject the project. This project adds no monetary value. Decision should be based on other criteria, e.g., strategic positioning or other factors not explicitly included in the calculation.

An alternative way of looking at Net Present Value is that at the given rate of Cost of Capital, whether the project can meet the cost of capital. For example, if the NPV is -$2.5 million (i.e.

negative NPV) for a given project, it may mean that at the given Weighted Average Cost of Capital (WACC), the project fails to meet the expectations of the suppliers of capital for the project. On the other hand, the NPV of $2.5 million would add $2.5 million to the wealth of the suppliers of funds over and above their expected returns.

Interpretation as Integral Transform

The time-discrete formula of the net present value,

$$\mathrm{NPV}(i, N) = \sum_{t=0}^{N} \frac{R_t}{(1+i)^t}$$

can also be written in a continuous variation,

$$\mathrm{NPV}(i) = \int_{t=0}^{\infty} (1+i)^{-t} \cdot r(t) dt$$

where:

$r(t)$ is the rate of flowing cash given in money per time, and $r(t) = 0$ when the investment is over.

Net present value can be regarded as Laplace- respectively Z-transformed cash flow with the integral operator including the complex number s which resembles to the interest rate i from the real number space or more precisely $s = \ln(1 + i)$.

$$F(s) = \{\mathcal{L}f\}(s) = \int_0^{\infty} e^{-st} f(t) dt$$

From this follow simplifications known from cybernetics, control theory and system dynamics. Imaginary parts of the complex number s describe the oscillating behaviour (compare with the pork cycle, cobweb theorem, and phase shift between commodity price and supply offer) whereas real parts are responsible for representing the effect of compound interest (compare with damping).

Example

A corporation must decide whether to introduce a new product line. The company will have immediate costs of 100,000 at $t = 0$. Recall, a cost is a negative for outgoing cash flow, thus this cash flow is represented as −100,000. The company assumes the product will provide equal benefits of 10,000 for each of 12 years beginning at $t = 1$. For simplicity, assume the company will have no outgoing cash flows after the initial 100,000 cost. This also makes the simplifying assumption that the net cash received or paid is lumped into a single transaction occurring *on the last day* of each year. At the end of the 12 years the product no longer provides any cash flow and is discontinued without any additional costs. Assume that the effective annual discount rate is 10%.

The present value (value at $t = 0$) can be calculated for each year:

Year	Cash flow	Present value
T = 0	$\dfrac{-100,000}{(1+0.10)^0}$	−100,000

T = 1	$\dfrac{10,000}{(1+0.10)^1}$	9,090.91
T = 2	$\dfrac{10,000}{(1+0.10)^2}$	8,264.46
T = 3	$\dfrac{10,000}{(1+0.10)^3}$	7,513.15
T = 4	$\dfrac{10,000}{(1+0.10)^4}$	6,830.13
T = 5	$\dfrac{10,000}{(1+0.10)^5}$	6,209.21
T = 6	$\dfrac{10,000}{(1+0.10)^6}$	5,644.74
T = 7	$\dfrac{10,000}{(1+0.10)^7}$	5,131.58
T = 8	$\dfrac{10,000}{(1+0.10)^8}$	4,665.07
T = 9	$\dfrac{10,000}{(1+0.10)^9}$	4,240.98
T = 10	$\dfrac{10,000}{(1+0.10)^{10}}$	3,855.43
T = 11	$\dfrac{10,000}{(1+0.10)^{11}}$	3,504.94
T = 12	$\dfrac{10,000}{(1+0.10)^{12}}$	3,186.31

The total present value of the incoming cash flows is 68,136.91. The total present value of the outgoing cash flows is simply the 100,000 at time $t = 0$. Thus:

$$\text{NPV} = PV(\text{benefits}) - PV(\text{costs})$$

In this example:

$$\text{NPV} = 68,136.91 - 100,000$$

$$\text{NPV} = -31,863.09$$

Observe that as t increases the present value of each cash flow at t decreases. For example, the final incoming cash flow has a future value of 10,000 at t = 12 but has a present value (at t = 0) of 3,186.31. The opposite of discounting is compounding. Taking the example in reverse, it is the equivalent of investing 3,186.31 at t = 0 (the present value) at an interest rate of 10% compounded for 12 years, which results in a cash flow of 10,000 at t = 12 (the future value).

$$NPV = \Sigma \frac{R(t)}{(1+i)^t}$$

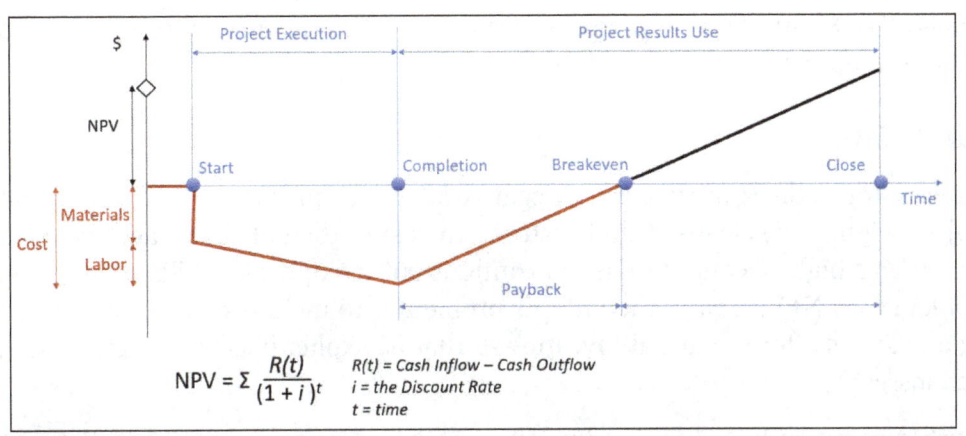

R(t) = Cash Inflow − Cash Outflow
i = the Discount Rate
t = time

A simplified cash flow model shows the expected cash flow. Each value is calculated with the discount rate. The simplified approach is used in project management simulation SimulTrain.

The importance of NPV becomes clear in this instance. Although the incoming cash flows (10,000 × 12 = 120,000) appear to exceed the outgoing cash flow (100,000), the future cash flows are not adjusted using the discount rate. Thus, the project appears misleadingly profitable. When the cash flows are discounted however, it indicates the project would result in a net loss of 31,863.09. Thus, the NPV calculation indicates that this project should be disregarded because investing in this project is the equivalent of a loss of 31,863.09 at t = 0. The concept of time value of money indicates that cash flows in different periods of time cannot be accurately compared unless they have been adjusted to reflect their value at the same period of time (in this instance, t = 0). It is the present value of each future cash flow that must be determined in order to provide any meaningful comparison between cash flows at different periods of time. There are a few inherent assumptions in this type of analysis:

- The *investment horizon* of all possible investment projects considered are equally acceptable to the investor (e.g. a 3-year project is not necessarily preferable vs. a 20-year project.)

- The 10% discount rate is the appropriate (and stable) rate to discount the expected cash flows from each project being considered. Each project is assumed equally speculative.

- The shareholders cannot get above a 10% return on their money if they were to directly assume an equivalent level of risk. (If the investor could do better elsewhere, no projects should be undertaken by the firm, and the excess capital should be turned over to the shareholder through dividends and stock repurchases.)

More realistic problems would also need to consider other factors, generally including: smaller time buckets, the calculation of taxes (including the cash flow timing), inflation, currency exchange fluctuations, hedged or unhedged commodity costs, risks of technical obsolescence, potential future competitive factors, uneven or unpredictable cash flows, and a more realistic salvage value assumption, as well as many others.

A more simple example of the net present value of incoming cash flow over a set period of time, would be winning a Powerball lottery of $500 million. If one does not select the "CASH" option they will be paid $25,000,000 per year for 20 years, a total of $500,000,000, however, if one does select the "CASH" option, they will receive a one-time lump sum payment of approximately $285 million, the NPV of $500,000,000 paid over time. See "other factors" above that could affect the payment amount. Both scenarios are before taxes.

Common Pitfalls

- If, for example, the R_t are generally negative late in the project (*e.g.*, an industrial or mining project might have clean-up and restoration costs), then at that stage the company owes money, so a high discount rate is not cautious but too optimistic. Some people see this as a problem with NPV. A way to avoid this problem is to include explicit provision for financing any losses after the initial investment, that is, explicitly calculate the cost of financing such losses.

- Another common pitfall is to adjust for risk by adding a premium to the discount rate. Whilst a bank might charge a higher rate of interest for a risky project, that does not mean that this is a valid approach to adjusting a net present value for risk, although it can be a reasonable approximation in some specific cases. One reason such an approach may not work well can be seen from the following: if some risk is incurred resulting in some losses, then a discount rate in the NPV will reduce the effect of such losses below their true financial cost. A rigorous approach to risk requires identifying and valuing risks explicitly, *e.g.*, by actuarial or Monte Carlo techniques, and explicitly calculating the cost of financing any losses incurred.

- Yet another issue can result from the compounding of the risk premium. R is a composite of the risk free rate and the risk premium. As a result, future cash flows are discounted by both the risk-free rate as well as the risk premium and this effect is compounded by each subsequent cash flow. This compounding results in a much lower NPV than might be otherwise calculated. The certainty equivalent model can be used to account for the risk premium without compounding its effect on present value.

- Another issue with relying on NPV is that it does not provide an overall picture of the gain or loss of executing a certain project. To see a percentage gain relative to the investments for the project, usually, Internal rate of return or other efficiency measures are used as a complement to NPV.

- Non-specialist users frequently make the error of computing NPV based on cash flows after interest. This is wrong because it double counts the time value of money. Free cash flow should be used as the basis for NPV computations.

STOCK VALUATION

In financial markets, stock valuation is the method of calculating theoretical values of companies and their stocks. The main use of these methods is to predict future market prices, or more generally, potential market prices, and thus to profit from price movement – stocks that are judged *undervalued* (with respect to their theoretical value) are bought, while stocks that are judged *overvalued* are sold, in the expectation that undervalued stocks will overall rise in value, while overvalued stocks will generally decrease in value.

In the view of fundamental analysis, stock valuation based on fundamentals aims to give an estimate of the intrinsic value of a stock, based on predictions of the future cash flows and profitability of the business. Fundamental analysis may be replaced or augmented by market criteria – what the market will pay for the stock, disregarding intrinsic value. These can be combined as "predictions of future cash flows/profits (fundamental)", together with "what will the market pay for these profits?" These can be seen as "supply and demand" sides – what underlies the supply (of stock), and what drives the (market) demand for stock?

In the view of John Maynard Keynes, stock valuation is not a *prediction* but a *convention,* which serves to facilitate investment and ensure that stocks are liquid, despite being underpinned by an illiquid business and its illiquid investments, such as factories.

Fundamental Criteria (Fair Value)

There are many different ways to value stocks. The key is to take each approach into account while formulating an overall opinion of the stock. If the valuation of a company is lower or higher than other similar stocks, then the next step would be to determine the reasons.

The first approach, Fundamental analysis, is typically associated with investors and financial analysts - its output is used to justify stock prices. The most theoretically sound stock valuation method, is called "income valuation" or the discounted cash flow (DCF) method. It is widely applied in all areas of finance. Perhaps the most common fundamental methodology is the P/E ratio (Price to Earnings Ratio). This example of "relative valuation" is based on historic ratios and aims to assign value to a stock based on measurable attributes. This form of valuation is typically what drives long-term stock prices.

The alternative approach - Technical analysis - is to base the assessment on supply and demand: simply, the more people that want to buy the stock, the higher its price will be; and conversely, the more people that want to sell the stock, the lower the price will be. This form of valuation often drives the short-term stock market trends; and is associated with speculators as opposed to investors.

Discounted Cash Flow

The discounted cash flow (DCF) method involves discounting of the profits (dividends, earnings, or cash flows) that the stock will bring to the stockholder in the foreseeable future, and a final value on disposal. The discounted rate normally includes a risk premium which is commonly based on the capital asset pricing model.

In July 2010, a Delaware court ruled on appropriate inputs to use in discounted cash flow analysis in a dispute between shareholders and a company over the proper fair value of the stock. In this case the shareholders' model provided value of $139 per share and the company's model provided $89 per share. Contested inputs included the terminal growth rate, the equity risk premium, and beta.

Earnings Per Share (EPS)

EPS is the Net income available to common shareholders of the company divided by the number of shares outstanding. Usually there will be two types of EPS listed: a GAAP (Generally Accepted Accounting Principles) EPS and a Pro Forma EPS, which means that the income has been adjusted to exclude any one time items as well as some non-cash items like amortization of goodwill or stock option expenses. The most important thing to look for in the EPS figure is the overall quality of earnings. Make sure the company is not trying to manipulate their EPS numbers to make it look like they are more profitable. Also, look at the growth in EPS over the past several quarters / years to understand how volatile their EPS is, and to see if they are an underachiever or an overachiever. In other words, have they consistently beaten expectations or are they constantly restating and lowering their forecasts?

The EPS number that most analysts use is the pro forma EPS. To compute this number, use the net income that excludes any one-time gains or losses and excludes any non-cash expenses like amortization of goodwill. Never exclude non-cash compensation expense as that does impact earnings per share. Then divide this number by the number of fully diluted shares outstanding. Historical EPS figures and forecasts for the next 1–2 years can be found by visiting free financial sites such as Yahoo Finance.

Price to Earnings (P/E)

Now that the analyst has several EPS figures (historical and forecasts), the analyst will be able to look at the most common valuation technique used, the price to earnings ratio, or P/E. To compute this figure, one divides the stock price by the annual EPS figure. For example, if the stock is trading at $10 and the EPS is $0.50, the P/E is 20 times. A complete analysis of the P/E multiple includes a look at the historical and forward ratios.

Historical P/Es are computed by taking the current price divided by the sum of the EPS for the last four quarters, or for the previous year. Historical trends of the P/E should also be considered by viewing a chart of its historical P/E over the last several years (one can find this on most finance sites like Yahoo Finance). Specifically consider what range the P/E has traded in so as to determine whether the current P/E is high or low versus its historical average.

Forward P/Es reflect the future growth of the company into the future. Forward P/Es are computed by taking the current stock price divided by the sum of the EPS estimates for the next four quarters, or for the EPS estimate for next calendar or fiscal year or two.

P/Es change constantly. If there is a large price change in a stock, or if the earnings (EPS) estimates change, the ratio is recomputed.

Growth Rate

Discounted cash flow based valuations rely (very) heavily on the expected growth rate of a company. An accurate assessment is therefore critical to the valuation.

Here, the analyst will typically look at the historical growth rate of both sales and income to derive a base for the type of future growth expected. However, since, companies are constantly evolving, as is the economy, solely using historical growth rates to predict the future will not be appropriate (the "problem of induction"). These, instead, are used as guidelines for what future growth "could look like" if similar circumstances are encountered by the company.

Calculating the future growth rate therefore requires personal investment research - familiarity with a company is essential before making a forecast. This may take form in listening to the company's quarterly conference call or reading a press release or other company article that discusses the company's growth guidance. However, although companies are in the best position to forecast their own growth, they are often far from accurate; further, unforeseen macro-events could cause impact the economy and/or the company's industry.

Regardless of research effort, a growth-rate based valuation therefore relies heavily on experience and judgement ("gut feel"), and analysts will thus (often) make inaccurate forecasts. It is for this reason, that analysts often model a range of forecast values. As an example here, if the company being valued has been growing earnings between 5 and 10% each year for the last 5 years, but believes that it will grow 15 –20% this year, a more conservative growth rate of 10–15% would be appropriate in valuations. Another example would be for a company that has been going through restructuring. It may have been growing earnings at 10–15% over the past several quarters or years because of cost cutting, but their sales growth could be only 0–5%. This would signal that their earnings growth will probably slow when the cost cutting has fully taken effect. Therefore, forecasting an earnings growth closer to the 0–5% rate would be more appropriate rather than the 15–20%.

Capital Structure Substitution - Asset Pricing Formula

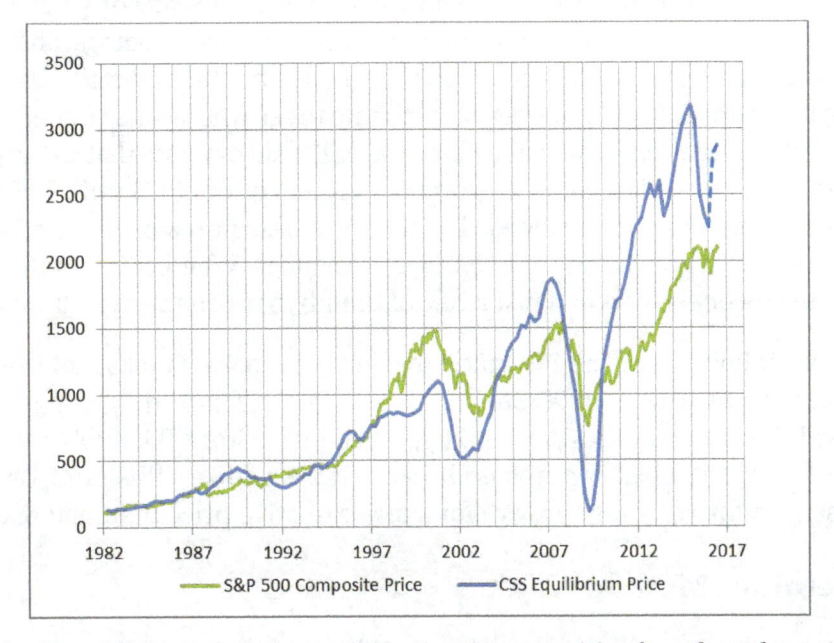

S&P 500 Composite Index compared to the CSS asset pricing formula - July 2016.

The capital structure substitution theory (CSS) describes the relationship between earnings, stock price and capital structure of public companies. The equilibrium condition of the CSS theory can be easily rearranged to an asset pricing formula:

$$P_x = \frac{E_x}{R_x[1-T]}$$

where:

- P is the current market price of public company x.
- E is the earnings-per-share of company x.

- R is the nominal interest rate on corporate bonds of company x.
- T is the corporate tax rate.

The CSS theory suggests that company share prices are strongly influenced by bondholders. As a result of active repurchasing or issuing of shares by company managements, equilibrium pricing is no longer a result of balancing shareholder demand and supply. The asset pricing formula only applies to debt-holding companies.

The asset pricing formula can be used on a market aggregate level as well. The resulting graph shows at what times the S&P 500 Composite was overpriced and at what times it was under-priced relative to the capital structure substitution theory equilibrium. In times when the market is under-priced, corporate buyback programs will allow companies to drive up earnings-per-share, and generate extra demand in the stock market.

Price Earnings to Growth (PEG) Ratio

This valuation technique has really become popular over the past decade or so. It is better than just looking at a P/E because it takes three factors into account; the price, earnings, and earnings growth rates. To compute the PEG ratio, the Forward P/E is divided by the expected earnings growth rate (one can also use historical P/E and historical growth rate to see where it has traded in the past). This will yield a ratio that is usually expressed as a percentage. The theory goes that as the percentage rises over 100% the stock becomes more and more overvalued, and as the PEG ratio falls below 100% the stock becomes more and more undervalued. The theory is based on a belief that P/E ratios should approximate the long-term growth rate of a company's earnings. Whether or not this is true will never be proven and the theory is therefore just a rule of thumb to use in the overall valuation process.

Here is an example of how to use the PEG ratio to compare stocks. Stock A is trading at a forward P/E of 15 and expected to grow at 20%. Stock B is trading at a forward P/E of 30 and expected to grow at 25%. The PEG ratio for Stock A is 75% (15/20) and for Stock B is 120% (30/25). According to the PEG ratio, Stock A is a better purchase because it has a lower PEG ratio, or in other words, you can purchase its future earnings growth for a lower relative price than that of Stock B.

Sum of Perpetuities Method

The PEG ratio is a special case in the sum of perpetuities method (SPM) equation. A generalized version of the Walter model (1956), SPM considers the effects of dividends, earnings growth, as well as the risk profile of a firm on a stock's value. Derived from the compound interest formula using the present value of a perpetuity equation, SPM is an alternative to the Gordon Growth Model. The variables are:

- *P* is the value of the stock or business.
- *E* is a company's earnings.
- *G* is the company's constant growth rate.
- *K* is the company's risk adjusted discount rate.

- is the company's dividend payment.

$$P = \left(\frac{E*G}{K^2}\right) + \left(\frac{D}{K}\right)$$

In a special case where K is equal to 10%, and the company does not pay dividends, SPM reduces to the PEG ratio.

Additional models represent the sum of perpetuities in terms of earnings, growth rate, the risk-adjusted discount rate, and accounting book value.

Return on Invested Capital (ROIC)

This valuation technique measures how much money the company makes each year per dollar of invested capital. Invested Capital is the amount of money invested in the company by both stockholders and debtors. The ratio is expressed as a percent and one looks for a percent that approximates the level of growth that expected. In its simplest definition, this ratio measures the investment return that management is able to get for its capital. The higher the number, the better the return.

To compute the ratio, take the pro forma net income (same one used in the EPS figure mentioned above) and divide it by the invested capital. Invested capital can be estimated by adding together the stockholders equity, the total long and short term debt and accounts payable, and then subtracting accounts receivable and cash (all of these numbers can be found on the company's latest quarterly balance sheet). This ratio is much more useful when comparing it to other companies being valued.

Return on Assets (ROA)

Similar to ROIC, ROA, expressed as a percent, measures the company's ability to make money from its assets. To measure the ROA, take the pro forma net income divided by the total assets. However, because of very common irregularities in balance sheets (due to things like Goodwill, write-offs, discontinuations, etc.) this ratio is not always a good indicator of the company's potential. If the ratio is higher or lower than expected, one should look closely at the assets to see what could be over or understating the figure.

Price to Sales (P/S)

This figure is useful because it compares the current stock price to the annual sales. In other words, it describes how much the stock costs per dollar of sales earned.

Market Cap

Market cap, which is short for market capitalization, is the value of all of the company's stock. To measure it, multiply the current stock price by the fully diluted shares outstanding. Remember, the market cap is only the value of the stock. To get a more complete picture, look at the enterprise value.

Enterprise Value (EV)

Enterprise value is equal to the total value of the company, as it is trading for on the stock market. To compute it, add the market cap and the total net debt of the company. The total net debt is equal to total long and short term debt plus accounts payable, minus accounts receivable, minus cash. The enterprise value is the best approximation of what a company is worth at any point in time because it takes into account the actual stock price instead of balance sheet prices. When analysts say that a company is a "billion dollar" company, they are often referring to its total enterprise value. Enterprise value fluctuates rapidly based on stock price changes.

EV to Sales

This ratio measures the total company value as compared to its annual sales. A high ratio means that the company's value is much more than its sales. To compute it, divide the EV by the net sales for the last four quarters. This ratio is especially useful when valuing companies that do not have earnings, or that are going through unusually rough times. For example, if a company is facing restructuring and it is currently losing money, then the P/E ratio would be irrelevant. However, by applying an EV to Sales ratio, one could compute what that company could trade for when its restructuring is over and its earnings are back to normal.

EBITDA

EBITDA stands for earnings before interest, taxes, depreciation and amortization. It is one of the best measures of a company's cash flow and is used for valuing both public and private companies. To compute EBITDA, use a company's income statement, take the net income and then add back interest, taxes, depreciation, amortization and any other non-cash or one-time charges. This leaves you with a number that approximates how much cash the company is producing. EBITDA is a very popular figure because it can easily be compared across companies, even if not all of the companies are profitable.

EV to EBITDA

This is perhaps one of the best measurements of whether or not a company is cheap or expensive. To compute, divide the EV by EBITDA. The higher the number, the more expensive the company is. However, remember that more expensive companies are often valued higher because they are growing faster or because they are a higher quality company. With that said, the best way to use EV/EBITDA is to compare it to that of other similar companies.

Approximate Valuation Approaches

Average Growth Approximation

Assuming that two stocks have the same earnings growth, the one with a lower P/E is a better value. The P/E method is perhaps the most commonly used valuation method in the stock brokerage industry. By using comparison firms, a target price/earnings (or P/E) ratio is selected for the company, and then the future earnings of the company are estimated. The valuation's fair price is simply estimated earnings times target P/E. This model is essentially the same model as Gordon's model, if k-g is estimated as the dividend payout ratio (D/E) divided by the target P/E ratio.

Constant Growth Approximation

The Gordon model or *Gordon's growth model* is the best known of a class of discounted dividend models. It assumes that dividends will increase at a constant growth rate (less than the discount rate) forever. The valuation is given by the formula:

$$P = D \cdot \sum_{i=1}^{\infty} \left(\frac{1+g}{1+k}\right)^i = D \cdot \frac{1+g}{k-g}.$$

and the following table defines each symbol:

Symbol	Meaning	Units
P	estimated stock price	$ or € or £
D	last dividend paid	$ or € or £
k	discount rate	%
g	the growth rate of the dividends	%

Dividend growth rate is not known, but earnings growth may be used in its place, assuming that the payout ratio is constant.

Limited High-growth Period Approximation

When a stock has a significantly higher growth rate than its peers, it is sometimes assumed that the earnings growth rate will be sustained for a short time (say, 5 years), and then the growth rate will revert to the mean. This is probably the most rigorous approximation that is practical.

While these DCF models are commonly used, the uncertainty in these values is hardly ever discussed. Note that the models diverge for $k = g$ and hence are extremely sensitive to the difference of dividend growth to discount factor. One might argue that an analyst can justify any value (and that would usually be one close to the current price supporting his call) by fine-tuning the growth/discount assumptions.

Implied Growth Models

One can use the Gordon model or the limited high-growth period approximation model to impute an implied growth estimate. To do this, one takes the average P/E and average growth for a comparison index, uses the current (or forward) P/E of the stock in question, and calculates what growth rate would be needed for the two valuation equations to be equal. This yields an estimate of the "break-even" growth rate for the stock's current P/E ratio.

Imputed Growth Acceleration Ratio

Subsequently, one can divide this imputed growth estimate by recent historical growth rates. If the resulting ratio is greater than one, it implies that the stock would need to experience accelerated growth relative to its prior recent historical growth to justify its current P/E (higher values suggest potential overvaluation). If the resulting ratio is less than one, it implies that either the market expects growth to slow for this stock or that the stock could sustain its current P/E with lower than historical growth (lower values suggest potential undervaluation). Comparison of the IGAR across stocks in the same industry may give estimates of relative value. IGAR averages across an industry may give estimates of relative expected changes in industry growth (e.g. the market's imputed expectation that an industry is about to "take-off" or stagnate). Naturally, any differences in IGAR between stocks in the same industry may be due to differences in fundamentals, and would require further specific analysis.

Market Criteria (Potential Price)

Some feel that if the stock is listed in a well-organized stock market, with a large volume of transactions, the market price will reflect all known information relevant to the valuation of the stock. This is called the efficient-market hypothesis.

On the other hand, studies made in the field of behavioral finance tend to show that deviations from the fair price are rather common, and sometimes quite large.

Thus, in addition to fundamental economic criteria, market criteria also have to be taken into account market-based valuation. Valuing a stock requires not just an estimate its fair value, but also to determine its potential price range, taking into account market behavior aspects. One of the behavioral valuation tools is the stock image, a coefficient that bridges the theoretical fair value and the market price.

Types of Stock Valuation

Stock valuation methods can be primarily categorized into two main types: absolute and relative.

Absolute

Absolute stock valuation relies on the company's fundamental information. The method generally involves the analysis of various financial information that can be found in or derived from a company's financial statements. Many techniques of absolute stock valuation primarily investigate the company's cash flows, dividends, and growth rates. Notable absolute stock valuation methods include the dividend discount model (DDM) and the discounted cash flow model (DCF).

Relative

Relative stock valuation concerns with the comparison of the investment with similar companies. The relative stock valuation method deals with the calculation of the key financial ratios of similar companies and derivation of the same ratio for the target company. The best example of relative stock valuation is comparable companies analysis.

An Example of Stock Valuation

If someone offered you a machine that was guaranteed to (legally) give you $10 per year, and the machine had zero maintenance costs, what would be a sensible amount of money to pay for this machine? It would depend on a few factors.

- The $10 represents owner's profit, or free cash flows. This is money you get free and clear.

- Due to the time value of money, $10 next year is not as valuable to you as $10 this year. Why? Because you could take $10 this year and probably invest it and turn it into $10.50 or $11 by next year.

This second point brings up the purpose of discounting. You have to discount the future money by an appropriate value in order to translate it into today's value. How much you discount it by can vary. You could, for example, use a "risk-free" rate of return, such as the yield on a U.S. Government Treasury Bill. Or, you could use Weighted Average Cost of Capital (WACC). More appropriately (and simply) in my view, what you should usually use is your targeted rate of return.

If you want to get, say, a 10% rate of return on your money, then you should use a discount rate of 10%. You may also alter it depending on your estimation of the level of risk involved. For a higher risk investment I'd use a higher discount rate (perhaps 12% or so), while in very defensive and reliable business I may use a discount rate of a bit under 10%. A famous quote by Buffett is that you can't compensate for risk with a high discount rate, and that's true in my view. I don't recommend using particularly high discount rates.

So how much is $10 a year from now, worth to you today, if you seek a 10% rate of return on your money? The answer is $9.09. If you had $9.09 right now, and you could invest that money at an annual rate of 10%, then you could turn that $9.09 into $10 in one year, since $9.09 multiplied by 1.1 equals $10. So $10 one year from now is only worth $9.09 to you today.

I calculated that via this equation: DPV = FV / (1 + r), where DPV means "discounted present value", and FV means "future value", and r is my discount rate (which in this case is 10% or 0.1). The $10 is future value, and I want to know the discounted present value of that ten dollars, so I divide the FV by (1 + 0.1) to get the DPV of that money.

If you wanted to know what $10 that you'll get in two years is worth today, you make a minor adjustment to that equation, and use DPV = FV / (1 + r)^2, since the discount rate must be applied for two years. The answer is that receiving $10 two years from now is worth $8.26 to you today, since you can take $8.26 and multiply it by 1.1, and then multiply it by 1.1 again, to get $10.

So we see that DPV = FV / (1 + r)^n, for a given future value.

If we have a sum of annual future cash flows, then the equation is this:

DPV = (FV1)/(1+r) + (FV2)/(1+r)^2 + ... + (FVn)/(1+r)^n

These are some of the well-known stock valuation equations.

Now, going back to the example, how much is the machine worth to you if it's guaranteed to give you $10 per year, forever, and you desire a 10% rate of return on your current money?

When it gives you $10 in one year, this money has a present value of $9.09.

When it again gives you $10 in two years, this money has a present value of $8.26.

When it again gives you $10 in three years, this money has a present value of $7.51.

The farther in the future the same $10 is, the less it's worth to you today, since it would take a smaller sum for you to compound to that amount.

The machine, therefore, is equal in value to all of its discounted future cash flows, which is a key aspect of stock valuation. In one year, it produces $10, which is worth $9.09 to you today. A year after that, it produces another $10, which is only worth $8.26 to you today. And so forth. If the machine operates forever, it technically produces an infinite amount of cash, but it's certainly not worth paying an infinite amount of money for, since you want a good rate of return on your current money.

If you sum up the next 25 years of discounted cash flows from this machine ($9.09 + $8.26 + $7.51...for 25 years), you'll calculate a value of $90.77. (The 25th year of $10 is only worth $0.92 to you today; the discounting makes the cash flows rather negligible over time). If, instead, you sum up the next 50 years of discounted cash flows from this machine, you'll calculate a value of $99.22. If, instead, you sum up the next 75 years of discounted free cash flows from this machine, you'll calculate a value of $99.92.

At this point, you should see that the answer is approaching $100, like a limit in calculus. A few decades was sufficient to show us this.

If you desire a 10% rate of return, and it's able to be proven that the machine works like it says it will, and will produce $10 per year forever with no maintenance costs, then it is an objective fact that this machine is worth $100 to you. If you were to buy it at that value, it would be appropriate, and you would meet your target rate of return. If you could buy the same machine for less than $100, even better! If those machines only sell for over $100, then you either need to reduce your expectations of rate of return on your money, or invest elsewhere. When it comes to stock valuation, investors unfortunately aren't that patient.

Suppose you made a side hobby out of buying those machines. Some machines produce $20 every year. Some produce $100 every year. Some produce $10 the first year, and then $11, and then $12, and then $13, and so on. Some even shrink, so perhaps they produce $50 the first year, then $49, then $48, and so forth. You could go around, finding people who are selling them, and take the time to inspect them to make sure they are legitimate and in good condition. Then you could perform discounted cash flow analysis on them with a target rate of return in mind, and then buy the machines and build a portfolio of them if you can get them for at-or-under my calculated fair price. And you calculate the fair price by summing up all future cash flows, and then discounting them based on your targeted rate of return. Each machine is worth to you a sum equal to the sum of all future discounted cash flows. The same is true for stock valuation.

It doesn't matter whether the machine produces the same amount each year, or produces a growing amount, or even a shrinking amount. You can add up all future cash flows, discount them to the current value of that money, sum those discounted cash flows up, and buy for an amount equal to or under that price. Of course, any growth or lack thereof in the cash flows affects the value of the discounted cash flows and therefore the total value of the investment itself.

We could even get more complicated, and say that a machine produces $10 in profits each year, but requires $1 in maintenance each year. In that case, only $9 is "free cash flow", and that's the number we'd have to use in our calculations.

We could apply this powerful equation of discounted cash flow to all sorts of machines, and make good money.

Suppose, however, that 1 in 20 of those machines actually breaks. In order to make sure you still get your desired 10% rate of return, you'll need to buy most of your machines at a mild discount, so that when the occasional machine breaks, you'll still do well overall with a diversified portfolio of these machines. That's the concept of a margin of safety, and that's how we build a collection of the best dividend stocks.

Stock Valuation Methods

Discounted Cash Flow Methods

The absolute valuation approach attempts to find intrinsic value of a stock by discounting future cash flows at an discount rate which reflects the risk inherent in the stock. Hence, it is also called discounted cash flow approach. Common discounted cash flow valuations model includes single-stage dividend discount model (also called Gordon Growth Model), multi-stage dividend discount model and free cash flow valuation.

Constant Growth Dividend Discount Model

The constant growth dividend discount model (DDM) (also called single-stage dividend discount model or Gordon Growth Model) is appropriate for valuation of a minority stake in mature dividend-paying companies. Stock value under the DDM equals the discounted present value of dividends per share expected to grow at a constant rate.

$$\text{Stock Value} = \frac{D_0 \times (1+g)}{r - g}$$

Where D_0 is current dividend per share per annum, r is the required return on equity (i.e. cost of equity) and g is the growth rate of dividends i.e. the sustainable growth rate which equals the product of retention ratio (1 − dividend payout ratio) and return on equity (ROE):

$$g = (1 - \text{Dividend Payout Ratio}) \times \text{ROE}$$

Multi-stage Dividend Discount Model

The multi-stage dividend discount model can be used to value minority stake in companies which are expected to have abnormal growth rate for some initial period, say 5 years, and the growth rate is expected to stabilize in the long-run. Dividend per share per annum are forecasted based on actual growth rate in initial years, the value of stock at the end of initial high-growth period (called terminal value) is determined using the single-stage dividend growth model or using some price multiple such as P/E ratio and the dividends and the terminal value are discounted at the required return on equity (i.e. cost of equity).

$$\text{Stock Value} = \frac{D_1}{(1+r)^1} + \frac{D_2}{(1+r)^2} + \ldots + \frac{D_n}{(1+r)^n} + \frac{V_n}{(1+r)^n}$$

Where D_1, D_2 and D_n are the dividend per share at the end of Year 1, Year 2 and Year n and V_n is the terminal value.

Free Cash Flow Models

The free cash flow valuation models can be used to value a majority i.e. controlling ownership based on free cash flows of the company which equals the cash flows from operating activities less any expected changes in working capital less any expected capital expenditure.

The single-stage free cash flow model discounts the expected free cash flows at the end of Year 1 at the weighted average cost of capital.

$$\text{Stock Value} = \frac{FCF_1}{WACC - g}$$

Where FCF_1 is the free cash flow at the end of Year 1, WACC is the weighted average cost of capital and g is the growth rate of free cash flows.

Stock value under the multi-stage free cash flow valuation model can be determined as follows:

$$\text{Stock Value} = \frac{FCF_1}{(1+W)^1} + \frac{FCF_2}{(1+W)^2} + \ldots + \frac{FCF_n}{(1+W)^n} + \frac{V_n}{(1+W)^n}$$

The value determined using the free cash flow models is the total firm value and the market value of debt must be subtracted to arrive at the equity value.

There are two other free cash flow models which discount free cash flow to equity (FCFE) (instead of the free cash flow to firm) using the required return on equity (instead of the weighted average cost of capital). The value determined using free cash flow to equity (FCFE) models is the equity value.

Chepakovich Valuation M

The Chepakovich valuation model is a specialized discounted cash flow valuation model, originally designed for the valuation of "growth stocks" (ordinary/common shares of companies experiencing high revenue growth rates), and subsequently applied to the valuation of high-tech companies even those that are (currently) unprofitable. Relatedly, it is a general valuation model and can also be applied to no-growth or negative growth companies. In fact, in the limiting case of no growth in revenues, the model yields similar (but not identical) results to a regular discounted cash flow to equity model. The model was developed by Alexander Chepakovich in 2000 and enhanced in subsequent years.

Features and Assumptions

The key distinguishing feature of the Chepakovich valuation model is separate forecasting of fixed (or quasi-fixed) and variable expenses for the valuated company Unlike other methods of valuation of loss-making companies, which rely primarily on use of comparable valuation ratios, and, therefore, provide only relative valuation, the Chepakovich valuation model estimates intrinsic (i.e. fundamental) value. Such companies initially have high fixed costs (relative to revenues) and small or negative net income. However, high rate of revenue growth insures that gross profit (defined here as revenues minus variable expenses) will grow rapidly in proportion to fixed expenses. This process will eventually lead the company to predictable and measurable future profitability.

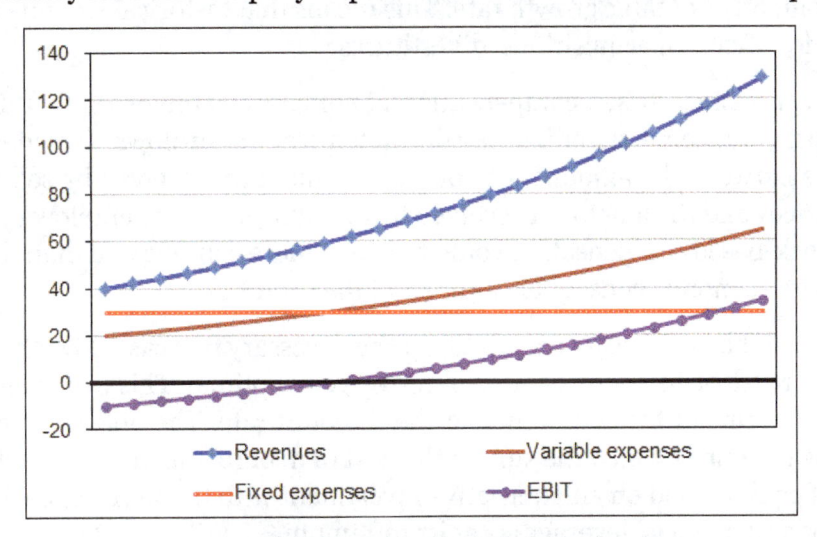

The model assumes that fixed expenses will only change at the rate of inflation or other predetermined rate of escalation, while variable expenses are set to be a fixed percentage of revenues (subject to efficiency improvement/degradation in the future – when this can be foreseen). Chepakovich suggested that the ratio of variable expenses to total expenses, which he denoted as variable cost ratio, is equal to the ratio of total expenses growth rate to revenue growth rate. This feature makes possible valuation of start-ups and other high-growth companies on a fundamental basis, i.e. with determination of their intrinsic values.

Other features of the model:

- Variable discount rate (depends on time in the future from which cash flow is discounted to the present) to reflect investor's required rate of return (it is constant for a particular investor) and risk of investment (it is a function of time and riskiness of investment). The base for setting the discount rate is the so-called risk-free rate, i.e. the yield on a corresponding zero-coupon Treasury bond. The riskiness of investment is quantified through use of a risk-rating procedure.

- Company's investments in means of production (it is the sum of tangible and intangible assets needed for a company to produce a certain amount of output – we call it 'production base') is set to be a function of the revenue growth (there should be enough production capacity to provide increase in production/revenue). Surprisingly many discounted cash flow (DCF) models used today do not account for additional production capacity need when revenues grow.

- Long-term convergence of company's revenue growth rate to that of GDP. This follows from the fact that combined revenue growth of all companies in an economy is equal to

GDP growth and from an assumption that over- or underperformance (compared to the GDP) by individual companies will be eliminated in the long run (which is usually the case for the vast majority of companies – so vast, indeed, that the incompliant others could be treated as a statistical error).

- Valuation is conducted on the premise that change in company's revenue is attributable only to company's organic growth rate. This means that historical revenue growth rates are adjusted for effects of acquisitions/divestitures.

- Factual cost of stock-based compensation of company's employees that does not show in the company's income statement is subtracted from cash flows. It is determined as the difference between the amount the company could have received by selling the shares at market prices and the amount it received from selling shares to employees (the actual process of stock-based compensation could be much more complicated than the one described here, but its economic consequences are still the same).

- It is assumed that, subject to availability of the necessary free cash flow, the company's capital structure (debt-to-equity ratio) will converge to optimal. This would also have an effect on the risk rating of the company and the discount rate. The optimal capital structure is defined as the one at which the sum of the cost of debt (company's interest payments) and its cost of equity (yield on an alternative investment with the same risk – it is a function of the company's financial leverage) is at its minimum.

Dividend Discount Model

The dividend discount model (DDM) is a method of valuing a company's stock price based on the theory that its stock is worth the sum of all of its future dividend payments, discounted back to their present value. In other words, it is used to value stocks based on the net present value of the future dividends. The equation most widely used is called the Gordon growth model (GGM). It is named after Myron J. Gordon of the University of Toronto, who originally published it along with Eli Shapiro in 1956 and made reference to it in 1959. Their work borrowed heavily from the theoretical and mathematical ideas found in John Burr Williams 1938 book "The Theory of Investment Value."

The variables are: P is the current stock price. g is the constant growth rate in perpetuity expected for the dividends. r is the constant cost of equity capital for that company. D_1 is the value of the next year's dividends.

$$= \frac{D_1}{r-g}$$

Derivation of Equation

The model uses the fact that the current value of the dividend payment $D_0(1+g)^t$ at (discrete) time t is $\frac{D_0(1+g)^t}{(1+r)^t}$, and so the current value of all the future dividend payments, which is the current price P, is the sum of the infinite series.

$$P_0 = \sum_{t=1}^{\infty} D_0 \frac{(1+g)^t}{(1+r)^t}$$

This summation can be rewritten as

$$P_0 = D_0 r'(1 + r' + r'^2 + r'^3 + ...)$$

where:

$$r' = \frac{(1+g)}{(1+r)}.$$

The series in parenthesis is the geometric series with common ratio r' so it sums to $\frac{1}{1-r'}$ if $r'^2 < 1$. Thus,

$$P_0 = \frac{D_0 r'}{1-r'}$$

Substituting the value for r' leads to

$$P_0 = \frac{D_0 \frac{1+g}{1+r}}{1 - \frac{1+g}{1+r}},$$

which is simplified by multiplying by $\frac{1+r}{1+r}$, so that

$$P_0 = \frac{D_0(1+g)}{r-g}$$

Income Plus Capital Gains Equals Total Return

The DDM equation can also be understood to state simply that a stock's total return equals the sum of its income and capital gains.

$$\frac{D_1}{r-g} = P_0 \text{ is rearranged to give } \frac{D_1}{P_0} + g = r$$

Dividend Yield (D_1 / P_0) plus Growth (g) equal Cost of Equity (r)

Consider the dividend growth rate in the DDM model as a proxy for the growth of earnings and by extension the stock price and capital gains. Consider the DDM's cost of equity capital as a proxy for the investor's required total return.

Income + Capital Gain = Total Return

Growth cannot Exceed Cost of Equity

From the first equation, one might notice that $r-g$ cannot be negative. When growth is expected to exceed the cost of equity in the short run, then usually a two-stage DDM is used:

$$P = \sum_{t=1}^{N} \frac{D_0(1+g)^t}{(1+r)^t} + \frac{P_N}{(1+r)^N}$$

Therefore,

$$P = \frac{D_0(1+g)}{r-g}\left[1 - \frac{(1+g)^N}{(1+r)^N}\right] + \frac{D_0(1+g)^N(1+g_\infty)}{(1+r)^N(r-g_\infty)},$$

where g denotes the short-run expected growth rate, g_∞ denotes the long-run growth rate, and N is the period (number of years), over which the short-run growth rate is applied.

Even when g is very close to r, P approaches infinity, so the model becomes meaningless.

Some Properties of the Model

- When the growth g is zero, the dividend is capitalized.

$$P_0 = \frac{D_1}{r}.$$

- This equation is also used to estimate the cost of capital by solving for r.

$$r = \frac{D_1}{P_0} + g.$$

- which is equivalent to the formula of the Gordon Growth Model.

$$P_0 = D_1 / (k - g)$$

where "P_0" stands for the present stock value, "D_1" stands for expected dividend per share one year from the present time, "g" stands for rate of growth of dividends, and "k" represents the required return rate for the equity investor.

Problems with the Model

- The presumption of a steady and perpetual growth rate less than the cost of capital may not be reasonable.
- If the stock does not currently pay a dividend, like many growth stocks, more general versions of the discounted dividend model must be used to value the stock. One common technique is to assume that the Modigliani-Miller hypothesis of dividend irrelevance is true, and therefore replace the stocks's dividend D with E earnings per share. However, this requires the use of earnings growth rather than dividend growth, which might be different.

This approach is especially useful for computing a residual value of future periods.

- The stock price resulting from the Gordon model is sensitive to the growth rate chosen.

Related Methods

The dividend discount model is closely related to both discounted earnings and discounted cash-flow models. In either of the latter two, the value of a company is based on how much money is made by the company. For example, if a company consistently paid out 50% of earnings as dividends, then the discounted dividends would be worth 50% of the discounted earnings. Also, in the dividend discount model, a company that does not pay dividends is worth nothing.

Dividend Discount Model Example

In this dividend discount model example, assume that you are considering the purchase of a stock which will pay dividends of $20 (Div 1) next year, and $21.6 (Div 2) the following year. After receiving the second dividend, you plan on selling the stock for $333.3 What is the intrinsic value of this stock if your required return is 15%?

Solution:

This dividend discount model example can be solved in 3 steps:

Step 1 – Find the present value of Dividends for Year 1 and Year 2.

- PV (year 1) = $20/((1.15)^1).
- PV(year 2) = $20/((1.15)^2).
- In this example, they come out to be $17.4 and $16.3 respectively for 1st and 2nd year dividend.

Step 2 – Find the Present value of future selling price after two years.

- PV(Selling Price) = $333.3 / (1.15^2).

Step 3 – Add the Present Value of Dividends and present value of Selling Price.

- $17.4 + $16.3 + $252.0 = $285.8.

	Year 0	Year 1	Year 2
Dividend payments	-	$20.0	$21.6
PV (Dividends) @ 15%		$17.4	$16.3
Stock Price			$333.3
PV (Stock) @ 15%			=H17/(1+0.15)^2
Intinsic Value	$0.0	$17.4	$268.4
Total Instrinsic Value	$285.8		

Types of Dividend Discount Models

Now that we have understood the very foundation of Dividend Discount Model, let us move forward and learn about three types of Dividend Discount Models.

- Zero Growth Dividend Discount Model – This model assumes that all the dividends that are paid by the stock remain one and same forever until infinite.

- Constant Growth Dividend Discount Model – This dividend discount model assumes that dividends grow at a fixed percentage annually. They are not variable and are constant throughout.

- Variable Growth Dividend Discount Model or Non Constant Growth –This model may divide the growth into two or three phases. The first one will be a fast initial phase, then a slower transition phase an then ultimately ends with a lower rate for the infinite period.

Zero-growth Dividend Discount Model

Zero-growth model assumes that the dividend always stays the same i.e. there is no growth in dividends. Therefore, the stock price would be equal to the annual dividends divided by the required rate of return.

Stock's Intrinsic Value = Annual Dividends / Required Rate of Return

This is basically the same formula used to calculate the Present Value of Perpetuity, and can be used to price preferred stock, which pays a dividend that is a specified percentage of its par value. A stock based on the zero-growth model can still change in price if the required rate changes when perceived risk changes, for instance.

Zero Growth Dividend Discount Model – Example

If a preferred share of stock pays dividends of $1.80 per year, and the required rate of return for the stock is 8%, then what is its intrinsic value?

Solution:

Here we use the dividend discount model formula for zero growth dividend,

Dividend Discount Model Formula = Intrinsic Value =Annual Dividends / Required Rate of Return

Intrinsic Value = $1.80/0.08 = $22.50.

The shortcoming of the model above is that you'd expect most companies to grow over time.

Constant-growth Rate DDM Model

The constant-growth Dividend Discount Model or the Gordon Growth Model assumes that dividends grow by a specific percentage each year,

Can you value Google, Amazon, Facebook, Twitter using this method? Ofcourse not as these companies do not give dividends and more importantly are growing at a much faster rate. Constant growth models can be used to value companies that are mature whose dividends increase steadily over the years.

Let us look at Walmart's Dividends paid in the last 30 years. Walmart is a mature company and we note that the dividends have steadily increased over this period. This company can be a candidate that can be valued using constant-growth Dividend Discount Model.

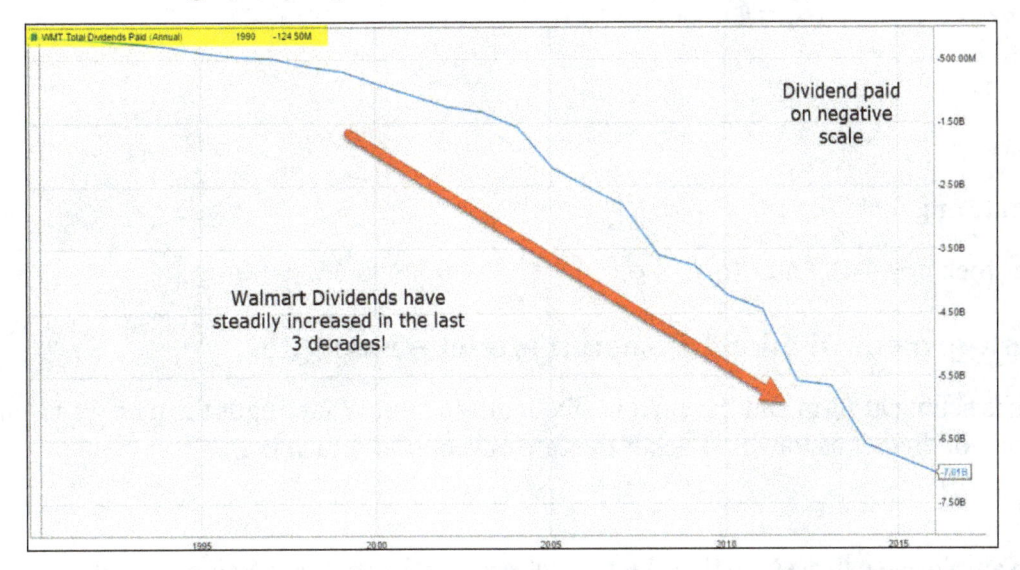

[Chart: Walmart Dividends have steadily increased in the last 3 decades! Dividend paid on negative scale]

Please note that in constant-growth Dividend Discount Model, we do assume that the growth rate in dividends is constant, however, the actual dividends outgo increases each year.

Growth rates in dividends is generally denoted as g, and the required rate is denoted by Ke. Another important assumption that you should note is the the required rate or Ke also remains constant every year.

Constant growth Dividend Discount Model or DDM Model gives us the present value of an infinite stream of dividends that are growing at a constant rate.

Constant-growth Dividend Discount Model formula is as per below:

$$Value\_stock = \frac{D_0(1+g)}{(K_e + g)} = \frac{D_1}{(K_e + g)}$$

Where:

- D_1 = Value of dividend to be received next year.
- D_0 = Value of dividend received this year.
- g = Growth rate of dividend.
- Ke = Discount rate.

Constant-growth Dividend Discount Model

Example:

If a stock pays a $4 dividend this year, and the dividend has been growing 6% annually, then what will be the intrinsic value of the stock, assuming a required rate of return of 12%?

Solution:

$$Value\_stock = \frac{D_0(1+g)}{(K_e-g)} = \frac{D_1}{(K_e-g)}$$

D1 = $4 x 1.06 = $4.24

Ke = 12%

Growth rate or g = 6%

Intrinsic stock price = $4.24 / (0.12 – 0.06) = $4/0.06 = $70.66

Constant-growth Dividend Discount Model – Example

If a stock is selling at $315 and the current dividends is $20. What might the market assuming the growth rate of dividends for this stock if the rate of required return is 15%?

Solution:

In this example, we will assume that the market price is the Intrinsic Value = $315.

This implies,

$315 = $20 x (1+g) / (0.15 – g)

If we solve the above equation for g, we get the implied growth rate as 8.13%.

Variable-growth Rate DDM Model (Multi-Stage Dividend Discount Model)

Variable Growth rate Dividend Discount Model or DDM Model is much closer to reality as compared to the other two types of dividend dicount model. This model solves the problems related to unsteady dividends by assuming that the company will experience different growth phases.

Variable growth rates can take different forms, you can even assume that the growth rates are different for each year. However, the most common form is one that assumes 3 different rates of growth:

- An initial high rate of growth,
- A transition to slower growth,
- Lastly, a sustainable, steady rate of growth.

Primarily, the constant-growth rate model is extended, with each phase of growth calculated using the constant-growth method, but using different growth rates for the different phases. The present values of each stage are added together to derive the intrinsic value of the stock.

Two stage Dividend Discount Model DDM

This model is designed to value the equity in a firm, with two stages of growth, an initial period of higher growth and a subsequent period of stable growth.

Two-stage Dividend Discount Model; best suited for firms paying residual cash in dividends while having moderate growth. For instance, it is more reasonable to assume that a firm growing at 12% in the high growth period will see its growth rate drops to 6% afterwards.

My take is that the companies with a higher dividend payout ratios may fit such a model. As we note below such two companies – Coca-Cola and PepsiCo. Both companies continue to pay dividends regularly and their dividend payout ratio is between 70-80%. In addition, these two companies show relatively stable growth rates.

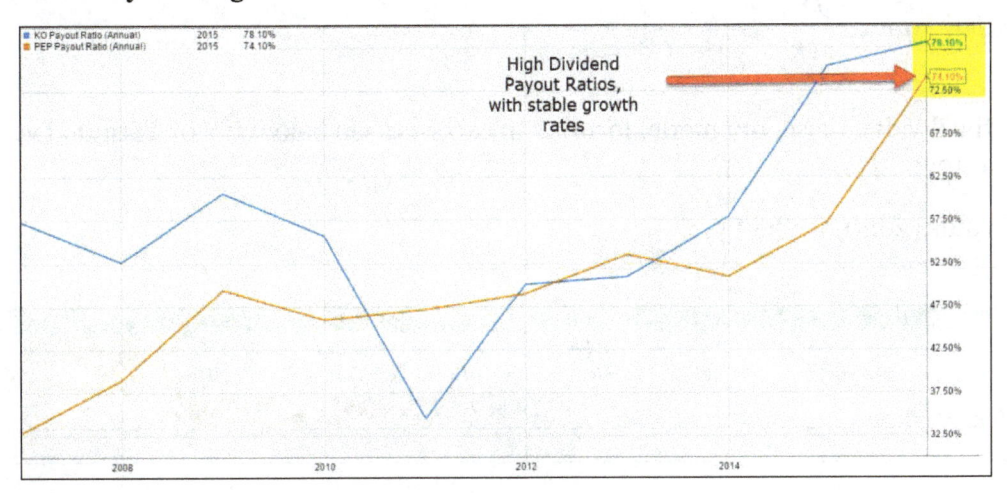

Assumptions

- Higher growth rate is expected the first period.
- This higher growth rate will drop at the end of the first period to a stable growth rate.
- The dividend payout ratio is consistent with the expected growth rate.

Two-stage DDM Model – Example

Check Mate forecasts that its dividend will grow at 20% per year for the next four years before settling down at a constant 8% forever. Dividend (current year,2016) = $12; Expected rate of return = 15%. What is the value of the stock now?

Step 1 : Calculate the dividends for each year till stable growth rate is reached.

The first component of value is the present value of the expected dividends during the high growth period. Based upon the current dividends ($12), the expected growth rate (15%) value of dividends (D1,D2,D3), can be computed for each year in the high growth period.

Stable growth rate is achieved after 4 years. Hence, we calculate the Dividend profile until 2010.

	Current				
	2016	2017	2018	2019	2020
Dividend	$12.0	=F85*(1+G86)	$17.3	$20.7	$24.9
Growth rate in dividends		20.0%	20.0%	20.0%	20.0%
Terminal Value					$0.0

Introduction to Asset Management

Step 2: Apply Dividend Discount Model to calculate the Terminal Value (Price at the end of high growth phase).

We can use the Dividend Discount Model at any point in time. Here, in this example the dividend growth is constant for first four years and then it decreases, so we can calculate the price that a stock should sell for in four years i.e. the terminal value at the end of the high growth phase (2020). This can be estimated using the Constant Growth Dividend Discount Model Formula:

$$Value\_stock = \frac{D_N(1+g)}{(K_e - g)} = \frac{D_{N+1}}{(K_e - g)}$$

We apply the dividend discount model formula in excel as seen below. TV or Terminal value at the end of year 2020.

Terminal value (2020) is $383.9.

	Current 2016	2017	2018	2019	2020	2021
Dividend	$12.0	$14.4	$17.3	$20.7	$24.9	$26.9
Growth rate in dividends	na	20.0%	20.0%	20.0%	20.0%	8.0%
Terminal Value			TV at 2020		=K85/(F95-K86)	

Step 3: Find the present value of all the projected dividends.

Present value of dividends during the high growth period (2017-2020) is given below. Please note that in this example, required rate of return is 15%.

	Current 2016	2017	2018	2019	2020	2021
Dividend	$12.0	$14.4	$17.3	$20.7	$24.9	$26.9
Growth rate in dividends	na	20.0%	20.0%	20.0%	20.0%	8.0%
Terminal Value					$383.9	
PV of Cash Flows		$12.5	$13.1 =I85/(1+F94)^3		$14.2	
PV of Terminal Value						
Sum						
Expected return	15.0%		Ke			

Step 4: Find the present value of Terminal Value.

Present value of Terminal value = $219.5

	Current 2016	2017	2018	2019	2020	2021
Dividend	$12.0	$14.4	$17.3	$20.7	$24.9	$26.9
Growth rate in dividends	na	20.0%	20.0%	20.0%	20.0%	8.0%
Terminal Value					$383.9	
PV of Cash Flows		$12.5	$13.1	$13.6	$14.2	
PV of Terminal Value					=I88/(1+F94)^4	
Sum						
Expected return	15.0%		Find the present value of Terminal value			

Step 5 : Find the Fair Value – the PV of Projeted Dividends and the PV of Terminal Value.

As we already know that Intrinsic value of the stock is the present value of its future cash flows. Since we have calculated the Present value of Dividends and Present value of Terminal Value, the sum total of both will reflect the Fair Value of the Stock.

Fair Value = PV(projected dividends) + PV(terminal value).

Fair Value come to $273.0.

	Current 2016	2017	2018	2019	2020	2021
Dividend	$12.0	$14.4	$17.3	$20.7	$24.9	$26.9
Growth rate in dividends	na	20.0%	20.0%	20.0%	20.0%	8.0%
Terminal Value					$383.9	
PV of Cash Flows		$12.5	$13.1	$13.6	$14.2	
					$219.5	
	=SUM(G90:J90,I91)		Intrinsic value or Fair Value			
Expected return	15.0%					

We can also find out the effect of changes in expected rate of return to the Fair Price of the stock. As we note from the graph below that the expected rate of return is extremely sensitive to the required rate of return. Due care should be taken to calculate the required rate of return. Required rate of return is professionally calculated using the CAPM Model.

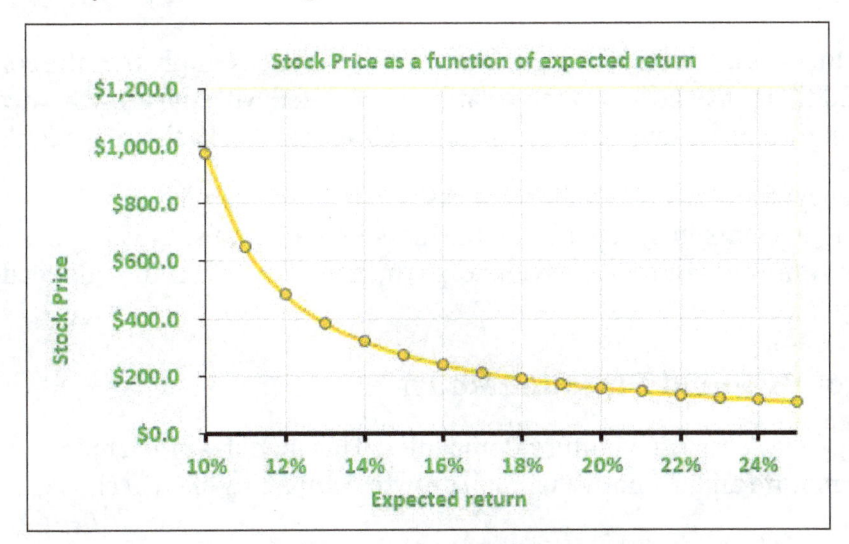

Three Stage Dividend Discount Model DDM

One improvement that we can make to the two-stage DDM Model is to allow the growth rate to change slowly rather than instantaneously.

The three-stage Dividend Discount Model or DDM Model is given by:

- First phase: there is a constant dividend growth (g1) or with no dividend.
- Second phase: there is a gradual dividend decline to the final level.

- Third phase: there is a constant dividend growth again (g3), i.e. the growth company opportunities are over.

The logic that we applied to two-stage model can be applied to three-stage model in a similar fashion. Below is the dividend discount model formula for applying three stage.

$$V_0 = \sum_{t=1}^{T} \frac{D_0(1+g)^t}{(1+k)^t} + \sum_{t=T+1}^{N} \frac{D_t}{(1+k)^t} + \frac{D_{N+1}}{(k-g_3)(1+k)^N}$$

My advise would be to not get intimidated by this dividiend discount model formulas. Just try and apply the logic that we used in the two stage dividend discount model. Only change will be that there will one more growth rate in between the high growth phase and the stable phase. For this growth rate, you need to find out the respective dividends and its present values.

If you want to find more examples of dividend paying stocks, you can refer to Dividend Aristocrat List. This list contains 50 stocks with dividend paying history of 25+ years.

Advantages of Dividend Discount Model

- Sound Logic: The dividend discount model tries to value of the stock based on all the future cash flow profile. Here the future cash flows is nothing but the dividends. In addition, there is very less subjectivity in the mathematical model, and hence, many analyst show faith in this model.

- Mature Business: The regular payment of dividends does imply that the company has matured and there may not be much volatility associated with the growth rates and earnings. This is important for investors who prefer to invest in stocks that pay regular dividends.

- Consistency: Since dividends in most cases is paid by cash, companies tend to keep their dividend payments in sync with the business fundamentals. This implies that companies may not want to manipulate dividend payments as they can directly lead to stock price volatility.

Limitations of Dividend Discount Model

- Can only be used to value Mature Companies: This model is efficient in valuing companies that are mature and cannot value high growth companies like Facebook, Twitter, Amazon and others.

- The sensitivity of Assumptions: As we saw earlier, fair price is highly sensitive to growth rates and required rate of return. 1 percent change in these two can affect the valuation of the company by as much as 10-20%.

- May not be related to earnings: In theory, dividends should be correlated to the earnings of the company. On the contrary, companies, however, try to maintain a stable dividend payout instead of the variable payout based on earnings. In many cases companies have even borrowed cash to pay dividends.

Earnings Multiple Approach

One of the quickest ways to check how highly valued a stock is, is to look at its price-to-earnings ratio (P/E), also known as an earnings multiple.

The earnings multiple is the stock price divided by earnings per share (EPS), and the units are expressed in years- how many years of those earnings it would take to equal that stock price.

For example, if a stock is $50, and its EPS is $2.50, then the earnings multiple is 20. The stock price is expressed in dollars, the EPS is expressed in dollars per year, so the earnings multiple of 20 is expressed in years- it would take twenty years of $2.50 each year to get $50.

Of course, the earnings multiple alone doesn't tell us much. If the company is growing its EPS each year, then in reality it will take less than that number of years for cumulative EPS to sum to the current stock price. Therefore, what constitutes a "fair" earnings multiple depends on several factors like growth and stability.

Proving a Fair Earnings Multiple

Often, earnings multiples are just used to compare two companies within the same industry, or used to compare for the same stock at two different points in time. It can also be used to check the valuation of the entire market, like with the Shiller P/E ratio.

However, using other valuation methods like the Dividend Discount Model or Discounted Cash Flow Analysis, you can determine an intrinsically fair stock price for a company, based on expected future profitability and a target rate of return. Playing around with those valuation methods, and checking the P/E ratios of those calculated fair values, provides an investor with experience about what earnings multiples are fair compared to certain amounts of growth and stability. Once an investor has that intuitive understanding, it's easy to do back-of-the-envelope calculations about stocks, easy to look at an earnings multiple, expected growth, and have a reasonable estimate of how fair is, etc.

The Earnings Multiple Valuation Approach

Having an intuitive understanding of what constitutes a "fair range" of earnings multiples for a stock, relative to stability and expected growth, allows an investor to calculate some scenarios about future stock price. This method can serve as an alternative to doing Discounted Cash Flow Analysis, and can be used whether or not the company pays a dividend.

The method is to estimate EPS growth over a period of years, then place a hypothetical earnings multiple on the EPS figure at the end of that period, and compare that hypothetical stock price to the current stock price, which can allow for quick calculation of expected rate of return over that period. There are three components to the final value:

- The final stock price at the end of the period.
- Cumulative dividends received over that period.
- The impact of cumulatively reinvesting those dividends.

An Example:

Suppose a railroad company, called "DM Rail" currently has EPS of $2, pays annual dividends of $1, and has a stock price of $40. Since 40/2 is 20, the earnings multiple is 20.

You think that's a little bit high, would rather see a lower earnings multiple, but decide to look at the track record of growth along with future company plans to make a 10-year estimate. Based on previous growth, management goals for EPS growth, explanations of how they'll reach those goals, and other factors, you estimate a 10% rate of EPS growth over the next ten years, and assume that the dividend payout will stay the same, so the dividend also grows by 10% per year.

The table of growth would like something like this:

Year	EPS	Dividend
0	$2.00	$1.00
1	$2.20	$1.10
2	$2.42	$1.21
3	$2.66	$1.33
4	$2.93	$1.46
5	$3.22	$1.61
6	$3.54	$1.77
7	$3.90	$1.95
8	$4.29	$2.14
9	$4.72	$2.36
10	$5.19	$2.59

The numbers of Year 0 are the trailing twelve month period that you're looking at, so the holding period, if you buy the stock, would be years 1-10 (for a ten year holding period).

You believe that the earnings multiple is a bit rich currently, but feel that the company has this fairly strong growth ahead, and would like to simulate what would happen if, over time, the market decides to lower the earnings multiple of the stock. You assume an earnings multiple of 16 is fair.

Ten years from now, if the company grows as expected, EPS will be about $5.19, and 16 * $5.19 = $83.04. That's the estimated stock price 10 years from now, but we still have to take into account dividends.

The cumulative dividend value over that ten year period (year 1 through year 10, just adding up ten years of dividends) was $17.52, which was calculated with a simple spreadsheet. But, assuming we didn't just collect dividends and leave them in an account, and instead reinvested them somehow (either back into the stock or into another investment), then those dividends have a time value and made more money during the decade, which we now have to take into account.

We can say, roughly, that dividends can be invested for an 8% rate of return, which is close to and a bit under the S&P 500 average rate of return, just to be on the conservative side. Assuming that, then these dividends, calculated with a fairly straightforward spreadsheet formula, mean that an additional $6.38 was generated over this period due to the money made from reinvesting those dividends. That calculation assumes dividends were reinvested annually- assuming a quarterly reinvestment rate will change the value by a few extra pennies.

If you're not using a spreadsheet, and you want to also use an 8% assumed rate of return for the dividends over a ten year period, then you can say that the amount generated from reinvested dividends was about a third of the total cumulative dividend value (in this case, $6.38/$17.52 = 36%). So, that's just a quick shortcut. Rather than calculating the effect of reinvested dividends each time, if you're assuming an 8% rate of return and a ten year period, you can just take cumulative dividends, and then add another 1/3rd of the cumulative dividends which represents the reinvested value of those dividends.

So, the total value at the end of this period is:

Final Stock Price) + (Cumulative Dividends) + (Value From Reinvested Dividends)

Using the shortcut, it's just:

(Final Stock Price) + (1.33 * Cumulative Dividends)

In this example, using the longer method, the final value is:

$83.04 + $17.52 + $6.38 = $106.94.

This means that over this ten year projected period, $40 turned into $106.94, which translates into an annualized rate of return of 10.3%, even though the earnings multiple dropped from 20 to 16. This simulation can be run in various ways for different rates of EPS/dividend growth, different final earnings multiples as assigned by the market at that time, in order to determine a range of scenarios that might happen. This can give you an idea of what some poor scenarios are, as well as some fair scenarios or particularly bullish scenarios.

References

- Valuing-of-assets, boundless-accounting: courses.lumenlearning.com, Retrieved 19 August, 2019
- Business-valuation-methods-2948478: thebalance.com, Retrieved 23 April, 2019
- Absolute-valuation-formula: investopedia.com, Retrieved 31 March, 2019
- Stock-valuation, trading-investing: corporatefinanceinstitute.com, Retrieved 15 May, 2019
- Dividend-discount-model: wallstreetmojo.com, Retrieved 18 January, 2019
- Earnings-multilple-approach-to-valuation: dividendmonk.com, Retrieved 26 June, 2019
- Stock-valuation, trading-investing: corporatefinanceinstitute.com, Retrieved 28 July, 2019

Diverse Aspects of Asset Management

CHAPTER 6

Some of the diverse aspects of asset management are funds management, infrastructure asset management, digital asset management and mobile enterprise asset management. This chapter closely examines these key concepts of asset management to provide an extensive understanding of the subject.

FUNDS MANAGEMENT

Funds management is the overseeing and handling of a financial institution's cash flow. The fund manager ensures that the maturity schedules of the deposits coincide with the demand for loans. To do this, the manager looks at both the liabilities and the assets that influence the bank's ability to issue credit.

Funds management – also referred to as asset management – covers any kind of system that maintains the value of an entity. It may be applied to intangible assets (e.g., intellectual property and goodwill), and tangible assets (e.g., equipment and real estate). It is the systematic process of operating, deploying, maintaining, disposing, and upgrading assets in the most cost-efficient and profit-yielding way possible.

A fund manager must pay close attention to cost and risk to capitalize on the cash flow opportunities. A financial institution runs on the ability to offer credit to customers. Ensuring the proper liquidity of the funds is a crucial aspect of the fund manager's position. Funds management can also refer to the management of fund assets.

In the financial world, the term "fund management" describes people and institutions that manage investments on behalf of investors. An would be investment managers who fix the assets of pension funds for pension investors.

Fund management may be divided into four industries: the financial investment industry, the infrastructure industry, the business and enterprise industry, and the public sector.

Financial Fund Management

The most common use of "fund management" refers to investment management or financial management, which are within the financial sector responsible for managing investment funds for client accounts. The fund manager's duties include studying the client's needs and financial goals, creating an investment plan, and executing the investment strategy.

Classifying Fund Management

Fund management can be classified according to client type, the method used for management, or the investment type.

When classifying fund management according to client type, the fund managers are either business fund managers, corporate fund managers, or personal fund managers who handle investment accounts for individual investors. Personal fund managers cover smaller investment portfolios compared to business fund managers. These funds may be controlled by one fund manager or by a team of many fund managers.

Some funds are managed by hedge fund managers who earn from an upfront fee and a certain percentage of the fund's performance, which serves as an incentive for them to perform to the best of their abilities.

Types of Fund Management

The types of Fund Management can be classified by the Investment type, Client type or the method used for management. The various types of investments managed by fund management professionals include:

- Mutual Funds,
- Trust Funds,
- Pension Funds,
- Hedge Fund,
- Equity fund management.

When classifying management of a fund by client, fund managers are generally personal fund managers, business fund managers or corporate fund managers. A personal fund manager typically deals with small quantum of investment funds and an individual manager can handle multiple lone funds.

Offering Investment management services includes extensive knowledge of:

- Financial Statement Analysis,
- Creation and Maintenance of Portfolio,
- Asset Allocation and Continuous Management.

Fund Management Styles

There are various fund management styles and approaches:

Growth Style

The managers using this style have a lot of emphasis on the current and future Corporate Earnings and are even prepared to pay a premium on securities having strong growth potential. The growth stocks are generally the cash-cows and are expected to be sold at prices in the northern direction.

Growth managers select companies having a strong competitive edge in their respective sectors. A high level of retained earnings is the expectation for such scripts to be successful as it makes the Balance Sheet of the firm very strong to attract investors. This can be coupled with a limited dividend distributed and low debt on the books making it a definite pick by the managers. The scripts which are part of such a style will have a relatively high turnover rate since as they are frequently traded in large quantities. The returns on the portfolio are made up of Capital gains resulting from stock trades.

The style produces attractive results when markets are bullish but the portfolio managers require to show talent and flair for achieving investment objectives during downward spirals.

Fidelity® Blue Chip Growth Fund (FBGRX)

Major Market Sectors (AS OF 6/30/2017)

Sector	Portfolio Weight	Russell 1000 Growth
Information Technology	42.95%	36.15%
Consumer Discretionary	27.10%	18.64%
Health Care	11.42%	13.66%
Consumer Staples	6.06%	7.63%
Industrials	4.97%	12.30%
Financials	3.87%	3.36%
Energy	1.64%	0.82%
Materials	1.52%	3.86%
Telecommunication Services	0.29%	0.95%
Real Estate	0.09%	2.60%
Utilities	0.01%	0.01%
Other	0.00%	0.00%

Growth at Reasonable Price

The Growth at Reasonable Price style will use a blend of Growth and Value investing for constructing the portfolio. This portfolio will usually include a restricted number of securities which are showing consistent performance. The sector constituents of such portfolios could be slightly different from that of the benchmark index in order to take advantage of growth prospects from these selected sectors since their ability can be maximised under specific conditions.

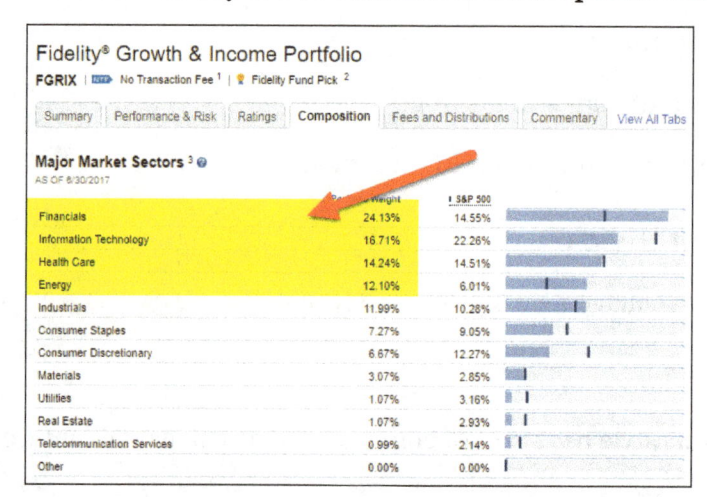

Fidelity® Growth & Income Portfolio (FGRIX)

Major Market Sectors (AS OF 6/30/2017)

Sector	Portfolio Weight	S&P 500
Financials	24.13%	14.55%
Information Technology	16.71%	22.26%
Health Care	14.24%	14.51%
Energy	12.10%	6.01%
Industrials	11.99%	10.28%
Consumer Staples	7.27%	9.05%
Consumer Discretionary	6.67%	12.27%
Materials	3.07%	2.85%
Utilities	1.07%	3.16%
Real Estate	1.07%	2.93%
Telecommunication Services	0.99%	2.14%
Other	0.00%	0.00%

Value Style

Managers following such a response will thrive on bargaining situations and offers. They are on the hunt for securities which are undervalued in relation to their expected returns. Securities could be undervalued even due to the fact they do not hold preference with the investors for multiple reasons.

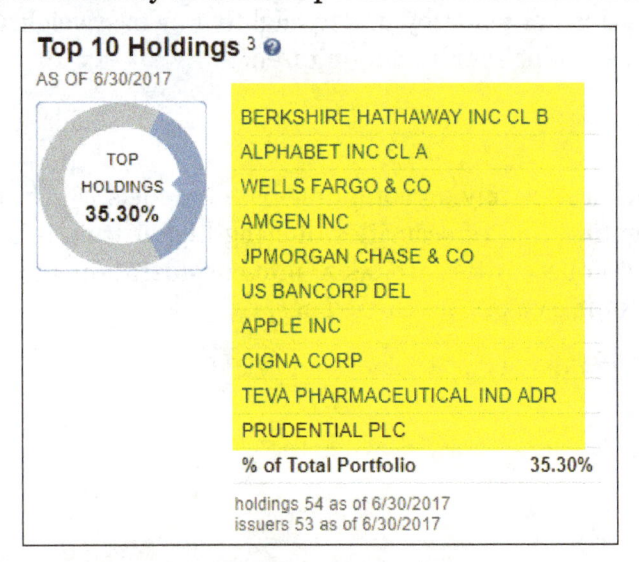

```
Top 10 Holdings 3
AS OF 6/30/2017

TOP HOLDINGS 35.30%

BERKSHIRE HATHAWAY INC CL B
ALPHABET INC CL A
WELLS FARGO & CO
AMGEN INC
JPMORGAN CHASE & CO
US BANCORP DEL
APPLE INC
CIGNA CORP
TEVA PHARMACEUTICAL IND ADR
PRUDENTIAL PLC

% of Total Portfolio          35.30%

holdings 54 as of 6/30/2017
issuers 53 as of 6/30/2017
```

The managers generally purchase the equities at low prices and tend to hold them till they reach their peak depending on the time frame expected and hence the portfolio mix will also stay stable. The value system performs at its peak during the bearish situation, although managers do take the benefits in situations of a bullish market. The objective is to extract the maximum benefit before it reaches its peak.

Fundamental Style

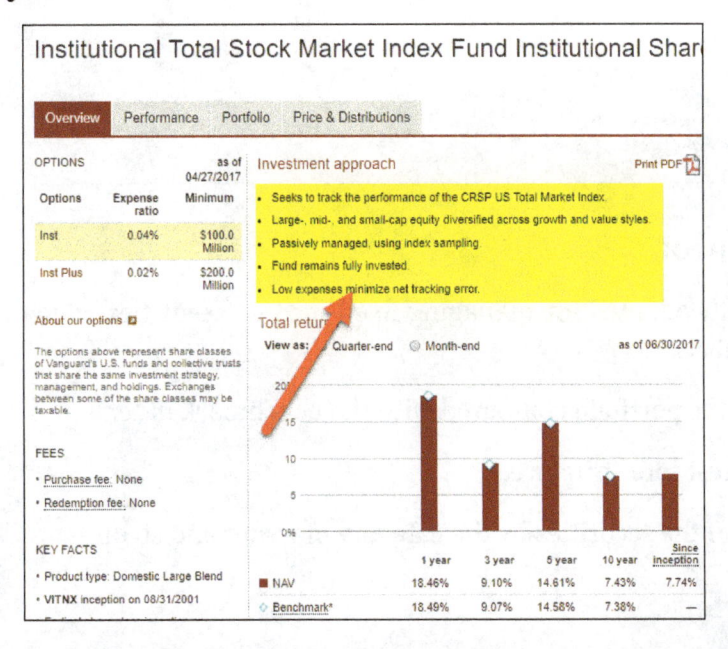

```
Institutional Total Stock Market Index Fund Institutional Shares

Overview | Performance | Portfolio | Price & Distributions

OPTIONS                  as of 04/27/2017      Investment approach                     Print PDF

Options    Expense    Minimum       • Seeks to track the performance of the CRSP US Total Market Index.
           ratio                    • Large-, mid-, and small-cap equity diversified across growth and value styles.
Inst       0.04%      $100.0        • Passively managed, using index sampling.
                      Million       • Fund remains fully invested.
Inst Plus  0.02%      $200.0        • Low expenses minimize net tracking error.
                      Million

About our options

The options above represent share classes
of Vanguard's U.S. funds and collective trusts
that share the same investment strategy,
management, and holdings. Exchanges
between some of the share classes may be
taxable.

                                    Total returns
                                    View as:   Quarter-end   Month-end            as of 06/30/2017

FEES
• Purchase fee: None
• Redemption fee: None

KEY FACTS                                         1 year   3 year   5 year   10 year   Since inception
• Product type: Domestic Large Blend    NAV       18.46%   9.10%    14.61%   7.43%     7.74%
• VITNX inception on 08/31/2001         Benchmark* 18.49%  9.07%    14.58%   7.38%     —
```

This is the basic and one of the most defensive styles which aim to match the returns of the benchmark index by replicating its sector breakdown and capitalization. The managers will strive to add value to the existing portfolio. Such styles are generally adopted by mutual funds to maintain a cautious approach since many retail investors with limited investments expect a basic return on their overall investment.

Portfolios managed according to this style are highly diversified and contains a large number of securities. The Capital gains are made by underweighting or overweighting certain securities or sectors with the differences being regularly monitored.

Quantitative Style

The managers using such a style rely on computer-based models which track the trends of price and profitability for identification of securities offering higher than market returns. Only basic data and objective criteria of securities are taken into consideration and no quantitative analysis of the issuer companies or its sectors are carried out.

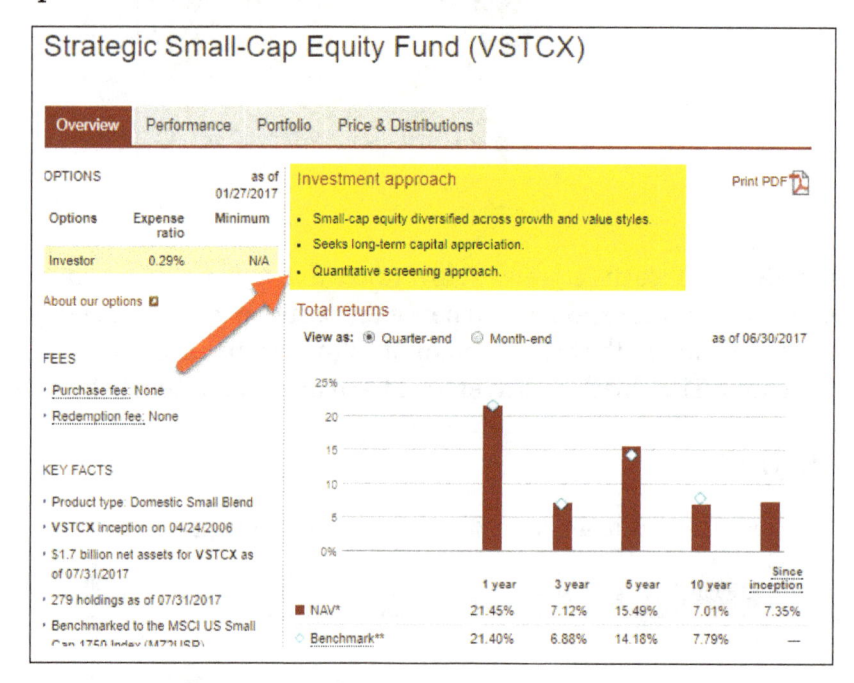

Risk Factor Control

This style is generally adopted for managing fixed-income securities which take into account all elements of risk such as:

- Duration of the portfolio compared with the benchmark index.
- Overall interest rate structure.
- Breakdown of the securities by the category of issuer and so on.

Bottoms-Up Style

The selection of the securities is based on the analysis of individual stocks with less emphasis on the significance of economic and market cycles. The investor will concentrate their efforts on a specific company instead of the overall industry or the economy. The approach is the company exceeding expectations despite industry or the economy not doing well.

The managers usually employ long-term strategies with a buy and hold approach. They will have a complete understanding of an individual stock and the long-term potential of the script and the company. The investors will take advantage of short-term volatility in the market for maximising their profits. This is done by quickly entering and exiting their positions.

Top-Down Investing

This approach of investment involves considering the overall condition of the economy and then further breaking down various components into minute details. Subsequently, analysts examine various industrial sectors for selection of those scripts which are expected to outperform the market.

Investors will look at the macroeconomic variables such as:

- GDP (Gross Domestic Product).
- Trade Balances.
- Current Account Deficit.
- Inflation and Interest rate.

Based on such variables the managers will reallocate the monetary assets for earning capital gains rather than extensive analysis on a single company or sector. For instance, if economic growth is doing well in South East Asia as compared to the domestic growth of the EU (European Union), investors may shift assets internationally by making a purchase of ETF's (Exchange-traded funds) that track the targeted countries in Asia.

INFRASTRUCTURE ASSET MANAGEMENT

Infrastructure asset management is the integrated, multidisciplinary set of strategies in sustaining public infrastructure assets such as water treatment facilities, sewer lines, roads, utility grids, bridges, and railways. Generally, the process focuses on the later stages of a facility's life cycle, specifically maintenance, rehabilitation, and replacement. Asset management specifically uses software tools to organize and implement these strategies with the fundamental goal to preserve and extend the service life of long-term infrastructure assets which are vital underlying components in maintaining the quality of life in society and efficiency in the economy.

Infrastructure asset management is a specific term of asset management focusing on physical, rather than financial assets. Sometimes the term infrastructure management is used to mean the same thing, most notably in title of The International Infrastructure Management Manual (2000, first edition). Where there is no problem of confusion, the term asset management is more widely used, as in the professional societies: the Asset Management Council in Australia, and the Institute of Asset Management in the UK. In this context, infrastructure is a wide term denoting road and rail, water, power, etc. assets. Road asset management is part of infrastructure asset management including all the physical assets on the road network such as roads, bridges, culverts and road furniture.

The first published use of the term asset management to refer to physical assets is not known for sure. The earliest adopter known for certain is Dr Penny Burns in 1984. The New Zealand Infrastructure Asset Management Manual published in 1996 is an early use of the specific term infrastructure asset management Home - NAMS NZ. The term "asset management" was first used in a document published in 1983 by the United States Department of Transportation, Federal Highway Administration entitled: Transportation Resource Management Strategies for Elected Officials of Rural Municipalities and Counties. That document consisted of seven chapters of resource management strategies for each of two types of transportation infrastructure - roads & bridges and public transportation. Each of these two parts of the document focused on the following seven categories: Planning, Prioritization, Contracting Out, Innovative Finance, Human Resource Management, Asset Management and Performance Measurement & Reporting.

After decades of capital investment in United States's infrastructure such as the Interstate Highway System, local water treatment facilities, electric transmission and utility lines, the need to sustain such infrastructure experiences mounting challenges. The current duress includes tight state and local budgets, deferral of needed maintenance funding, and political pressures to cut public spending. Today, shrinking federal appropriations, progressively aging capital stock, and parochial statuses and interest groups have inhibited flexible procurement strategies. And with the rise of design firms, professional societies, licensures, construction and industry associations, and related specialties the management of the infrastructure system has dramatically altered. As a result, the life cycle of a facility, including Planning, Design, Construction, Operations, Maintenance, Upgrading, and Replacement, has become bifurcated between agencies and firms where Design and Construction becomes contracted separately from Operations and Maintenance. The push for more dual-track strategies and not segmented ones such as Design-Build and Build-Operate-Transfer helps in maintaining public facilities. Yet, over time, the government apparatus focused more on start-up capital expenses for constructing public assets without focused monies on maintenance.

After World War II, with the policies of the Roosevelt Administration, economic boom of the 1950s, and rise in Federalism, public projects became financed through direct government funding. Additionally, the federal government began setting criteria and procedures for architects and engineers to comply on federal construction and related projects. State and local statutes soon followed suit. Over the years, a large bureaucratic machine began administering infrastructure projects through Design-Bid-Build and debt financing methods. This led to hyper-competition of federal, states, and localities over scant federal resources and overall fostered a limited approach in life-cycle attention (namely, no account of operation and maintenance). Asset management attempts to fill in the gaps of such fragmentation for better performance in infrastructure assets.

In Canada, the majority of municipal assets were built between 1960s to 1970s. The average age of municipal infrastructure has increased since the end of the late 1970s, because investment has been insufficient to replace deteriorating assets. This deficit could be the result a shift in financing policy at the end of 1970s, which made the local governments responsible to fund the municipal assets. Recently, in Ontario municipalities are required to develop an asset management plan to receive provincial fund.

Processes and Activities

The basic premise of infrastructure asset management is to intervene at strategic points in an asset's normal life cycle to extend the expected service life, and thereby maintain its performance. Typically, a long-life-cycle asset requires multiple intervention points including a combination of repair and maintenance activities and even overall rehabilitation. Costs decrease with planned maintenance rather than unplanned maintenance. Yet, excessive planned maintenance increases costs. Thus, a balance between the two must be recognized. While each improvement raises an asset's condition curve, each rehabilitation resets an asset's condition curve, and complete replacement returns condition curve to new level or upgraded level. Therefore, strategically timing these interventions will aid in extending an asset's life cycle. A simple working definition of asset management would be: first, assess what you have; then, assess what condition it is in; and lastly, assess the financial burden to maintain it at a targeted condition.

Essential processes and activities for infrastructure asset management include the following:

- Maintaining a systematic record of individual assets (an inventory)—e.g., acquisition cost, original service life, remaining useful life, physical condition, repair and maintenance consistency.

- Developing a defined program for sustaining the aggregate body of assets through planned maintenance, repair, and replacement.

- Implementing and managing information systems in support of these systems—e.g., Geographic Information Systems.

These processes and activities are interrelated and interdependent aspects that usually cross organizational boundaries including finance, engineering, and operations. Hence, asset management is a comprehensive approach in handling an immense portfolio of public and private capital stock. As example, in 2009, the IBM Maximo software was adopted to manage the maintenance of rolling stock and facilities for three railway systems: the Long Island Rail Road, San Francisco BART system, Washington metrorail. Also, recently, wireless sensors, totaling 663, have been installed on South Korea's Jindo Bridge to detect structural cracks and corrosion. Though in a testing phase among three universities in South Korea, United States, and Japan, the use of wireless technology to may lend itself to future, cost-efficient asset management.

In 2014, ISO published an international management system standard for asset management. The ISO 55000 series provides terminology, requirements and guidance for implementing, maintaining and improving an effective asset management system.

Work Practices

Politically, many legal and governmental initiatives have emphasized proactive asset management given the current state of an aging infrastructure and fiscal challenges. Recent developments include the Governmental Accounting Standards Board Statement No. 34 that required state and local entities to report in their accounting *all* infrastructure assets not only the privately financed ones such as water supply and utilities paid by user fees. This helps to determine an agency's overall infrastructure asset inventory, timely assessment of physical condition, and annual projection of financial requirements. Additionally, the United States Environmental Protection Agency's Capacity, Management, Operation, and Maintenance (CMOM) initiative works to move away from the compliance-mandate enforcement to proactive partnership with public managers to self-audit their infrastructure systems in assessing capacity, management, and operations/maintenance.

Still other proponents for proactive management include judicial consent decrees for facility managers to resolve noncompliance with environmental standards set by EPA or state environmental protection departments (i.e., laws against sewer overflows); post-9/11 security vulnerability analyses; funding legislation that specifies asset management as qualifying condition to receive/keep award; and professional organizations that are moving the industry to asset management through education, research, and workshops.

Despite the current challenges of the time's financial constraints, one advantage is the growing availability of methodology and technology to employ asset management. But while municipalities have made significant investments and use of software tools in the last 20 years, they are mostly stand-alone systems with limited to no capability for sharing or exchanging information with other tools. Consequently, they operate in isolated silos of information across municipal departments. Data has to be re-interpreted, transformed, and reentered into different software tools several times leading to time-consuming, prone-to-error inefficiencies. Many in academia and industry recognize the need for integrated, multidisciplinary asset management that involves:

- Systemization and coordination of work processes.
- Development of centralized share data repositories.
- Organization of distributed software tools into modular, extensive-wide software environments.

IIAM Approach

The Institute of Infrastructure Asset Management (IIAM), a U.S.-based transportation consultancy, works to promote the same issues and collaborates with other organizations, such as in the INFRAASSETS2010 conference in Malaysia, in management of public assets.

The IIAM approach to infrastructure asset management is based upon the definition of a Standard of Service (SoS) that describes how an asset will perform in objective and measurable terms. The SoS includes the definition of a "minimum condition grade", which is established by considering the consequences of a failure of the infrastructure asset.

The key components of "Infrastructure Asset Management" are:

- Definition of a Standard of Service:
  - Establishment of measurable specifications of how the asset should perform.
  - Establishment of a minimum condition grade.
- Establishment of a whole-life cost approach to managing the asset.
- Elaboration of an Asset Management Plan.

GIS System

Public asset management expands the definition of Enterprise Asset Management (EAM) by incorporating the management of all things which are of value to a municipal jurisdiction and its citizen's expectations. Public Asset Management is the term that considers the importance that public assets affect other public assets and work activities which are important sources of revenue for municipal governments and has various points of citizen interaction. The versatility and functionality of a GIS system allow for the control and management of all assets and land-focused activities. All public assets are interconnected and share proximity, and this connectivity is possible through the use of GIS. GIS-centric public asset management standardizes data and allows interoperability, providing users the capability to reuse, coordinate, and share information in an efficient and effective manner.

Among the GISs in use for infrastructure management in the USA are GE Smallworld and ESRI. An ESRI GIS platform combined with the overall public asset management umbrella of both physical *hard* assets and *soft* assets helps remove the traditional silos of structured municipal functions which serves the citizens. While the hard assets are the typical physical assets or infrastructure assets, the soft assets of a municipality includes permits, license, code enforcement, right-of-ways and other land-focused work activities.

DIGITAL ASSET MANAGEMENT

Operations on a collection of digital assets require the use of a computer application implementing digital asset management (DAM) to ensure that the owner, and possibly their delegates, can perform operations on the data files.

Management Operations on Digital Assets

Creation

To make a data object into a digital asset it must first be brought into the digital domain as a computer file, or digital object.

Applications implement digital asset management by importing them from the analog and/or digital domains (by encoding, scanning, optical character recognition, etc.) or by authoring them as new objects.

Indexing

A primary function of a DAM system is to make assets easily available to its users by providing a searchable index that supports retrieval of assets by their content and/or metadata. The cataloging function is usually part of the ingestion process for new assets.

Workflow

Digital assets will typically have a lifecycle, which may include various states such as creation, approval, live, archived and deleted. Many systems allow custom workflows to be created, modelling different asset lifecycles depending on their use within the organisation.

Version Control

Often a DAM system will store earlier versions of a digital asset and allow those to be downloaded or reverted to. Therefore, a DAM system can operate as an advanced type of version control system.

Access Control

Finally, a DAM system typically includes security controls ensuring relevant people have access to assets. This will often involve integration with existing directory services via a technology such as single sign-on.

Categorization

Smaller DAM systems are used in a particular operational context, for instance in video production systems. The key differentiators between them are the types of input encoders used for creating digital copies of assets to bring them under management, and the output decoders and/or formatters used to make them usable as documents and/or online resources. The metadata of a content item can serve as a guide to the selection of the codec(s) needed to handle the content during processing, and may be of use when applying access control rules to enforce authorization policy.

Assets that require particular technology to be used in a workflow need to have their requirements for bandwidth, latency, and access control considered in the design of the tools that create or store them, and in the architecture of the system that distributes and archives them. When not being worked on assets can be held in a DAM in a variety of formats including blob (binary large object in a database) or as a file in a normal file system, that are "cheaper" to store than the form needed during operations on them. This makes it possible to implement a large scale DAM as an assembly of high performance processing systems in a network with a high density storage solution at its centre.

Media Asset Issues

An asset can exist in several formats and in a sequence of versions. The digital version of the original asset is generally captured in as high a resolution, colour depth, and (if applicable) frame rate as will be needed to ensure that results are of acceptable quality for the end-use. There can also be thumbnail copies of lower quality for use in visual indexing.

Metadata for an asset can include its packaging, encoding, provenance, ownership and access rights, and location of original creation. It is used to provide hints to the tools and systems used to work on, or with, the asset about how it should be handled and displayed.

Types of Systems

Digital asset management systems fall into the following classifications:

- Brand management system to enforce brand presentation within an organization by making the approved logos, fonts, and product images easily available.

- Library or archive for bulk storage of infrequently changing video or photo assets.

- Production management systems for handling assets being created on the fly for use in live media production or as visual effects for use in gaming applications, TV, or films.

- Streaming for on-demand delivery of digital content, like TV shows or movies, to end users on behalf of digital retailers.

All of these types will include features for work-flow management, collaboration, project-management, and revision control.

MOBILE ENTERPRISE ASSET MANAGEMENT

Mobile enterprise asset management (or mobile EAM) refers to the mobile extension of work processes for maintenance, operations and repair of corporate or public-entity physical assets, equipment, buildings and grounds. It involves management of work orders (planned, break/fix or service requests) via communication between a mobilized workforce and computer systems to maintain an organization's facilities, structures and other assets.

The idea behind mobile EAM as a business practice is that it enables remote workers – employees who spend part or all of their time away from a central office – access to data from the organization's computer application software for enterprise asset management (commonly referred to as an enterprise system, EAM system or backend system), typically using a handheld or other mobile computer. This is to distinguish from the term mobile asset management, which refers more broadly to the actual tools, instruments and containers organizations use to track and secure equipment and other such assets frequently on the move.

In the mobile EAM process, the organization eliminates a need for paper forms or other data reporting and communication methods (push-to-talk and radio) to move work order information to and from the point where the work is being performed.

While enterprise asset management encompasses the management of an organization's entire asset portfolio across processes including equipment addition/ reduction, replacement, over-hauling, redundancy setup and maintenance budgets, mobile enterprise asset management is focused, by definition, strictly on the wireless automation of asset management data for such processes.

Mobile EAM Technology

When viewed and used on a handheld device, mobile work order applications provide details such as location, stepwise job plans, safety alerts, lock-outs and prior work history on the asset, giving a maintenance technician or other remote worker more detailed asset information as well as the ability to transmit work data to the organization's enterprise system when completed – through a wireless network, docking station or other synchronization method.

Using computer software to achieve standard mobile EAM practices, organizations often report such advantages as an increase in timely, accurate data flow between their remote workers and central management such as planners and schedulers, which thereby improves capital and labor allocation decision processes (including an ability to schedule more planned/preventive maintenance work).

With the proliferation of smartphone and other mobile computing technologies, asset managers can expect an ever more tech-savvy workforce, lower costs in mobile devices and a higher propensity of feature-rich, workflow-specific mobile applications.

Challenges

Nearly all challenges in mobile EAM practices can be traced to two factors: time and labor resources (including IT or information technology management) and investment costs.

Developing and implementing a mobile application architecture on the enterprise scale is not an easy undertaking by any means, as mobile applications are faced with a diversity of device operating systems, output media (voice and data) and connectivity methods, contrasting with a PC (personal computer) environment where in most cases software requires relatively few, if major, updates and lower upfront costs. Organizations looking to implement mobile EAM applications often seek the help of technology consulting firms and spend months researching, planning and selecting an implementation strategy.

Industries using Mobile EAM

The use of mobile enterprise application platforms (MEAPs), designed around service-oriented architecture principles for multiple systems integration and custom modification, and other forms of wireless computing technology for mobile EAM solutions is growing rapidly, particularly in industries where physical assets form a significant cost proportion of organizations' total assets. These industries can include:

- Facilities management.
- Utilities.
- Life sciences.
- Government organizations.
- Manufacturing.
- Oil and gas industry.
- Transportation industry.

In such high-value asset scenarios, the asset lifecycle improvements introduced by the increase in enterprise data flow of mobile EAM processes can bring significant savings, particularly when part of an enterprise-wide capital and labor management strategy that integrates multiple systems in an enterprise architecture (EAM system, mobile EAM application, labor dispatch / scheduling software, GIS, etc.).

Market Growth

In a 2009 study, market analyst Gartner, Inc. forecasted, "for the MEAP and packaged mobile application market. We now expect market growth annually of 15 to 20% through 2013." Gartner attributes this anticipated growth to enterprises' increasing willingness (and ability) to extend decision-relevant information to employees, who are themselves increasingly mobile.

For EAM practices as a whole, this means that an increasing proportion of organizations in capital-intensive industry sectors (such as those above) are adopting mobile technology as an integral part of their enterprise asset management strategy – corresponding with an enterprise-wide emphasis on whole life planning, life cycle costing, planned and proactive maintenance and other industry best practices.

CAPITAL APPRECIATION

Capital appreciation is an increase in the price or value of assets. It may refer to appreciation of company stocks or bonds held by an investor, an increase in land valuation, or other upward revaluation of fixed assets.

Capital appreciation may occur passively and gradually, without the investor taking any action. It is distinguished from a capital gain which is the profit achieved by selling an asset. Capital appreciation may or may not be shown in financial statements; if it is shown, by revaluation of the asset, the increase is said to be "recognized". Once the asset is sold, the appreciation since the date of initially buying the asset becomes a "realized" gain.

When the term is used in reference to stock valuation, capital appreciation is the goal of an investor seeking long term growth. It is growth in the principal amount invested, but not necessarily an increase in the current income from the asset.

In the context of investment in a mutual fund, capital appreciation refers to a rise in the value of the securities in a portfolio which contributes to the growth in net asset value. A capital appreciation fund is a fund for which it is its primary goal, and accordingly invests in growth stocks.

EVENT STUDY

An event study is a statistical method to assess the impact of an event on the value of a firm. For example, the announcement of a merger between two business entities can be analyzed to see whether investors believe the merger will create or destroy value. The basic idea is to find the abnormal return attributable to the event being studied by adjusting for the return that stems from the price fluctuation of the market as a whole. The event study was invented by Ball and Brown (1968).

As the event methodology can be used to elicit the effects of any type of event on the direction and magnitude of stock price changes, it is very versatile. Event studies are thus common to various research areas, such as accounting and finance, management, economics, marketing, information technology, law, political science, operations and supply chain management.

One aspect often used to structure the overall body of event studies is the breadth of the studied event types. On the one hand, there is research investigating the stock market responses to economy-wide events (i.e., market shocks, such as regulatory changes, or catastrophic events). On the other hand, event studies are used to investigate the stock market responses to corporate events, such as mergers and acquisitions, earnings announcements, debt or equity issues, corporate reorganisations, investment decisions and corporate social responsibility.

Methodology

The general event study methodology is explained in, for example, MacKinlay or Mitchell and Netter. In MacKinlay, this is done "using financial market data" to "measure the impact of a specific event on the value of a firm". He argues that "given rationality in the marketplace, the effects of an event will be reflected immediately in security prices. Thus a measure of the event's economic impact can be constructed using security prices observed over a relatively short time period". It is important to note that short-horizon event studies are more reliable than long-horizon event studies as the latter have many limitations. However, Kothari and Warner were able to refine long-horizon methodologies in order to improve the design and reliability of the studies over longer periods.

Empirical Methods

Methodologically, event studies imply the following: Based on an estimation window prior to the analyzed event, the method estimates what the normal stock returns of the affected firm(s) should be at the day of the event and several days prior and after the event (i.e., during the event window). Thereafter, the method deducts this 'normal returns' from the 'actual returns' to receive 'abnormal returns' attributed to the event.

Event studies, however, may differ with respect to their specification of normal returns. The most common model for normal returns is the 'market model'. Following this model, the analysis implies to use an estimation window (typically sized 120 days) prior to the event to derive the typical relationship between the firm's stock and a reference index through a regression analysis. Based on the regression coefficients, the normal returns are then projected and used to calculate the abnormal returns. Alternative models for the normal returns include the CAPM model, or more simplistic approaches such as mean returns.

Calculation of Abnormal Returns

Depending on the model chosen for the 'normal return', conducting event studies requires the researcher to implement a distinct sequence of steps. For the most common model, the 'market model', the steps are as follows:

- Retrieve and match time series of financial returns of the focal firm's stock and its reference index.

- For each event, identify the sequences of firm and market returns that need to be included in the estimation window.

- Using regression analysis, calculate the alpha, beta and sigma coefficients that explicate the typical relationship between the stock and the reference index.

- With these three parameters, predict the 'normal returns' for all days of the event window.
- Deducting these 'normal returns' from the 'actual returns' gives you the 'abnormal returns' which are the metrics of interest.

Significance of Abnormal Returns

To specify if individual abnormal returns differ from zero with some statistical validity, test statistics need to be applied. Various test statistics at the different levels of analysis (i.e., AR-, CAR-, AAR- and CAAR-level) exist for this purpose. The most common test, the t-test, divides the abnormal returns through the root mean square error of the regression. Resulting t-values need then to be compared with the critical values of the Student's t-distribution. There is some evidence that during times of high volatility (e.g. financial crisis of 2007–2008), too many companies tend to show significantly abnormal returns using the t-test, which makes it more difficult to determine which returns are truly "abnormal".

Software for Conducting Event Studies

Event studies can be implemented with various different tools. Single event studies can easily be implemented with MS Excel, event studies covering multiple events need to be built using statistical software packages (e.g., STATA, Matlab). Besides of these multi-use tools, there are solutions tailored to conducting event study analyses (e.g., Eventus, Event Study Metrics, EventStudyTools).

Application to Merger Analysis

The logic behind the event study methodology (within the specific context of mergers) is explained in Warren-Boulton and Dalkir (2001):

> Investors in financial markets bet their dollars on whether a merger will raise or lower prices. A merger that raises market prices will benefit both the merging parties and their rivals and thus raise the prices for all their shares. Conversely, the financial community may expect the efficiencies from the merger to be sufficiently large to drive down prices. In this case, the share values of the merging firms' rivals fall as the probability of the merger goes up. Thus, evidence from financial markets can be used to predict market price effects when significant merger-related events have taken place.

Warren-Boulton and Dalkir (2001) apply their event-probability methodology to the proposed merger between Staples, Inc. and Office Depot (1996), which was challenged by the Federal Trade Commission and eventually withdrawn.

Findings

Warren-Boulton and Dalkir (2001) find highly significant returns to the only rival firm in the relevant market. Based on these returns, they are able to estimate the price effect of the merger in the product market which is highly consistent with the estimates of the likely price increase from other independent sources.

ASSET/LIABILITY MODELING

Asset/liability modeling is the process used to manage the business and financial objectives of a financial institution or an individual through an assessment of the portfolio assets and liabilities in an integrated manner. The process is characterized by an on-going review, modification, and revision of asset and liability management strategies so that sensitivity to interest rate changes are confined within acceptable tolerance levels. There are different models used and some use different elements, according to specific needs and contexts. For instance, an individual or an organization may keep parts of the ALM process and outsource the modeling function or adapt the model according to the requirements and capabilities of relevant institutions such as banks, which often have their in-house modeling process. For pensioners, asset/liability modeling is all about determining the best allocation for specific situations. There is a vast array of models available today for practical asset and liability modeling and these have been the subject of several research and studies.

Asset/Liability Modeling (Pension)

The ongoing financial crisis drove the 100 largest corporate pension plans to a record $300 billion loss of funded status in 2008. In the wake of these losses, many pension plan sponsors have been led to re-examine their pension plan asset allocation strategies, to consider the risk exposures to the plans and to the sponsors. A recent study indicates that many corporate defined benefit plans fail to address the full range of risks facing them, especially the ones related to liabilities. Too often, the study says, corporate pensions are distracted by concerns that have nothing to do with the long-term health of the fund. Asset/liability modeling is an approach to examining pension risks and allows the sponsor to set informed policies for funding, benefit design, and asset allocation.

Asset/liability modeling goes beyond traditional, asset-only analysis of the asset allocation decision. Traditional asset-only models analyze risk and reward in terms of investment performance. Asset/liability models take a comprehensive approach to analyze risk and reward in terms of the overall pension plan impact. An actuary or investment consultant may look at expectations and downside risk measures on the present value of contributions, plan surplus, excess returns (asset return less liability return), asset returns, and any number of other variables. The model may consider measures over 5, 10 or 20 year horizons, as well as quarterly or annual value at risk measures.

Pension plans face a variety of liability risks including price and wage inflation risk, interest rate risk and longevity risk. While some of these risks materialize slowly over time, others – such as interest rate risk – are felt with each measurement period. Liabilities are the actuarial present value of future plan cash flows, discounted at current interest rates. Thus, asset/liability management strategies often include bonds and swaps or other derivatives to accomplish some degree of interest rate hedging (immunization, cash flow matching, duration matching, etc.). Such approaches are sometimes called "liability-driven investment" (LDI) strategies. In 2008, plans with such approaches strongly outperformed those with traditional "total return" seeking investment policies.

Asset/Liability Studies

Successful asset/liability studies: Increase a plan sponsor's understanding of the pension plan's current situation and likely future trends:

- Highlight key asset and liability risks that should be considered.
- Help establish a cohesive risk management framework.
- Analyze surplus return, standard deviation, funded status, contribution requirements and balance sheet impacts.
- Consider customized risk measures based on the plan sponsor, plan design and time horizon.
- Help design an appropriate strategic investment strategy.
- Provide insight into current market dislocations and practical implications for the near term.

Historically, most pension plan sponsors conducted comprehensive asset/liability studies every three to five years or after a significant change in demographics, plan design, funded status, sponsor circumstances, or funding legislation. Recent trends suggest more frequent studies, and/or a desire for regular tracking of key asset/liability risk metrics in between formal studies.

Additional Challenges

In the United States, the Pension Protection Act of 2006 (PPA) has introduced stricter standards on pension plans, requiring higher funding targets and larger contributions from plan sponsors. With growing deficits and PPA funding requirements looming large, there is an unprecedented need for asset/liability modeling and overall pension risk management.

Asset/Liability Modeling for Individuals

Some financial advisors offer Monte Carlo simulation tools aimed at helping individuals model the odds they will be able to retire when they want with the amount of money they want. These tools are designed to model the individual's likelihood of assets surpassing expenses (liabilities).

Proponents of Monte Carlo simulation contend that these tools are valuable because they offer simulation using randomly ordered returns based on a set of reasonable parameters. For example, the tool can model retirement cash flows 500 or 1,000 times, thus reflecting a range of possible outcomes.

Some critics of these tools claim that the consequences of failure are not laid out and argue that these tools are no better than typical retirement tools that use standard assumptions. Recent financial turmoil has fueled the claims of critics who believe that Monte Carlo simulation tools are inaccurate and overly optimistic.

ASSET CLASSES

In finance, an asset class is a group of financial instruments which have similar financial characteristics and behave similarly in the marketplace. We can often break these instruments into those having to do with real assets and those having to do with financial assets. Often, assets within the same asset class are subject to the same laws and regulations; however, this is not always true. For instance, futures on an asset are often considered part of the same asset class as the underlying instrument but are subject to different regulations than the underlying instrument.

Many investment funds are composed of the two main asset classes which are securities: equities (stocks) and fixed-income (bonds). However, some also hold cash and foreign currencies. Funds may also hold money market instruments and they may even refer to these as cash equivalents; however, that ignores the possibility of default. Money market instruments, being short-term fixed income investments, should therefore be grouped with fixed income.

In addition to stocks and bonds, we can add cash, foreign currencies, real estate, infrastructure and commodities to the list of commonly held asset classes. In general, an asset class is expected to exhibit different risk and return investment characteristics, and to perform differently in certain market environments.

Asset classes and asset class categories are often mixed together. In other words, describing large-cap stocks or short-term bonds asset classes is incorrect. These investment vehicles are asset class categories, and are used for diversification purposes.

Stocks - Also called equities:

- Represent shares of ownership in publicly held companies.
- Historically have outperformed other investments over long periods (keep in mind that past performance does not guarantee future results).
- Most volatile in the short term.
- Returns and principal will fluctuate so that accumulations, when redeemed, may be worth more or less than original cost.

Fixed income - Fixed income, or bond investments, generally pay a set rate of interest over a given period, then return the investor's principal.

- Set rate of interest.
- More stability than stocks.
- Value fluctuates due to current interest and inflation rates.
- Includes "guaranteed" or "risk-free" assets.
- Also includes money market instruments (short-term fixed income investments).

Cash

Foreign Currencies - Also called FX, or foreign exchange:

- Cryptocurrencies such as bitcoin are an emerging asset class.
- No bearish periods, as when one currency's value falls, others' will in turn rise.

- The only truly 24-hour tradeable asset class.
- Highly speculative (97%) market.

Real estate - Your home or investment property, plus shares of funds that invest in commercial real estate.

- Helps protect future purchasing power as property values and rental income run parallel to inflation.
- Values tend to rise and fall more slowly than stock and bond prices. It is important to keep in mind that the real estate sector is subject to various risks, including fluctuation in underlying property values, expenses and income, and potential environmental liabilities.

Infrastructure as an Asset Class

- Broad category including highways, airports, rail networks, energy generation (utilities), energy storage and distribution (gas mains, pipelines etc.)
- Provides a longer duration (facilitating cash flow matching with long-term liabilities), protection against inflation, and statistical diversification (low correlation with 'traditional' listed assets such as equity and fixed income investments), thus reducing overall portfolio volatility.

Commodities - Physical goods such as gold, copper, crude oil, natural gas, wheat, corn, and even electricity.

- Helps protect future purchasing power as values have fixed utility and thus run parallel to inflation.
- Values tend to exhibit low correlations with stock and bond prices.
- Price dynamics are also unique: commodities become more volatile as prices rise. Thus a commodity with a 20% volatility might have a 50% volatility if prices doubled.

Most financial experts agree that some of the most effective investment strategies involve diversifying investments across broad asset classes like stocks and bonds, rather than focusing on specific securities that may or may not turn out to be "winners." Diversification is a technique to help reduce risk. However, there is no guarantee that diversification will protect against a loss of income.

The goal of asset allocation is to create a balanced mix of assets that have the potential to improve returns, while meeting your:

- Tolerance for risk (market volatility).
- Goals and investment objectives.
- Preferences for certain types of investments within asset classes.

Being diversified across asset classes may help reduce volatility. If you include several asset classes in your long-term portfolio, the upswing of one asset class may help offset the downward movement of another as conditions change. But keep in mind that there are inherent risks associated with investing in securities, and diversification doesn't protect against loss.

ASSET RECOVERY

Asset recovery, also known as investment or resource recovery, is the process of maximizing the value of unused or end-of-life assets through effective reuse or divestment. While sometimes referred to in the context of a company undergoing liquidation, Asset recovery also can describe the process of liquidating excess inventory, refurbished items, and equipment returned at the end of a lease.

Asset recovery can also refer to the task of recovery of assets that have been wrongfully taken either stolen, fraudulently misappropriated or otherwise disposed of to remove them from their rightful owner.

Asset recovery has three main elements—identification, redeployment, and divestment. Specialized asset recovery software may assist any of these steps.

Identification

Because unproductive assets cost money, it is important to classify them as such by investment recovery personnel. Later, a decision can be made whether to redeploy or divest. Surplus assets could be in any form, including fixed equipment, mobile equipment, buildings, or land. Idle or surplus assets can be either capital assets or non-capital surplus.

Redeployment

Redeploying an idle asset to another part of an organization is often the most productive use for the asset. Asset redeployment also saves the organization money by eliminating the need to purchase a new asset at current market rates. For effective reuse, another part of the company needs to require an asset of that kind. It must also be practical to transfer and deploy the asset at the new location.

One form of internal redeployment is cannibalization of usable spare parts from one asset to another. For example, a taxicab company has two non-running cabs with different non-working parts in each. By taking a working part from one non-running cab and placing it in the other, the company has reduced its number of non-running cabs by 50%.

Disposition

Disposition of surplus or idle assets is the process of either selling, scrapping, recycling, donating, or disposing an asset. The process involves removing the asset from an organization's books. When this is done effectively, the organization obtains capital that can be placed back into the business. In addition, a good asset sale produces revenue and boosts profits. Donations also build goodwill and deliver tax benefits. The type of disposition method employed will depend on the type of asset, its fair value, and market demand.

ASSET PROTECTION

Asset protection (sometimes also referred to as *debtor-creditor law*) is a set of legal techniques and a body of statutory and common law dealing with protecting assets of individuals and business entities from civil money judgments. The goal of asset protection planning is to insulate assets from claims of creditors without perjury or tax evasion.

Asset protection consists of methods available to protect assets from liabilities arising elsewhere. It should not be confused with limiting liability, which concerns the ability to stop or constrain liability to the asset or activity from which it arises. Assets that are shielded from creditors by law are few (common examples include some home equity, certain retirement plans and interests in LLCs and limited partnerships [and even these are not always unreachable]). Assets that are almost always unreachable are those to which one does not hold legal title. In many cases it is possible to vest legal title to personal assets in a trust, an agent or a nominee, while retaining all the control of the assets. The goal of asset protection is similar to bankruptcy, and the two practice areas go hand-in-hand. When a debtor has none to few assets, the bankruptcy route is preferable. When the debtor has significant assets, asset protection may be the solution.

The four threshold factors that are either expressly or implicitly analyzed in each asset protection case are:

- The identity of the person engaging in asset protection planning:
    - If the debtor is an individual, does he or she have a spouse, and is the spouse also liable? If the spouse is not liable, is it possible to enter into a transmutation agreement? Are the spouses engaged in activities that are equally likely to result in lawsuits or is one spouse more likely to be sued than the other?
    - If the debtor is an entity, did an individual guarantee the entity's debt? How likely is it that the creditor will be able to pierce the corporate veil or otherwise get the assets of the individual owners? Is there a statute that renders the individual personally liable for the obligations of the entity?
- The nature of the claim:
    - Are there specific claims or the asset protection is taken as a result of a desire to insulate from lawsuits?
    - If the claim has been reduced to a judgement, what assets does the judgement encumber?
    - Is the claim dischargeable?
    - What is the statute of limitations for bringing the claim?
- The identity of the creditor:
    - How aggressive is the creditor?
    - Is the creditor a government agency? Taxing authority? Some government agencies possess powers of seizure that other government agencies do not.

- The nature of the assets:
  - To what extent are the assets exempt from the claims of the creditors? For example, the degree of protection offered by the homestead exemption, the exemption of the assets in a qualified plan, i.e. assets in a plan under the Employee Retirement Income Security Act (ERISA) etc.

Whilst the aforementioned use of Trusts will be of benefit in a number of cases, the question of ownership can still arise, as although legal ownership may have been transferred to the trustees, beneficial ownership may still in many cases lie with the settler of the Trust. A Private Placement Life Insurance contract (PPLI), can provide a greater degree of protection and privacy than most Trusts, and can also be integrated with an existing trust if necessary. Whilst Trusts may not be recognised in many Jurisdictions, Life insurance also has the advantage of being Multi jurisdictional.

ASSET TRACKING

In information technology, asset tracking is the process of keeping track of the movement of one or more IT assets throughout the organization.

It is practiced by IT administrators and managers to have administrative control and insight into the movement of the entire IT infrastructure.

IT asset tracking generally utilizes an IT inventory database that records and maintains inventory data for all:

- Devices.
- Software.
- Network configuration.
- Cloud assets.
- IT documentation.
- Other IT infrastructure-related data.

Asset tracking is generally performed through asset tracking software that scans the entire IT infrastructure network and compiles an inventory of all IT assets. Any change in the movement of devices is recorded for future reference. The change in movement can include:

- IP address change.
- Physical relocation of device.
- Device removed from network.
- Software installation/uninstallation.
- Software license expiration.

Methods of Asset Tracking

While asset tracking can be time consuming and expensive, there are methods of asset tracking that can save your organization time and money. The goal of any asset tracking system, therefore, is to maximize asset control efficiency and minimize equipment loss. Through the use of mobile computers, barcode labels, handheld barcode scanners, and asset management software, you can track your assets in real time, resulting in more efficient production planning and reduced downtime. The proper management software also enables organizations to schedule necessary maintenance or service, or even preventive maintenance. Complete asset tracking solutions include barcode technology, enabling organizations to scan their fixed assets to track them accurately and efficiently. Barcodes are the standard for data collection and asset tracking, giving each asset a unique identifier so that they may be individually recognized and tracked. Barcodes include information that is critical to business, such as project name, asset category, and more. Barcode scanners read each barcode, allowing organizations to count assets more quickly and accurately without the risk of introducing human error.

Benefits of Asset Tracking

The benefits of asset tracking are numerous, and nearly all contribute to a healthier bottom line for the organizations that properly implement effective asset management processes. We highlight some of the most beneficial advantages of employing asset tracking here:

- Improve efficiency and trim costs.
- Adjust company records as equip.ment is reassigned between departments, and use the updated information when calculating taxes and costs for each department.
- Quickly and easily locate assets at any time, and in real time.
- Conduct asset tracking using fewer resources, with the aid of an asset tracking system.
- Lower administrative costs, since administrators do not need to track or locate assets manually.
- Track and reduce asset loss and utilize assets more effectively.
- Grow your company and scale your asset tracking as necessary.
- Improve customer service through improved asset tracking and management practices.
- Ensure accountability and accuracy with asset loss and management.
- Immediately know where your assets have been allocated.
- Proper asset tracking is required for regulatory compliance in certain industries.
- Increase the efficiency and organization of your company's physical space by identifying which items are accessed together and creating a better structure of your physical system.
- Get real-time reports on the position of each asset and increase the accuracy of your asset management.

ASSET SWAP

An asset swap is similar in structure to a plain vanilla swap with the key difference being the underlying of the swap contract. Rather than regular fixed and floating loan interest rates being swapped, fixed and floating assets are being exchanged.

All swaps are derivative contracts through which two parties exchange financial instruments. These instruments can be almost anything, but most swaps involve cash flows based on a notional principal amount agreed upon by both parties. As the name suggests, asset swaps involve an actual asset exchange instead of just cash flows.

Swaps do not trade on exchanges, and retail investors do not generally engage in swaps. Rather, swaps are over-the-counter contracts between businesses or financial institutions.

Asset swaps can be used to overlay the fixed interest rates of bond coupons with floating rates. In that sense, they are used to transform cash flow characteristics of underlying assets and transforming them to hedge the asset's risks, whether relate to currency, credit, and/or interest rates.

Typically, an asset swap involves transactions in which the investor acquires a bond position and then enters into an interest rate swap with the bank that sold him/her the bond. The investor pays fixed and receives floating. This transforms the fixed coupon of the bond into a LIBOR-based floating coupon.

It is widely used by banks to convert their long-term fixed rate assets to a floating rate in order to match their short-term liabilities (depositor accounts).

Another use is to insure against loss due to credit risk, such as default or bankruptcy, of the bond's issuer. Here, the swap buyer is also buying protection.

Whether the swap is to hedge interest rate risk or default risk, there are two separate trades that occur.

First, the swap buyer purchases a bond from the swap seller in return for a full price of par plus accrued interest (called the dirty price).

Next, the two parties create a contract where the buyer agrees to pay fixed coupons to the swap seller equal to the fixed rate coupons received from the bond. In return, the swap buyer receives variable rate payments of LIBOR plus (or minus) an agreed upon fixed spread. The maturity of this swap is the same as the maturity of the asset.

The mechanics are the same for the swap buyer wishing to hedge default or some other event risk. Here, the swap buyer is essentially buying protection and the swap seller is also selling that protection.

As before, the swap seller (protection seller) will agree to pay the swap buyer (protection buyer) LIBOR plus (or minus) a spread in return for the cash flows of the risky bond (the bond itself does not change hands). In the event of default, the swap buyer will continue to receive LIBOR plus (or minus) the spread from the swap seller. In this way, the swap buyer has transformed its original risk profile by changing both its interest rate and credit risk exposure.

There are two components used in calculating the spread for an asset swap. The first one is the value of coupons of underlying assets minus par swap rates. The second component is a comparison between bond prices and par values to determine the price that the investor has to pay over the lifetime of the swap. The difference between these two components is the asset swap spread paid by the protection seller to the swap buyer.

Example of an Asset Swap

Suppose an investor buys a bond at a dirty price of 110% and wants it hedge the risk of a default by the bond issuer. She contacts a bank for an asset swap. The bond's fixed coupons are 6% of par value. The swap rate is 5%. Assume that the investor has to pay 0.5% price premium during the swap's lifetime. Then the asset swap spread is 0.5% (6- 5 -0.5). Hence the bank pays the investor LIBOR rates plus 0.5% during the swap's lifetime.

References

- Fund-management: wallstreetmojo.com, Retrieved 29 May, 2019
- Halfawy, M. (2008). "Integration of Municipal Infrastructure Assets Management Processes". Journal of Computing in Civil Engineering, vol. 22, no. 6.
- Asset-tracking- 29984: techopedia.com, Retrieved 02 June, 2019
- "Business Management Magazine no 39- Optimizing Digital Asset Management (page 86)". Archived from the original on July 14, 2009. Retrieved July 25, 2019.
- What-is-asset-tracking, asset-tags: camcode.com, Retrieved 28 January, 2019
- Spillane, Chris (8 September 2011). "U.K. Homeowners Shouldn't Count on Capital Gains, Minister Says". Bloomberg. London. Retrieved 2012-06-02. 'Gone are the days where you buy a house for capital appreciation,' Shapps... said
- "Asset Liability Modeling". Finance Training Course. Retrieved 2018-07-25

PERMISSIONS

All chapters in this book are published with permission under the Creative Commons Attribution Share Alike License or equivalent. Every chapter published in this book has been scrutinized by our experts. Their significance has been extensively debated. The topics covered herein carry significant information for a comprehensive understanding. They may even be implemented as practical applications or may be referred to as a beginning point for further studies.

We would like to thank the editorial team for lending their expertise to make the book truly unique. They have played a crucial role in the development of this book. Without their invaluable contributions this book wouldn't have been possible. They have made vital efforts to compile up to date information on the varied aspects of this subject to make this book a valuable addition to the collection of many professionals and students.

This book was conceptualized with the vision of imparting up-to-date and integrated information in this field. To ensure the same, a matchless editorial board was set up. Every individual on the board went through rigorous rounds of assessment to prove their worth. After which they invested a large part of their time researching and compiling the most relevant data for our readers.

The editorial board has been involved in producing this book since its inception. They have spent rigorous hours researching and exploring the diverse topics which have resulted in the successful publishing of this book. They have passed on their knowledge of decades through this book. To expedite this challenging task, the publisher supported the team at every step. A small team of assistant editors was also appointed to further simplify the editing procedure and attain best results for the readers.

Apart from the editorial board, the designing team has also invested a significant amount of their time in understanding the subject and creating the most relevant covers. They scrutinized every image to scout for the most suitable representation of the subject and create an appropriate cover for the book.

The publishing team has been an ardent support to the editorial, designing and production team. Their endless efforts to recruit the best for this project, has resulted in the accomplishment of this book. They are a veteran in the field of academics and their pool of knowledge is as vast as their experience in printing. Their expertise and guidance has proved useful at every step. Their uncompromising quality standards have made this book an exceptional effort. Their encouragement from time to time has been an inspiration for everyone.

The publisher and the editorial board hope that this book will prove to be a valuable piece of knowledge for students, practitioners and scholars across the globe.

INDEX

A
Accounts Payable, 22, 30-31, 191-192
Accounts Receivable, 1, 10-11, 22-24, 31, 33, 36, 39, 112, 191-192
Active Management, 56, 64-65, 68, 73-76, 78, 87-88
Amortization Expense, 41-42
Asset Allocation, 56, 63, 68-74, 80, 88, 215, 230, 233
Asset Inventory, 8, 221

B
Balance Sheet, 1, 10-11, 13, 22-23, 25, 28, 30, 33, 35-38, 43, 45, 51, 55, 111, 114, 117, 128, 143, 158, 175-179, 191-192, 216, 231
Batch Control, 17-18
Benchmark Error, 79
Bond Investments, 36, 232
Book Value, 35-36, 41, 44, 46-47, 51, 54, 111, 113-114, 122, 141, 143, 145, 171, 175-178, 191
Bottoms-up Style, 218
Bull Market, 93

C
Capital Asset Pricing Model, 79, 109, 118-119, 158, 187
Capital Assets, 35, 176, 234
Capital Expenditure, 42-43, 134, 144-145, 198
Cash and Cash Equivalents, 1, 11-13, 32, 36, 69
Cash Flow, 1, 35, 43, 47, 57, 109-110, 116-117, 120, 122, 124, 129, 131, 133-134, 138, 145, 147, 153-155, 157-165, 171-173, 183-188, 192, 194, 196, 230, 233, 238
Cash Ratio, 13, 32-34
Commercial Paper, 11, 27, 176
Contrarian Investment, 67
Corporate Bonds, 2, 105, 190
Current Assets, 1, 10-13, 22, 25-26, 30-32, 35-38, 50, 57, 112
Current Liabilities, 12-13, 30-33, 38, 45, 112
Current Ratio, 13, 30-31, 34, 38, 112

D
Debt Instruments, 12, 26
Debt Securities, 11, 26
Deposit Account, 69
Depreciation, 2, 35, 37-38, 44, 46-47, 50-55, 57, 110-111, 113-114, 118, 122, 134, 143-145, 175, 177-178, 192
Dividends, 26-27, 47, 50, 67, 77, 106-107, 125, 131, 162-163, 165, 171-172, 177-178, 185, 187, 190-191, 193-194, 197, 200, 202-213

E
Economic Analysis, 3, 127
Equity Markets, 59-60, 66, 94
Exchange-traded Funds, 27, 81, 219

F
Financial Accounting, 37, 39-40, 44
Financial Assets, 2, 38, 103, 110, 176, 219, 232
Financial Statements, 1, 7, 12, 23, 36, 39-40, 99, 116-117, 132, 139, 178, 194, 227
Fiscal Year, 10-11, 43, 188
Fixed Asset Turnover, 45-47
Fixed Assets, 1-2, 35-36, 38, 42-50, 52, 57, 110, 112-113, 163, 227, 237
Fixed Income, 2, 59-60, 69, 73, 77, 86, 91, 94, 232-233
Foreign Currency, 10, 12, 60, 70
Fund of Funds, 79-81

G
Generally Accepted Accounting Principles, 2, 28, 187
Goodwill, 2, 36-38, 40-42, 112-113, 122, 175-176, 178-179, 187-188, 191, 214, 234
Government Grants, 42

H
Hedge Fund, 74, 79-81, 83, 90-91, 93-104, 215

I
Income Statement, 28, 40, 55, 114, 177-179, 192, 200
Indexing, 64, 66-67, 81, 88, 223-224
Intangible Assets, 1-2, 35-41, 43, 122, 170, 175-176, 199, 214
Intellectual Property, 36, 41, 118, 124, 214
Investment Management, 56-58, 83, 85, 90, 96, 214-215
Investment Portfolio, 56, 58, 61-62, 66, 68, 74
Investment Risk, 57, 59, 61-62, 85-86, 88, 121

L
Life Cycle Cost, 3-4
Liquid Assets, 10, 12-13, 28, 31-32, 35, 57, 90

M

Market Sentiment, 59-60
Marketable Securities, 10-11, 13, 24-28, 31-34, 37
Maturity Date, 11-12, 25, 27
Modern Portfolio Theory, 63, 69, 79, 121
Money Market Fund, 2-3, 69
Mutual Funds, 2, 56, 62-63, 65, 72, 74-77, 80, 83, 89-90, 122, 128, 157, 215, 218

O

Offshore Funds, 99-101
Operating Expenses, 10, 42, 81, 159

P

Paper Assets, 56
Passive Investing, 81-82
Pension Funds, 56, 58, 80-81, 96, 104, 214-215
Portfolio Management, 56, 61-66, 73, 77, 79
Preferred Equity, 2, 176
Preferred Shares, 12, 27, 177
Prepaid Expenses, 1, 28-31, 36
Private Equity, 70, 76, 79, 83, 90, 96, 104-105, 117, 162-166

Q

Quality Management, 19
Quick Ratio, 13, 31, 34, 38

R

Radio Frequency Identification, 17-21
Return On Investment, 27, 90, 141, 149

S

Stock Control, 14, 16-21
Stock Inventory, 10
Stock Security, 19-21
Straight-line Depreciation, 52
Supply Chain, 14, 18-19, 227

T

Tangible Asset, 24, 36-37
Treasury Bills, 11, 27, 33-34

V

Venture Capital Funds, 81

W

Working Capital, 12, 23-24, 134, 145, 163, 198

CPSIA information can be obtained
at www.ICGtesting.com
Printed in the USA
BVHW051702180820
586707BV00003B/77

9 781641 723701